Appeasement in Crisis

Appeasement in Crisis

From Munich to Prague, October 1938–March 1939

David Gillard

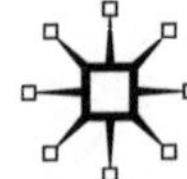

First published 2007 by
PALGRAVE MACMILLAN
Houndmills, Basingstoke, Hampshire RG21 6XS and
175 Fifth Avenue, New York, N.Y. 10010
Companies and representatives throughout the world

PALGRAVE MACMILLAN is the global academic imprint of the Palgrave Macmillan division of St. Martin's Press, LLC and of Palgrave Macmillan Ltd. Macmillan® is a registered trademark in the United States, United Kingdom and other countries. Palgrave is a registered trademark in the European Union and other countries.

ISBN-13: 978-0-230-50040-2 hardback
ISBN-10: 0-230-50040-4 hardback

This book is printed on paper suitable for recycling and made from fully managed and sustained forest sources. Logging, pulping and manufacturing processes are expected to conform to the environmental regulations of the country of origin.

A catalogue record for this book is available from the British Library.

A catalog record for this book is available from the Library of Congress.

10 9 8 7 6 5 4 3 2 1
16 15 14 13 12 11 10 09 08 07

Printed and bound in Great Britain by
Antony Rowe Ltd, Chippenham and Eastbourne

To My Family

Contents

Acknowledgments viii

1. Diplomacy by Guarantee 1
2. The Outlook from Whitehall 14
3. The Challenge of Barbarism 35
4. The Prospect of War 56
5. Resolving to Resist 74
6. Continental Commitment 95
7. The Challenge of Annexation 116
8. The Quest for Coalition 137
9. The Guaranteeing of Poland 157
10. Diplomacy by Drama 178

List of Abbreviations 188

Notes 189

Bibliography 201

Index 210

Acknowledgments

I am grateful for the assistance afforded me by staff and the following institutions, holding official and private papers.

Birmingham University Library
Bodleian Library, Oxford
Cambridge University Library
Churchill College, Cambridge
India Office Library
Kend Archives, Maidstone
National Archives of Scotland, Edinburgh
National Library of Scotland, Edinburgh
National Maritime Museum
Public Record Office
Robinson Library, University of Newcastle

1
Diplomacy by Guarantee

At the end of March 1939, those responsible for British foreign policy took a decision which none of them had anticipated a fortnight earlier. They committed their country to war in support of Poland if the latter fought to preserve its independence. The commitment was public and it was not hedged round by conditions offering an escape. Even what cynical observers thought to be half-hidden escape routes had been explicitly ruled out by ministers in private exchanges prior to the announcement. One lay in the absence of any reference to the integrity of Poland's frontiers. Certainly, their eventual revision by diplomatic means was still anticipated in London, but Neville Chamberlain told his Cabinet that confining the guarantee thus to Poland's independence was not intended to limit its effect. If German military action against, say, the disputed territory of Danzig was viewed by Polish leaders as a threat to their country's independence which they had to resist, the British Government should accept that interpretation and go to Poland's aid.[1] Similarly, Lord Halifax had turned down the suggestion of his Ambassador in Warsaw that only an 'unprovoked' action by Germany should trigger British intervention. The Foreign Secretary told Sir Howard Kennard that 'the German technique of aggression is so varied and so insidious that it might well be that Poland might in certain circumstances be driven to commit a technical act of provocation'.[2]

This readiness to fight for Poland's independence appeared to mark a radical break with the traditions of British foreign policy. In the past, British governments had been very sparing of pledges to fight, and then only if the obligations could be met by direct use of military and especially naval power. Nor had they ever been at ease in using the 'guarantee' as a diplomatic device. That particular unease had been manifest only six months before during the Commons debate on the Munich

Agreement. An Annex to the Agreement had referred to an international guarantee of Czechoslovakia, which had been proposed by France and Great Britain on 19 September 1938. The two Powers had recognised that if President Eduard Benes made the sacrifices required of him, he would be entitled to some assurance as to his country's future security. They were ready, therefore, to join in an international guarantee of the new boundaries of Czechoslovakia against unprovoked aggression. This 'general guarantee' would safeguard Czechoslovakia's independence in place of 'existing treaties which involved reciprocal obligations of a military character' with France and Russia.[3] At Munich, the British and French governments had stood by this offer. The Annex also claimed that when 'the question of the Polish and Hungarian minorities in Czechoslovakia has been settled, Germany and Italy, for their part, will give a guarantee to Czechoslovakia'.[4] It was the implications for Great Britain of this guarantee which were explored, to the government's discomfort, by a score of critics from both sides of the House.

The questions and criticisms were directed at the uncertain nature of the guarantee. Speakers pointed out that an unprecedented commitment had been made to defend a frontier in Central Europe. That frontier was of a state surrounded by enemies and largely deprived by the Munich Agreement of its means of defence. The projected German and Italian guarantees were seen as worthless even if they were ever given. The line of the frontier to be guaranteed was still uncertain, as further changes to the advantage of Germany, Poland and Hungary were anticipated. At what point, therefore, would the guarantee come into effect, and under what circumstances would Great Britain be committed to act? Would it be only on an actual violation of the frontier, or would actions which deprived Czechoslovakia of its political freedom and independence be sufficient cause? German broadcasts were already advocating the severance of Ruthenia and Slovakia; if foreign intrigue accomplished that, would Great Britain intervene? Moreover, the guarantee having now been offered, the strategic inaccessibility of Czechoslovakia could not be used as an excuse next time. The means to honour it must, therefore, be provided. An army on continental lines would be required and other guarantors would be needed, notably Russia. Or had the British and French guarantees been offered to Benes without serious intent, merely to sugar-coat the bitter pill of Munich? Ministers and their supporters responded to all this evasively and with mounting embarrassment.[5] The government, observed Sir Alexander Cadogan, Permanent Under-Secretary at the Foreign Office, 'are getting rather knocked about in this Debate'.[6]

The difficulty for ministers in trying to frame a response was that they broadly shared these concerns. The international guarantee had not been a British initiative. It had been proposed by the French Premier, Edouard Daladier, and his Foreign Minister, Georges Bonnet, during conversations at 10 Downing Street on 18 September. It was strongly resisted by Chamberlain and Halifax, who had been anticipating something of the sort. A Foreign Office memorandum had already, in June, spelled out the complications which would be involved in framing a guarantee even if the reconstructed Czechoslovakia was neutralised on the lines of Belgium or Luxembourg.[7] Chamberlain had told the French ministers, as his critics in the Commons were to tell him, that their proposal was 'a very grave departure' which would be 'a great liability and a serious source of embarrassment' since, for reasons of military geography, Great Britain could scarcely be expected to fulfil the guarantee if the occasion arose. Halifax had said that he was prepared to contemplate a guarantee only if there were 'some understanding on the part of the Czech Government that in issues involving peace and war they should accept the advice of His Majesty's Government, and that if they did not accept it His Majesty's Government would then be automatically absolved of their guarantee'. The French ministers insisted, however, that the guarantee was for them a vital matter on which their co-operation depended, and eventually the British gave way. Bonnet assured them that the main value of the guarantee would be 'moral', so that Czechoslovakia's strategic inaccessibility was not a crucial consideration. Daladier argued that a British guarantee 'would help to stop the German march to the East'.[8] What they meant by either remark was far from clear and was quite unhelpful to ministers coping with sceptical MPs.

Having heard the initial speeches on the afternoon of Monday 3 October, Sir Samuel Hoare, Home Secretary and a former Foreign Secretary, sought the help of three senior members of the Foreign Office – Cadogan, Sir William Malkin and William Strang – in preparing the speech he was to give at the end of the first day.[9] Whether on their advice or not, he tried to blur the issue of the guarantee by some optimistic speculation. First, Hoare argued that, with its minorities problem solved, Czechoslovakia would simply cease to be in danger. Second, he expected all the Great Powers, including Russia, to participate in the guarantee 'in one way or another', perhaps with Great Britain, France, Russia, Germany and Italy making non-aggression pacts as well with the new Czechoslovakia. This attempt to reduce the British guarantee to insignificance through an imagined and rosy future failed to carry conviction. Demands for clarification persisted on the following day, and another Cabinet minister, Leslie Burgin, was challenged about the guarantee during his praise of the overall settlement. He refused to answer, but promised that the matter would be dealt with later. It was left to Sir Thomas Inskip, Minister for Co-ordination of Defence, to do so at the end of the evening's debate. Inskip tried to blunt at least one of the criticisms of the guarantee:

> The question has been raised whether our guarantee to Czechoslovakia is already in operation. The House will realise that the formal Treaty of guarantee has yet to be drawn up and completed in the normal way, and, as the Foreign Secretary has stated in another place, there are some matters which must await settlement between the governments concerned. Until that has been done, technically the guarantee cannot be said to be in force. His Majesty's Government, however, feel under a moral obligation to Czechoslovakia to treat the guarantee as being now in force. In the event, therefore, of an act of unprovoked aggression against Czechoslovakia, His Majesty's Government would certainly feel bound to take all steps in their power to see that the integrity of Czechoslovakia is preserved.[10]

Inskip refused to elaborate on what he described as a 'deliberately framed answer', and the use of the words 'unprovoked' and 'all steps in their power' were presumably chosen with care. Given the government's insistence that it had not been in their power to preserve Czechoslovakia's integrity the previous week, Winston Churchill and Harold Nicolson were scathingly incredulous about the 'steps' which Inskip implied were readily available just a few days later. Nicolson claimed that aggressive moves against Czechoslovakia by Poland and Hungary had been in progress while Inskip was speaking, and that Great Britain had already been snubbed by the Polish Government when trying to protest.[11]

The Foreign Secretary, acutely aware that British diplomacy had, indeed, been able to do nothing for Czechoslovakia during the days since Munich, understood more clearly than Chamberlain the need to pre-empt criticism. The Prime Minister, opening the Commons debate, had invited trouble by making only a brief and ill-judged reference to the guarantee, citing it as one of the advantages of the Munich terms over those demanded earlier at Godesberg.[12] In the Lords, Halifax reduced the flow of awkward questions to which there could be no satisfactory answers by candidly listing, at the beginning of his speech, the disadvantages and obscurities of the guarantee, and by confessing that its actual form was still to be determined in exchanges with other governments.[13] This did not, of course, prevent some of his fellow peers from complaining that such should be the case. In both Houses, the government were left in no doubt that the guarantee had heightened their difficulties in dealing with the aftermath of a controversial settlement. Their misgivings had been justified. Their guarded attempt to define the position had merely confused the issue still further.

Guarantees had never been a straightforward matter for British governments, though one Foreign Secretary, George Canning, had tried in 1823 to make them so. He had regarded a guarantee as 'one of the most onerous obligations which one state can contract towards another', because, in contrast to a defensive alliance, it was unlimited in its duration and in the degree of sacrifice required of the guarantor. As such, guarantees of either territories or institutions were best avoided altogether.[14] Canning was right as to the original principle of the guarantee as a diplomatic device, but arguably wrong as to what was, by then, its current practice. In the seventeenth century, guarantees had been the normal means by which major European governments had tried to ensure lasting observance of the treaties they had negotiated. According to Sir Ernest Satow, in his study of their origins, 'a guarantee properly speaking involves an understanding that force will be employed by the guarantor to ensure the fulfilment of a treaty, whenever he is applied to by one of the parties for assistance against the other who has been guilty of its violation.'[15] Given the rapidity with which international circumstances and the interests of guarantors were liable to change, it is not surprising that most governments had become disinclined to rely much upon guarantees by the time Canning made his pronouncement.

Canning's predecessor, Castlereagh, had abandoned an attempt to persuade allied governments to bestow a general guarantee on the Vienna settlement of 1815. He subsequently explained the practical difficulties preventing this in terms which the founders of the League of Nations should have realised were still valid a hundred years later:

> There is no doubt that a breach of the Covenant by any one State is an Injury, which all the other States may, if they shall think fit, either separately or collectively resent, but the Treaties do not impose, by express stipulation, the doing so, as a matter of positive obligation. So solemn a Pact, on the faithful execution and observance of which all Nations should feel the strongest Interest, may be considered, as under the protection of a moral guarantee, of the highest Nature, but as those who framed these acts did not probably see how the whole Confederacy could, without the utmost

> Inconvenience, be made collectively to enforce the observance of these Treaties, the execution of this duty seems to have been deliberately left to arise out of the Circumstances of the Time and of the Case, and the offending State to be brought to reason by such of the injured States, as might, at the moment think fit to charge themselves with the Task of defending their own rights, thus invaded.[16]

It was for these reasons that guarantees, while still found occasionally convenient as a form of reassurance or menace, acquired during the nineteenth century much the same status in international politics as in the world of commerce. They might mean what they appeared to say, or they might not. Inskip was echoing Castlereagh when he described the latest guarantee as a 'moral obligation'.

In Great Britain, the cases of Belgium (1839) and Luxembourg (1867) had given rise to conflicting views and to confusion about the nature of guarantees which were still apparent in the debate of October 1938. The territory, independence and neutrality of Belgium had been guaranteed by the Great Powers since 1839. Given Great Britain's traditionally strategic and commercial interests there, it would have been reasonable to assume that the British Government, at least, would be determined to see that this guarantee did mean what it said. Yet there was recurrent uncertainty in London as to whether the British would ever actually go to war in defence of Belgium. Gladstone more than once questioned the strength of the obligation;[17] Salisbury was significantly silent about it when asked in 1887; Crowe and Hardinge disputed the matter within the Foreign Office in 1908; and, while to some members of the Cabinet, German violation of Belgium's frontiers was crucial to the decision for war in 1914, it is uncertain what would have been their attitude had such an action been initiated by the French.[18] Like their continental counterparts, British political leaders would not allow this kind of obligation, then commonly accepted as provisional and imprecise, to override considerations deemed more important to the national interest. They were, however, much more prone to agonise over verbal distinctions by which evasion might be justified to Parliament.

When Derby's Government reluctantly agreed in 1867 to participate in an international guarantee of Luxembourg, the British negotiators irritated their partners by the distinction they made between a 'collective' and a 'joint and several' guarantee. In the British view, a collective, or joint, guarantee obliged all the guarantors to enforce it in concert; if they did not unanimously agree so to act, which was only too probable, then individual guarantors would be relieved of their obligation. Faced with popular dislike of any intervention in continental affairs, they claimed that the new guarantee of Luxembourg was of this kind. A joint and several, or several, guarantee, on the other hand, would have obliged each guarantor to act regardless of the attitude of the other governments involved. That guarantees had to be so distinguished from one another was denied by the other Great Powers. It was not that they had any more intention than the British of fulfilling the guarantee if it proved to be, as Castlereagh had put it, 'of the utmost Inconvenience', but the form of words constituting a guarantee might carry advantages which the British interpretation would dilute or dispel. There could be long-term diplomatic advantages, such as providing an excuse for intervention or for putting pressure on a partner in some future crisis. There could be an immediate political or 'moral' advantage in the apparent strengthening of an agreement which had aroused unease at home. It was this which was sought by Bismarck in April 1867, when he had to reassure public opinion over withdrawal of the Prussian garrison from Luxembourg. His doing so was not at odds with his remark earlier in the month that a guarantee was in those days of little value.[19] That little value it did have was of use to him in the short term, as it was to Daladier and Bonnet after Munich, and it might have been undermined in each case by the British zeal for definition. Yet Great Britain's honouring of the Belgian guarantee in 1914 appeared to A.L. Kennedy of *The Times* to have made a lasting impression in Europe. When he interviewed Benes at the time of the *Anschluss*, he found it distressing that 'the one thing he wants is a British guarantee'; 'his face fell every time I advanced an argument showing the difficulties ....'[20]

The British interpretation may not have found favour among international jurists, but it became an established doctrine in British political and diplomatic circles. It was still being aired, by Halifax himself among others, during the parliamentary debates of October 1938. In the Lords debate, for example, Lord Lloyd argued that the distinction was all-important:

> If you are guaranteeing her only jointly, let me remind you what one of the greatest authorities on diplomatic usage has said. Headlam-Morley said: 'If you have a joint guarantee alone it is a mere rhetorical flourish of the pen at the end of a document.' Is yours jointly or is it jointly and severally? If it is jointly and severally and two of the contracting parties, Germany and Italy let us say – the axis – break the guarantee, what then?[21]

Lloyd demanded to know whether the guarantee had any real meaning at all or whether it was only 'adding to our obligations and reducing our power to fulfil them?' In the Commons, Geoffrey Mander, the Liberal MP, had made the same point, and when Inskip defined the government's position, Mander reminded him that he had still failed to mention which of these two kinds of guarantees had been given. Inskip evaded the question:

> If the hon. Gentleman had done me the courtesy to listen to me, he would have realised that I said that His Majesty's Government feel under a moral obligation to see that the integrity of Czechoslovakia is preserved.
>
> Mander: It is several.
>
> Inskip: It is a guarantee by His Majesty's Government in these circumstance which I have stated in that deliberately framed answer.[22]

Mander was wrong to claim that Inskip's words implied that the guarantee was 'several'. The word 'moral' at least hinted at the other meaning. There was no need, however, for Inskip to be so cautious, since the Foreign Secretary had already told the Lords that whether it was to be a joint or a several guarantee had simply not yet been decided. The government did realise that they could not get away with a guarantee that was 'a mere rhetorical flourish', but they were nevertheless determined not to be left to act alone. They were certainly not willing to follow the advice of the authority to whom Lloyd had alluded. Sir James Headlam-Morley rejected altogether the distinction made by Derby and Stanley in 1867. He wanted a return to the straightforward and unambiguous guarantees of the seventeenth century, as described, but not recommended, by Canning. Speaking in February 1926, he had welcomed the guarantees in the recent Treaty of Locarno, somewhat surprisingly given their conditional wording.[23] The wording was not, however, conditional enough for Chamberlain and Halifax because the Powers had agreed to act 'collectively and severally', and they rejected Bonnet's argument that the Locarno guarantees should be the model for an international guarantee of Czechoslovakia. At their conversations in Paris on 24 November 1938, they proposed instead a third kind of guarantee.

The British proposal was that the Four Munich Powers should guarantee the new frontiers of Czechoslovakia, but that in the event of their unprovoked violation no one government would be obliged to act unless at least two of the others were prepared to do so. This was a variation of the joint guarantee, previously regarded by British governments as requiring the active participation of all the guarantors. It would, however, have the same effect of ensuring that Great Britain would act only as part of a formidable alliance and, in the current circumstances, of reducing almost to nil the likelihood of it having to act at all. The French strongly resisted this interpretation of what the two governments had undertaken to do. In fact, neither the British nor the French leaders seriously envisaged fighting for Czechoslovakia at all, but their lengthy discussion serves to indicate why it was the form of an apparently useless guarantee which was important to both governments.

The British view was that Czechoslovakia would be relatively safe once the frontiers had been redrawn. The point of the proffered guarantee had been to reassure the suspicious Czechs, though in practice it would not help them against determined aggression by Germany or their other neighbours. If Germany and Italy joined in the guarantee, this might make it more difficult for them to preside over the absorption of what remained of Czechoslovakia. If Czechoslovakia was, nevertheless, attacked, British and French intervention on its behalf would be even less feasible than in September last. Yet it would be humiliating for them to be unable to fulfil a stated obligation. The British Government had publicly acknowledged their moral obligation to defend the integrity of the reconstituted Czechoslovakia, but the guarantee of 19 September had been of a very general kind and they now wanted a precise text to define what they were actually obliged to do. They would not undertake any liability in Central Europe which Great Britain might be left to fulfil alone, nor would it be sensible for Great Britain and France to get themselves involved in war against both Germany and Italy on behalf of a state whose conquest they could not prevent. Hence they would not accept a joint and several guarantee for Czechoslovakia. Such a guarantee might, moreover, encourage the Czechs to rely mistakenly on British and French support for behaviour which Germany might deem provocative. A guarantee by which each signatory would judge whether aggression had been provoked or not, and which would come into force only through a decision of three of the Four Powers would at least conform to the letter of the 19 September declaration. Such a decision was even possible, since German and Italian interests in Central Europe did not always coincide and Italy might side with Great Britain and France.

The Czech Government should, therefore, be told that Great Britain and France were willing to give a guarantee along with Germany and Italy. The Czechs themselves seemed to realise that the original plan of including Russia among the guarantors was scarcely practicable since Germany, from whom they had most to fear, would then refuse to participate. It was more important for the Czechs to have a guarantee given by both Germany and Italy, and if the Czechs themselves were satisfied with the British proposal, that should satisfy everyone.

It did not. The French representatives were not at all satisfied with such an arrangement. It might be in accordance with the letter of the declaration of 19 September, but not with its spirit. The Czechs had been led to expect that in future they would be guaranteed by Great Britain, France and Russia. A guarantee by the Four Munich Powers, operative only when at least three of them were in agreement, would be of far less value because, in practice, they would be either equally divided on such an issue or, improbably, unanimous. If the British Government had not wanted a joint and several guarantee of the Locarno kind, they should not have agreed to make a guarantee part of the Munich settlement. France was already in a very difficult moral position, because the actual loss of territory suffered by its Czech ally since 30 September was more substantial than what Great Britain and France had persuaded the Czechs to cede at Munich. A manifestly inoperable guarantee for even these less favourable frontiers would make matters worse. The Czech Government should be told straightaway that France and Great Britain were willing to give a guarantee without waiting to see whether Germany and Italy would do so. Those two Powers might well be unwilling to do so until they were sure that their arbitration between Hungary and Czechoslovakia, announced on 2 November, was really going to end disputes over Ruthenia. The Czechs could then be asked if they wanted a Four Power guarantee, about Russia as a guarantor, and finally about guarantees from neighbours other than Germany. France would certainly not tell Russia that its guarantee was unwanted, nor should Great Britain. Only the Czechs could do that.

In response to Halifax's enquiry as to how the sort of guarantee favoured by France could be acted upon, when the Western Powers were even less able to save Czechoslovakia than in September, Daladier replied that in practice they would never be called upon to do so. The Czech Government could now do nothing without Germany's consent. In a recent dispute with Hungary, they had, significantly, sought the arbitration of Germany and Italy, not that of France and Great Britain. The guarantee they were discussing had only moral value.[24] This was, of course, what Bonnet had told the British ministers on 19 September. Yet it was also what Inskip had told the Commons on 4 October. Neither government intended to go to war over Czechoslovakia. Each wished to restore a damaged moral position by giving the impression that support for the Czechs might just possibly go that far.

Their leaders, nevertheless, differed because domestic opinion in each country had different, though equally illusory, expectations. In Great Britain, politicians and journalists, regardless of whether they wanted a greater or lesser commitment, had demanded to know exactly what the Munich guarantee would entail if acted upon. Their French counterparts, on the other hand, would be worried as to what such a diluted guarantee, to meet British requirements, would imply about France's already damaged credibility as a Great Power and as, still, Czechoslovakia's ally. To convey the necessary assertiveness, the guarantee would have for them to be at least ostensibly unequivocal. In each case the wording was important. For Chamberlain and Halifax, it was essential that the means of escape from the guarantee were made explicit. For Daladier and Bonnet, it was essential that they were not. Since no agreement proved possible on this, it was decided to put off a decision by asking the Czechs what kind of guarantee they wanted. 'Had some trouble about guarantee to Czecho', noted Cadogan, 'but slid out of it'.[25]

The new Czech Foreign Minister, Frantisek Chvalkovsky, was understandably less concerned about the actual form of any guarantee. On 11 December, the British Minister at Prague, Basil Newton, reported, with sympathetic irony, that he 'seemed hardly to have appreciated the importance of distinctions between an individual guarantee and various forms of collective guarantee' which Newton had been instructed to explain to him. Chvalkovsky made clear that what he wanted above all, and as quickly as possible, was a German guarantee; other guarantees would, of course, be welcome, but a British guarantee, whatever form it took, would be 'more of the nature of a confirmatory and reassuring gesture'.[26] He politely returned the problem to Newton, who understood Chvalkovsky's predicament. Newton had already, on 6 December, suggested to the Foreign Office that the assumptions underlying Inskip's statement were no longer valid because of the extent to which Czechoslovakia had lost its independence and because of the prospect of the state's disintegration through growing discord between Czechs and Slovaks. Only Germany could militarily guarantee Czechoslovakia, and it was 'largely a matter for Germany's own convenience whether she occupies Czechoslovakia. A triumphal march into Prague, often claimed by Germans as one of the oldest and most beautiful of German cities, would be a cheap way of raising his prestige, should Herr Hitler ever feel the necessity.'[27]

The Czech wish for a German guarantee did not, of course, betoken any faith in Hitler's word, but it did show a proper awareness of what his unwillingness to pledge even that was likely to mean. While guarantees had not normally ranked very high in the scale of diplomatic indicators, the explicit refusal of a guarantee by a powerful and aggressive neighbour, previously pledged to offer one, would be a very strong signal indeed of impending danger. During his visit to Paris on 6 December, Joachim von Ribbentrop had made it clear that a German guarantee was unlikely.[28] From the British Embassy in Berlin, Sir George Ogilvie-Forbes, the Chargé d'Affaires, reported on 22 December that 'in their present anti-British temper' the German Government would not be responsive to proposals for a guarantee. That same morning, at the German Foreign Ministry, a reference to the guarantee by the French Ambassador had been studiously ignored.[29] Given the Czech and German attitudes, the French Government lost interest in the form which the ever elusive guarantee might take. They left further initiatives to the British leaders, who tried to win Italian support during a visit to Rome. On 12 January 1939, Chamberlain put to Mussolini the British proposal, with its implicit prospect of Italy joining with Great Britain and France against Germany. Unsurprisingly, Mussolini did not take up the suggestion. He argued that a guarantee by distant governments would be moral rather than material; only the limitrophe states could offer an effective guarantee; even that must await a final settlement of Czechoslovakia's internal constitution, neutral status and frontiers.[30] Yet a settlement of that kind would presumably be to the benefit of Germany, Poland and Hungary, those very limitrophe states whose further predatory activities Chamberlain's proposed guarantee was designed to prevent. The British did, however, find a use for these three conditions as the pretext for a formal enquiry to Germany about the promised guarantee.

Ogilvie-Forbes was told on 26 January 1939 to concert with his French colleague in making the enquiry.[31] The French Government showed no sense of urgency in instructing Robert Coulondre, and puzzled the Foreign Office by conflicting remarks as to whether they now accepted the British form of guarantee or not.[32] Not that it any longer mattered. The British and French enquiries were made on 8 February, and the German reply, dated 28 February, was received at their embassies on 3 March, less than a fortnight before the German occupation of Prague. Germany, they were told, regarded a guarantee as inopportune, not only because Czech disputes with Poland and Hungary persisted but because the guarantees offered by Great Britain and France, 'whether seriously meant or otherwise', had exacerbated

Czechoslovakia's internal difficulties in 1938 by encouraging the government in Prague to resist demands by their national minorities. Fresh guarantees could be expected only to intensify current tensions. In any case, these developments were occurring 'within the sphere of the most important interests of the German Reich, not only from the historical point of view, but in the light of geographical and above all economic necessity'.[33] Despite this unmistakable and uncompromising refusal by Germany, Chamberlain confirmed as late as the afternoon of 14 March 1939 Great Britain's moral obligation to guarantee the Czech frontiers.[34]

Such avowals had become a well-established routine ever since Inskip's statement and especially since the news in November that the Germans were to build a road across Czech territory linking Breslau and Vienna as part of their system of military communications.[35] Questions as to progress in formulating the guarantee and as to how this road and other German activities affected Czechoslovakia's neutral status, and hence the force of the guarantee, were repeatedly asked by Opposition MPs, notably Philip Noel-Baker, Ellen Wilkinson, William Wedgwood Benn and Geoffrey Mander, until Wednesday 15 March, when Seymour Cocks, who was scheduled to make the usual enquiry, announced that in the circumstances 'it would be kinder and more dignified not to ask the question'.[36] Chamberlain's apparent indifference to the plight of the Czechs on 15 March, both in Cabinet in the morning and at the Commons in the afternoon, was ill-judged and insensitive, though understandable. He would be troubled no longer by the political and diplomatic irritant which the guarantee had become once it had served its immediate purpose at Munich and during the Commons debate on Munich. As had been the case since the 1860s, Parliament took guarantees too seriously, continental governments too casually. The scope for dangerous misunderstanding in the Europe of 1938–39 was immense. 'There must be no repetition', Cadogan had warned the Foreign Policy Committee on 6 December 1938, when explaining why such a peculiar form of joint guarantee was being proposed by Great Britain, 'of the situation of last September, when France and ourselves had been faced with the alternatives of fighting, without any hope of saving Czechoslovakia, or of defaulting on the guarantee'.[37]

Yet a few days after Hitler had demonstrated his disregard for Great Britain's oft-repeated guarantee of Czechoslovakia, ministers and officials in London were actively planning to deter him by new guarantees for Poland and other countries in Eastern Europe, which could place them in exactly the same dilemma.

Why?

2
The Outlook from Whitehall

The Munich Agreement was signed in the early hours of Friday 30 September 1938. Any illusion that it would transform international politics should have been dispelled by early on Saturday afternoon.

Throughout the second half of September, Poland and Hungary had been insisting that their territorial demands on Czechoslovakia should be considered alongside those of Germany. Diplomats warned of mounting popular excitement and military preparations in both countries. With their attention centred on the threat of German action, Halifax and his officials had tried to be at once reassuring, non-committal and admonitory.[1] Provision was made in the Agreement for a further meeting of the Four Powers if Poland and Hungary had failed to settle with Czechoslovakia after three months. That the demands would have to be broadly met even sooner had by then been accepted by the Czechs; only the conditions attaching to the surrender of territories and to the actual line of the new frontiers were thought to require negotiation.[2]. Poland's leaders were not, however, prepared to negotiate at all. Incensed by their exclusion from the Munich conference and by the inferior ranking which that implied, they demanded the immediate and unconditional transfer of Trans-Olza, one of those parts of Teschen Silesia denied to them by the Spa Conference in 1920.[3] Before midnight on 30 September they delivered an ultimatum to that effect, requiring the Czech government to accept the terms in full by noon on the following day.[4]

British leaders were mystified, as usual, at the preference for getting by threats what would be available by negotiation. They were fresh from having persuaded even Hitler to take the latter course and they noted that the Hungarian government was responding to appeals for patience. A burst of diplomatic activity was, therefore, immediately initiated in

London to bring Warsaw into line with Berlin and Budapest. At 10 p.m. on 30 September, Halifax told Kennard to offer mediation between Warsaw and Prague. The Ambassador was to tell the Polish Foreign Minister, Colonel Jozef Beck, that, in the light of the Munich Agreement, his government would be 'very short-sighted and ill-advised to take the law into their own hands instead of basing their policy on the fact that the four Powers have undertaken to see that justice is done'. They would 'put themselves entirely in the wrong if they occupied any Czech territory before agreement to do so had been reached as in the case of the Sudeten territory'.[5] At 11.50 p.m., Newton was instructed to tell the Czech government of this move, but at the same time to urge them not 'to risk an armed clash with Poland over lesser questions of detail', such as the date of transferring territory they had already expressed a willingness to cede.[6]

Around 9.30 on Saturday morning Kennard made the offer of mediation to Count Michal Lubienski, Beck's *chef de cabinet*. Beck was said to be in bed and unavailable. While he was waiting for an answer, Kennard was instructed by telephone to get action on the ultimatum postponed and to warn the Polish government that they must confine themselves to discussion with the Czechs, referring the matter to the International Commission if discussion produced no result. At 11 a.m. Lubienski brought Kennard the Foreign Minister's response that it was now too late for mediation. The Ambassador, who had been given to understand unofficially by Lubienski that a request for postponement of military action by a few hours to allow for rapid diplomacy would be an acceptable means of averting conflict, refused to take Beck's answer seriously. He forecast international outrage if it became known that mediation had been rejected on such trivial grounds. During this exchange Beck himself phoned for him to call round. Kennard thought he was making some impression on Beck when another telephone call told the latter of a Czech request for the deadline to be postponed for an hour; a favourable reply, with some reservations, could then be expected. Beck, thereupon, became cordial, expressed appreciation of the British offer, and assured Kennard he would let him know if it could be of use.[7]

Unaware of this, ministers and officials in London were intensifying their efforts to get the post-Munich era off to a good start. They joined France and Italy in appeals for Germany to exercise its influence, and they responded to a French suggestion, backed by the American Ambassador in Paris, that Chamberlain should forestall Polish use of force by proposing a conference. Halifax and Cadogan worked out with Chamberlain a personal message from the Prime Minister to Beck, which was sent off at 11.30 a.m. Chamberlain did not suggest a conference, but he repeated the warning which had accompanied the offer of mediation and he told Beck how sure he was that 'while pressing Polish claims you must personally wish to contribute towards the development of the procedure of settlement by consultation and agreement which was initiated at Munich'. The message reached Kennard after his conversation with Beck. He sent it round by hand. Czechoslovakia accepted the Polish ultimatum shortly after midday; the only reservation was that details of transfer should be worked out jointly by military representatives. News of the surrender reached the Foreign Office at 1.30 p.m. It appeared that Czech understanding of what the post-Munich era really meant for weaker states corresponded with that in Warsaw rather than with that in London.[8] Count Edward Raczynski, the Polish Ambassador at London, was disturbed to find how cold and hostile the atmosphere became in the aftermath of this episode.[9]

It was, nevertheless, possible to seize on some slight uncertainty within this rapid sequence of events and remain optimistic. Kennard was inclined to think that Beck had been less intransigent than he afterwards claimed, and that mediation might have been welcomed had the Czechs stood firm; resentment at reports in the Polish press that his approach to Beck had been contemptuously brushed aside may have coloured his view. At the same time he did stress that Beck had been 'endeavouring to free himself from the control of the Great Powers as far as he could, and the mere mention of any Four Power Pact or Conference infuriates him'.[10] Ministers in London so inclined could ignore this latter observation and hope that the Teschen episode would prove an exception to the supposed Munich rule that peaceful discussion presided over by those Four Powers would henceforth prevail in European disputes. A month later, in Cabinet, Chamberlain was, indeed, still able to repeat that British foreign policy was 'one of appeasement: we must aim at establishing relations with the Dictator Powers which will lead to a settlement in Europe and to a sense of stability.'[11]

No one challenged the assertion, nor would it have occasioned much dissent in the country at large, even among critics of Chamberlain's recent diplomacy. In British political discourse, appeasement was still simply a goal which would have been achieved when all European governments accepted that treaty revision and other changes to the international system must be brought about only by discussion and negotiated compromise, not by force nor by open threats of force. It did not yet mean the futile use of conciliatory words and deeds to ward off aggression. Since the word still referred to the end sought rather than to the means employed, it was used uncontroversially in that sense by people with quite conflicting views as to what those means should be. Nor did any Minister challenge Chamberlain's implied assumption that further revision of the peace settlement in collaboration with the 'Dictator Powers' was an element of British foreign policy. Implicit, too, was the assumption that preference for peaceful change of that kind was an element in the foreign policies of Germany and Italy.

Hope that foreign policy could be left thus unchanged in dealing with a Europe which had been so radically changed was due to the absence of any convincing alternative course. Ever since the emergence in the later nineteenth century of new imperialist powers capable of building big navies, British policy-makers had been seeking means to lessen the vulnerability of their own scattered empire to any coalition of predators. Although divisions and rivalry among their potential enemies tended to inhibit such coalition-building, reluctance to rely upon that had understandably prevailed. From 1885 until the empire's dismantling, there appeared to be only two solutions which did not involve defence expenditure on a scale destructive of the British way of life. The preferred course was to settle old disputes and anticipate new ones by deals with other imperial powers, such as were negotiated with Germany (1890), the United States (1901), France (1904), Russia (1907) and which were still being sought with Germany on the eve of the First World War. This solution presupposed an accepted international order which facilitated the peaceful resolution of disputes. Such an order had prevailed during much of the nineteenth century, but it had broken down at intervals and finally collapsed between 1914 and 1918. Its post-war replacement, illusively reinforced by the League of Nations, faced renewed disruption in the 1930s by states essential to its working. Unless the British Government could restore international order by conventional diplomacy, their only serious alternative was to follow Bismarck's maxim, namely to ensure that one's own country formed part of the majority grouping among the Great Powers. As a partner in such a grouping, Great Britain was able to emerge victorious in both world wars. These two solutions to the problem could, of course, be attempted simultaneously, as before 1914 in the settlements mentioned and in alignment with former enemies France and Russia, and after 1945 through organisations such as UNO on the one hand and NATO on the other.

The problem was thus an old one. Both ways of solving it were well understood but very difficult to implement in the circumstances of the 1930s. If the embryonic coalition of Germany, Italy and Japan became a military reality, it could threaten simultaneously the United Kingdom, its Mediterranean communications and allies, its Asian empire and the Australasian dominions. Since all three Powers had broken with the League and had pursued their aims by force, the chances of their reverting more than occasionally to negotiated settlements were slim. The British Government could, therefore, place only little reliance on the first solution yet there was even less prospect of their combining with the governments of the three other Great Powers – France, Russia and America – to constitute the superior grouping in terms of manpower and resources. The governments in Paris, Moscow and Washington were, whatever their rhetoric, as shy of precise commitments which might draw them into general war as were Chamberlain and his colleagues.

Nor, if it came to war, were British leaders confident that even victory would solve for long this fundamental problem of defending their world-wide empire from a distant and relatively small island base. That island base might simply find itself endangered for a third time by the seemingly irrepressible power of Germany. In a conversation with the Russian Ambassador on 11 October 1938, Halifax had tried to counter Ivan Maisky's argument that the policy represented by the Munich Agreement would once more open the way to German domination of Central Europe and the Balkans, which the Kaiser's armies had come so close to securing. He said that the alternative policy of combined resistance to the point of war, which the Russian government had claimed to favour, 'suggested the necessity of having a war with Germany every fifteen or twenty years to prevent worse things happening'.[12] Halifax thereby implied that Germany's capacity and will to dominate much of Europe, and hence be in a position to threaten the British Isles, were independent of the aggressive inclinations of its present dictator. That capacity had survived defeat in 1918 and could be expected to do so again under Hitler's successors. Cadogan thought that he detected a comparable will to expand German territory and power among those opponents of Hitler who hinted at their readiness to organise his overthrow. He described a programme secretly transmitted to the Foreign Office in December 1938 by Karl Goerdeler as 'too much like *Mein Kampf*'.[13]

The essential problem, therefore, was how to convince Hitler or any post-Nazi leadership that it was in Germany's long-term interests to exercise restraint in its use of power and to rely on negotiated change within the international order, despite Germany's undoubted power to disrupt that order. Success would constitute 'European appeasement', the fashionable term for the traditional preference of British governments for a diplomacy of deals rather than one of alliances. After Munich, Chamberlain believed that the prospects for this were good.

Although the Prime Minister soon qualified the words he had used on returning from Munich about 'peace in our time',[14] he had no such reservations about the importance of the statement he had persuaded Hitler to join him in signing. He was convinced that Hitler had thereby committed himself to a process of consultation with him on matters which might affect the peace of Europe. He accepted that his goal of general appeasement and disarmament was still in the distance, and that it would require a protracted diplomatic process liable to be interrupted by dictatorial tantrums, but Hitler's readiness to put his name to the statement had made Chamberlain confident of reaching that goal. He assumed that, in any major crisis involving further revision of the Versailles settlement, Hitler would accept that Great Britain had an essential role to play. He did not seek to contain Germany by threats. He believed that Hitler had already realised the need for a sufficient degree of self-containment to avert a general war, and that his immediate and unqualified consent to the statement drafted by Strang and Chamberlain, with no German input, was gratifying evidence of this.

His optimism did have some rational basis. There were grounds for thinking that time was on his side and that, as Great Britain's strength steadily grew, Germany would be increasingly weakened by the economic problems associated with over-rapid rearmament. Hitler, as Chamberlain liked to say, would have missed the bus. The value which he attached to the statement of 30 September was, however, misplaced from the start. Even assuming that any pledge by Hitler could be relied upon, much less had been agreed than Chamberlain thought. The two men were 'resolved that the method of consultation shall be the method adopted to deal with any other questions that may concern our two countries'.[15] To Chamberlain it was obvious that changes to the distribution of power and territory in Central Europe were a British as well as a German concern. To Hitler, bent on unilaterally dismantling the Versailles settlement by displays of German power, it was equally obvious that they were not. He quickly regretted the Munich Agreement as inconsistent with his chosen course. He was determined to reject in future British claims to a role in the region and to confine consultation to matters more manifestly of mutual concern like the bilateral Naval Agreement of 1935. Chamberlain had incautiously inserted a reference to that into Strang's draft as an example of the type of agreement he would be seeking with Germany.[16] That was, indeed, the only kind of agreement which Hitler was at all likely to concede, and then only at the unacceptable price of Great Britain's self-exclusion from European affairs. As he had reiterated to Chamberlain at Godesberg, Anglo-German relations should rest on the formula 'you take the sea and we the land'.[17]

Chamberlain, quite unable to take seriously the implications of that, tried to push on quickly with the process of appeasement which he believed the Declaration embodied. He had been disappointed by Hitler's failure to make more than an offhand and unenthusiastic reference to him in public on 5 October, just when the sort of glowing tribute he had expected might have helped to still the criticism to which he was being subjected in the Commons. In another speech on 9 October, at Saarbrucken, Hitler's references to Great Britain were directly offensive. At the time Chamberlain was on holiday in Scotland. Soundings were made on his behalf at the German Embassy to try and stimulate more positive exchanges and, before the end of October, two of his Cabinet colleagues, Sir Samuel Hoare and Leslie Burgin, had informal discussions with the German Ambassador, Herbert von Dirksen.

On Wednesday 12 October von Dirksen reported to Berlin on the first of these approaches. He forwarded a memorandum by Dr. Fritz Hesse, a German press representative in London who assisted the Embassy's Press Attache. This recounted Hesse's conversation with George Steward, Chamberlain's Press Relations Officer, who routinely maintained this form of contact with the German Embassy on Chamberlain's behalf.[18] Steward told Hesse that the crucial decisions in September had been made by Chamberlain himself in consultation with his most intimate advisers, that at the end he had sought the opinion of none of his Cabinet colleagues, and that the Foreign Office had in the final days tried to sabotage Chamberlain's plans and commit Great Britain to war. He suggested that the German government should in future bypass the Foreign Office on major issues and deal directly with Chamberlain.

Steward's specific role in these approaches seems to have been to secure a change in the way German spokesmen and journalists covered relations with Great Britain. Instead of giving publicity to the opponents of Munich by their attacks, which smacked of interference in British affairs, they should stress German trust in Chamberlain as the man who reciprocated Germany's desire for friendship and who had gone to Munich in the interests of justice and not out of military weakness. Instead of boasting about the outcome of the Czech crisis and about Germany's military strength, they should help Chamberlain to remove the impression in Great Britain that the country's prestige had been damaged. By proclaiming that they never wished to go to war again with Great Britain or France, by keeping quiet about the colonial question for the time being and, above all, by enabling Chamberlain to claim some credit in the matter of arms reduction, they could stabilise pro-German tendencies in Britain and promote a climate of opinion suitable for a general election.[19] Steward's overture had no chance of success. Ribbentrop's object in instigating a hostile press campaign had been to polarise opinion in Great Britain and thereby ensure that demands for increased rearmament would be matched by opposition to it.[20] The State Secretary, Ernst Weizsacker, chose not to irritate Ribbentrop by passing on Hesse's memorandum[21] and he warned von Dirksen that a rapprochement with Britain was not currently on the cards.[22] This would have surprised Chamberlain who was assuming that the Munich Agreement had constituted a rapprochement.

During the last two weekends in October von Dirksen accepted separate invitations to meet with Hoare and Burgin. Hoare could reliably transmit Chamberlain's views while, according to Inskip, Burgin acted in Cabinet as 'a sort of chorus to the P.M.'[23] What they were reported as having told the Ambassador echoed Steward as regards the government's electoral prospects should Germany be persuaded to give low priority to colonies and high priority to arms limitation, but their main object was to pave the way for imminent proposals from Chamberlain himself. The Prime Minister wanted prompt action to halt advances in the range possible for bombers and to ban poison gas and the bombing of cities. This could lead on to a general settlement for which he believed the time was ripe. He was uncertain only whether to propose direct talks with Germany immediately or to wait until Czechoslovakia's other frontier disputes had been resolved. Von Dirksen did not disillusion them.[24]

At the Foreign Office Sir Alexander Cadogan, too, initially thought that some diplomatic advantage might accrue from the Munich Conference. 'Mustn't let this drop', he noted after talking at length with Sir Horace Wilson about the prospects. 'I've seen so many failures by letting initiatives cool off.'[25] During October he and some other senior officials set down their ideas as to what the outcome of the Czech crisis signified for British policy. Although Cadogan complained that this plethora of 'bright or dark ideas' was getting him muddled[26], on three important issues there was complete agreement or only one dissenting voice. First, all took for granted that German predominance in the countries which lay between Germany and Russia, and in much of the Balkans, would be henceforth unchallengable as far as Great Britain was concerned. Secondly, with the possible exception of Laurence Collier, Head of the Northern Department, they assumed that its manifest military superiority meant that Germany would have no need of war to enforce its economic demands on these neighbouring states. Largely informal economic imperialism was the form German predominance was expected to take. Thirdly, with the possible exception of Frank Ashton-Gwatkin, Head of the Economic Section within the Western Department, they saw accelerated rearmament as urgently necessary to restore Great Britain's diplomatic weight in the Iberian peninsula and in all countries bordering the Mediterranean. There, German predominance would constitute a direct threat to Great Britain's imperial communications and to its primacy in the Middle East. Apart from this common advocacy of a loosely defined diplomatic containment, they assessed the consequences for Great Britain of recent German aggrandisement in a variety of ways.[27]

The most divergent assessments were offered by Collier and Ashton-Gwatkin. Collier (29 October 1938) took the view that, under their present rulers, Germany and Italy were predatory states which were not susceptible to the give and take of normal diplomatic practice. Concessions merely encouraged them and gave momentum to their expansionist policies. It was too late to restore a balance of power in East and Central Europe, but they must both be forced to abandon hope of realising their wider ambitions, just as Russia's leaders had been forced to realise that world revolution was unobtainable. British policy should henceforth be directed to this end. Any colonial demands, for example, should be rejected and Great Britain should try to prevent a victory by Franco in Spain. If they pursued such a 'national' foreign policy, the Government could unite the country and dispel the popular suspicion that they were influenced by press barons, bankers and businessmen. Ashton-Gwatkin, by contrast, was ready to welcome German domination of the Danubian states. It would be their opportunity to be developed by German enterprise and organisation with a consequent rise in their living standards. He interpreted the German victory in relation to Czechoslovakia as a decisive historical event, foreshadowing a German United States of Middle Europe from which only Yugoslavia, Greece and Turkey might be able to stand aside. He saw no need for political alarm. Göring should be invited to London as representing the reasonable wing of the Nazi leadership, so that the colonial issue could be discussed as part of a broad economic plan for freer trade.

Despite their conflicting interpretations both men were optimists in their confidence that British interests could be protected by clear-cut and relatively simple policies. From a different viewpoint William Strang (10 October 1938) was equally confident that a policy of limited diplomatic containment would be successful. He believed that Germany was in no position to start a war against the two Western Powers and he saw no need to initiate any deals with Berlin. Cadogan, initially hopeful, took a gloomier view and quickly resigned himself to more modest objectives than either forcing Hitler to abandon his plans or to luring him into economic partnership. In his view British rearmament had not even reached the point whereby an effective foreign policy could be pursued at all. The most that could be done was to consider what policy would be appropriate when it did. Nor did he find that easy. 'I only know the one we have followed is wrong.'[28] International policing in defence of the Versailles settlement or at the behest of the League was obsolete. 'We are back in the old lawless Europe and have got to look out for ourselves.'[29] Pre-emptive war against Germany or Japan was not an option. Even when rearmament had restored Great Britain's diplomatic weight, Germany's inherently greater military strength meant that only a defensive policy based on naval and air power would be feasible. Nor must measures essential to keeping Germany away from direct access to the Mediterranean be so ostentatious as to provoke accusations of encirclement. Yet he was hopeful that eventually Germany would have to revert to a normal economy and that, meanwhile, its autarky need not threaten Great Britain's trading position. He wondered, though less hopefully, whether the idea, which he had entertained since returning to the Foreign Office in 1936, of a conference to revise what remained of the post-war treaty system might now be realised. Asking Hitler what he wanted and responding with reasonable concessions, broadcast to the German people, might cramp the dictator's style and undermine popular support for further expansion.

Thus, like his three colleagues, Cadogan was relatively relaxed in his post-Munich anticipations. A great crisis had passed, a premature war had been avoided and Germany was now expected to concentrate for some time on exploiting its newly won hegemony in Central Europe. More badly needed time had thereby become available for political, military and diplomatic preparations against a strengthened Germany. The threat from Germany, as with that from Japan, was serious but not imminent.

By contrast, the assessment by Gladwyn Jebb, Cadogan's Private Secretary, had a strong underlying pessimism despite its jaunty style. After glimpsing a possible future much on the lines of what was actually to obtain in the middle of 1942, Jebb considered four possible lines which policy might take in trying to avert such disaster. He was dismissive of collective security as currently impracticable, and of yielding to Hitler's European and colonial claims as an abdication of status which would risk imperial disintegration. A third possibility was simply the preservation of post-Munich Europe by giving what support was possible to France's remaining allies in Eastern Europe, by providing the Balkan states with economic aid on a scale which might encourage them to resist German diplomatic pressure, and by abandoning attempts to woo Hitler. He thought that this would appeal to the United States and to the smaller states, but he questioned whether Great Britain and France possessed the requisite strength to impose restraint on Germany. (His doubt was shown to have substance after the two allies tried to implement that kind of policy six months later.) The policy which he preferred, as offering the best chance of a real balance of power, was concentrating on the defence of the West. This would entail French renunciation of the pact with Russia, leaving Germany to expand into the Ukraine, and gradually enticing Mussolini away from his bond with Hitler. He characterised this as Machiavellian, but thought that the policy could be justified as being in defence of the empire, of freedom of thought and of Christian Europe. Presumably Jebb realised that this, the only option he deemed likely to succeed, was politically out of the question since he concluded by recommending a flexible and opportunistic approach little different from that of Cadogan. The pessimistic implication of his analysis was that the realities of power did not allow of a politically acceptable solution.

Also available to the makers of policy was the advice offered by the Secret Intelligence Service (SIS) during the Czech crisis. Dated 18 September 1938 and assumed to represent the views of its Chief, Admiral Sir Hugh Sinclair, it had provided reinforcement for Chamberlain's immediate policy but its bleak assessment of the future was altogether at odds with the Prime Minister's post-Munich optimism. It took for granted that Hitler's aim, during a temporary rapprochement with Great Britain, was to amass such military power that a network of vassal states would be created, beginning with those of Eastern and South-Eastern Europe and including thereafter the Baltic states and the Low Countries. Further vassal states would emerge when Germany had brought about the disintegration of Russia. From this position Germany would penetrate the Middle East and foment trouble for the British there and in the rest of their empire. As with Jebb's analysis, pessimism and Machiavellianism went hand in hand in the SIS memorandum. No other government could be accorded unqualified trust, so that rearmament must be pursued until Great Britain could fight a war regardless of its scale and with a minimum of reliance on outside help.

At the same time there must be built a rival network of states allied to Great Britain, or at least detached from Germany. This meant a permanent alliance with France and a relationship almost as close with Turkey, providing direct bulwarks against Germany. Great Britain must play on the pride of the fickle and unscrupulous Italians, and mediate between them and the French so as to draw Mussolini away from Hitler. As it was too early to spot the winner in Spain, it was important to be on good terms with both sides. There could be no banking on Russia, but it was necessary to keep on the right side of its leaders. The Palestine problem must be resolved in such a way as to satisfy the Arab world. The closest possible relations with the United States must be developed and, to this end, emotions aroused there by the fate of the Czechs should be exploited. Japan's special position in East Asia had to be recognised and friction kept to a minimum in an effort to restore the old friendship. Meanwhile it made sense to cultivate friendship with Germany as long as no sacrifice of principle or of vital interest was involved. There was, however, no point in offering Hitler colonies in return for good behaviour as his promises were worthless.[30]

Given its gloomy prognosis and its tone of ruthless realism, the SIS memorandum was inappropriately sanguine in at least two respects. It ignored the difficulties inherent in trying to be equally friendly towards states fundamentally at odds with one another, like France and Italy or Japan and the United States; and it shared the optimism of politicians and diplomats alike in assuming that, whatever the scale of Hitler's ambitions, there would now be the time and the opportunities to contain them without unleashing general war.

Thus, despite so many variations in the advice offered to Halifax from the worlds of diplomacy and intelligence, there was agreement as to the sphere of predominant influence which must be yielded to Germany and as to the urgency with which Great Britain must promote its own influence almost everywhere else. There was a vaguer consensus that British influence must not be excluded altogether from the German sphere. Halifax shared these views and the vagueness. The carefully drafted exposition of British policy sent on 1 November 1938 to Sir Eric Phipps, the British Ambassador at Paris, tends to confirm that a breezily colloquial report by the American Ambassador in London had not distorted the views expressed to him by Halifax less than a fortnight after Munich. In a conversation lasting an hour and a half on the afternoon of 12 October, Halifax conveyed to Joseph Kennedy the basic idea that Hitler should be left to dominate Central Europe, while British diplomacy concentrated its efforts in the maritime states of Europe and the Middle East and on relations with the Dominions, America and Russia. At the same time he advanced a notably optimistic interpretation of how international politics were likely to develop, with implications which were much less clear-cut.

In the first place, he assumed that further revision of the frontiers established by the peace treaties would be by consent and would not occasion international crises. He expected a relatively early transfer to Germany of Danzig and Memel by agreement with Poland and Lithuania, respectively. The recent British entanglement, with such risk of war, had been on account of France's alliances in Eastern Europe which, he implied, would now fade away or at least would no longer involve Great Britain. In the aforementioned letter to Phipps, Halifax assumed that Poland would 'fall more and more into the German orbit'. According to Kennedy, even if Hitler decided 'to go into Rumania it is Halifax's idea that England should mind her own business'. Halifax did not believe that Hitler wanted war with Great Britain and saw no reason why Great Britain should fight Germany as long as there was no direct threat to its imperial interests. Secondly, he saw the future of war as lying with the defensive. States would protect themselves on land with fortifications such as the Maginot Line, and Great Britain and France must similarly equip their countries against air attack, which the world would come to realise need never be decisive. Like his officials, Halifax obviously expected to have the time to create this degree of security while Hitler was consolidating his sphere of influence.[31]

The remark about Roumania was either quoted inaccurately by Kennedy or was misleadingly vague on Halifax's part, or perhaps both. The obvious meaning of 'to go into' Roumania was that of invasion, but Halifax shared the prevailing assumption in 1938 that even if there was any resort by Hitler to conquest and annexation, it would be confined, at least for the foreseeable future, to immediately neighbouring territories inhabited by Germans. The substantial but more distant German minority in Roumania was currently discounted as a pretext for military action. An alternative meaning was that of German economic penetration, but that was nothing new and its extent was thought to be very much Great Britain's business. A meaning consistent with the ideas in circulation at the Foreign Office was that even Roumania was part of that area of Europe in which German pre-eminence would not be contested. He certainly meant no more than that, since on the following day he wrote to Chamberlain urging the purchase, on explicitly political grounds, of 200,000 tons of Roumanian wheat. Both the Treasury and the Board of Trade were opposed to the purchase as uneconomic, but Halifax thought it 'very important at the present time that we should not appear disinterested in the Danubian countries'. It was not a matter of blocking German economic expansion but of maintaining 'a small foothold' in the Balkans.[32] He wanted immediate action ahead of a visit to Bucharest by the German Economics Minister. Otherwise the Roumanian government, in despair at Great Britain's indifference, might make concessions to Walter Funk disastrous for British trade.[33] The undefined extent of that small foothold and the reason why it was Great Britain's business to maintain it were part of the vagueness about South-Eastern Europe present in an otherwise clear re-statement of British policy. Kennedy might well have been confused.

This vagueness has appeared more important in retrospect than it did at the time, and has occasioned disputes as to whether British commercial policy was designed to resist Germany's advance in the region.[34] With regard to Turkey and Greece this was undoubtedly the case, but the 'small foothold' sought in Hungary, Roumania, Bulgaria and Yugoslavia did not constitute resistance. There was consensus as to the impossibility of resisting German political and commercial predominance in these four countries. At the same time there was consensus as to the importance of promoting British trade and influence in them. There was no contradiction in this. As is clear from the Foreign Office and SIS papers there was still near unanimity that beyond areas populated by Germans, Hitler intended to control neighbouring states in Central and Eastern Europe by forms of economic imperialism familiar to other Great Powers. On this interpretation, other Powers could expect some share in the trade of these regions, just as Germany had access to countries within their orbits. It made economic sense for Great Britain to maximise its commercial stake in the emerging German order. At the same time that commercial stake was expected to have political value as well.

This is clear from a Foreign Office memorandum of 10 November. Halifax had told the Cabinet on 19 October that this was being prepared, observing that over the previous fortnight there had been a number of claims that, unless the British Government financed some transaction or other, this or that Balkan country would fall under German domination. At that meeting he had, with Chamberlain's prior backing, secured approval for his plan to 'steady the position' by buying unwanted Roumanian wheat; the Food (Defence Plans) Department was to put it in storage.[35] With the 10 November memorandum he made the political case for pursuing such deals anywhere in the region whether they made commercial sense or not. He did stress how limited in scope such a policy must be. Even in May 1938, when it was still hoped that governments in South-Eastern Europe might look to the Western Powers rather than Germany, it had been realised that an actual anti-German bloc was out of the question unless the British and, perhaps, the French government had been ready to grant military guarantees, which they were clearly not prepared to do. Six months later it was obvious that nothing could prevent Germany from getting 'all she materially requires in these areas' with immense benefits for Germany's economy, diplomatic position and military potential. Nevertheless a moderate and reasonable aim for Great Britain would still be to encourage these countries to believe that a possible *point d'appui* other than Berlin did exist and that Great Britain's political and economic interests were going to be maintained and developed there.[36]

Halifax was taking it for granted that German economic predominance in a state would not mean the end of its political independence. The European system of highly unequal states had always meant that lesser governments were to varying degrees dependent on the good will of more powerful neighbours, while the major Powers had traditionally competed with one another in coralling minor Powers into their orbits. That competition had at times led to war, as in 1914, out of which a revamped system would emerge, as it had done in 1919. That such a system should persist was tacitly conceded. Lenin's attempt to supplant it with an entirely new international order had been successfully resisted and his successors had resigned themselves to working within the traditional system for the indefinite future. An unspoken assumption, to use James Joll's invaluable term, was that annexation of even a very minor state would be regarded as an attack on the States System itself, intolerable to other Powers unless they had conceded it by negotiation or had been forced to do so by military defeat. The consternation and hostility provoked in 1908 by Austria–Hungary's formal annexation of territory she had actually occupied and administered by international treaty for 30 years had been an example of how important the distinction was normally deemed to be between the finality of annexation and movable degrees of predominance. (Cadogan's diplomatic career began with clerical duties arising from this event.[37]) Even the ambitious sketch of Germany's war aims drawn up by its Chancellor in September 1914 had envisaged continental predominance through a system of economic control and vassal states, with relatively few annexations. While

Hitler had violated international treaties, his principal act of annexation so far had appeared to be welcome to most of Austria's inhabitants and hence arguably consistent with the principle of national self-determination which the European States System was now supposed to reflect. It could, though with dangerous ambiguity, be regarded as an exception to the rule.

Neither the British nor the French government expected predominant German economic and political influence in Hungary, Roumania, Bulgaria and Yugoslavia, or even in the newly truncated and militarily helpless Czechoslovakia, to foreshadow the end of their status as technically independent countries within the European system. As the various British memoranda showed, it was anticipated that Germany would continue to demand revision of the Versailles settlement by the mixture of threats and bargaining which had characterised the Sudeten crisis. Yet, more or less violent revision of treaties a decade or so after their conclusion was so familiar a feature of European history that this was only moderately alarming to those unconvinced by the assumptions of the League. The Treaties of Vienna (1815), Paris (1856) and Berlin (1878) had undergone forcible revision in 1830, 1871 and 1887, respectively, but in each case the Powers had, by skilful diplomacy, managed to accommodate within the system changes they were not prepared to resist by war, a process which Bismarck had described as drowning the question in ink.[38] It was a process recalled in the 1930s through major works of diplomatic history by Webster, Temperley, Seton-Watson, Medlicott and others, with whose gist, at least, Chamberlain and his colleagues were familiar. The Munich Agreement was only the most recent example. It was not surprising, though shocking to those who aspired to a different kind of normality, that Chamberlain and Halifax expected further such episodes involving Memel, Danzig and the Polish Corridor, and that these could be similarly concluded without war. The basic system of states which had emerged from war and revolution 20 years earlier was expected to survive territorial adjustments and shifts in the distribution of power, even such a major redistribution as Hitler was in the process of accomplishing. As long as that basic system survived, the promotion of British political and economic influence within it seemed a reasonable enough objective, even allowing for Germany's currently autarkic practices.

Halifax had concluded in the weeks immediately after Munich that in South-Eastern Europe 'we are not in a position to prevent Germany realising the greater part of her ambitions'. This was, he argued, because a diplomatic offensive in the region, involving alliances, military conversations and the supply of arms, would almost certainly lead to war and would, in any case, be feasible only in the case of Turkey and possibly of Greece. It would be 'folly to enter into an unequal race'. Yet while Great Britain could not prevent German preponderance in the region, it might be possible to modify its effects if British political influence was strengthened there 'by the judicious encouragement of trade, industry and capital investment'. This would require unorthodox use of financial and economic power, such as encouraging private business interests to develop trade somewhat in the manner of Germany, even if it meant guaranteeing them against financial loss. Companies should be encouraged and helped to buy oil, wheat and tobacco even if the reason for doing so was more political than commercial, and the law should be changed to allow credits when exporting munitions. Predictable German complaints of encirclement would simply have to be met by reassurance and, eventually, by offers of co-operation as part of the 'general economic appeasement in Europe', but the matter was too urgent to allow German protests to deter British efforts.[39]

Vagueness was present less in the way British policy in the region was conceived than in the actual measures by which it was to be implemented. For example, Halifax suggested helping British firms to buy Roumanian oil and wheat, and to participate in the construction of a Black Sea naval base, but in practice he intended to wait for King Carol to identify Roumanian needs during his forthcoming visit to Great Britain. Inability to help Roumania in face of any German threats would, he pointed out, limit Great Britain's role in any case. Yugoslavia's problems in relation to Germany seemed to him less urgent and were more likely to be dealt with by its government leaning towards Italy rather than towards Great Britain. In the case of Bulgaria, it was probably too late to do much in face of offers already made by Germany, but any opportunities arising from Turkey's relationship with Bulgaria would be taken. Hungary's spirit of independence should be encouraged, though reducing duty on the import of Hungarian turkeys was the only example Halifax could bring to mind for promoting British influence there. Much, then, remained vague in the sphere of action, but the importance which Halifax attached to even a small political foothold through some undramatic but useful economic role was unquestionable. In the conclusion to the memorandum he contended that '... it may well be essential to our ultimate security to promote our political influence by economic measures in South-Eastern Europe to-day; or perhaps it would be fairer to say that to permit our political influence in these countries now to go by the board may well have, in the long run, a most serious effect upon that security'. As in other pronouncements in the first six weeks after Munich, Halifax shared the view that there was a long run in which to operate.[40]

This redefinition of Great Britain's role in South-Eastern Europe was the only marked innovation in policy immediately following the Munich Agreement, and even this had been long in the making. The full restoration of Germany as a Great Power had now been accomplished, but this had been anticipated since the autumn of 1933; defence policy and diplomacy had thereafter been devised with this in mind, and the various Foreign Office appraisals of October 1938 were the fruit of lively internal debates in the intervening years.[41] Important moves in relation to Portugal and Palestine during October may indicate an added impetus given by the crisis to business already in hand, but these developments would have been unsurprising had there been no crisis in Central Europe.

The traditional alliance with Portugal had acquired added importance since the outbreak of civil war in Spain. It was recognised in London that a 'nationalist' victory giving rise to a regime like that of Italy might cost Great Britain the use of Gibraltar, in which case Portuguese air and naval facilities in Madeira, the Azores and Cape Verde would become crucial to the defence of British shipping.[42] Yet the eagerness of Germany to supply the arms sought by the Portuguese government in case the outcome in Spain threatened their own security was in sharp contrast to the hesitancy of the British, whose support Antonio Salazar preferred but whose own shortages left them with little to spare. At the end of June 1938, the Committee of Imperial Defence (CID) had reflected that 'our efforts to keep Portugal within our orbit have not hitherto been too successful.'[43] More definite offers of support were needed; even deferred payment for arms, traditionally distasteful to the Treasury, might be considered if this would 'turn the scale between keeping Portugal within our own orbit or the partial surrender of our position to Germany'.[44] The military mission, sent to Portugal at its government's request in February 1938, made an interim report in September. Their recommendations of political, military and financial help were backed in a report of the Chiefs of Staff on 14 October and accepted by the CID on 20 October.[45] On 28 October the news was passed to the Portuguese government, whose reported alarm at the prospect of a general European war had been conveyed to London.[46] This may have contributed to the timing of the reassurance but the decision itself had arisen out of much earlier concern at the developing situation in Europe.

In the case of Palestine, the Munich crisis similarly gave added point to a reappraisal already deemed necessary by the Foreign Office. As the Mandatory Power, Great Britain had tried unsuccessfully to reconcile Arab and Jewish aspirations with the result that an unanticipatedly large number of British troops was required to deal with the violence of militant elements from both communities. A Royal Commission had in July 1937 recommended partition. Jewish reaction was at best lukewarm, the Palestinian Arabs opposed it, and there was acute awareness in the Foreign Office of the hostility displayed by neighbouring Arab rulers who were the targets of German and Italian diplomacy. At the Colonial Office, officials retained their enthusiasm for partition but that of the Colonial Secretary, Malcolm MacDonald, began to fade.[47] A Cabinet decision in December 1937 to despatch another commission to Palestine signalled a likely retreat. This did not prevent renewed Arab insurgency, which was at its height during the European crisis of September 1938. In the event of war, control of Palestine could have been crucial to the defence of Britain's position in the Middle East, which was in turn crucial to imperial defence as a whole.[48] That partition would not pacify Palestine had been clear before the events of September underlined the case for its abandonment. In November, the government reverted to attempts at reconciliation and compromise.[49]

There was also enhanced anxiety about German influence on the governments of Italy and France. A premature concession to Italy was one consequence of this. Mussolini's contribution to the Munich settlement had encouraged Chamberlain to believe that Italian influence might be brought to bear upon Hitler with regard to other European problems, while Halifax wanted at least to draw Mussolini back to a more intermediary stance between Germany and the Western Powers. Great Britain's continued refusal to bring into force the Anglo-Italian Agreement of 16 April 1938, dealing with sources of tension between the two Powers, seemed to stand in the way of further co-operation. Of particular value to Italy had been Great Britain's willingness at last to give official recognition of the Italian empire in Ethiopia. The British Government had, however, made it clear that 'a settlement of the Spanish question' was a prerequisite for the coming into force of the Agreement. What would constitute a settlement was left unclear, though one element was to be acceptance of a British plan for the withdrawal of foreign 'volunteers'. At the time of signing the Agreement, the victory of Franco's forces had appeared imminent, but, as this prospect faded, the matter of definition became important. In June, Chamberlain had interpreted 'settlement' to mean merely 'something which could be shown to have eliminated or to be in a process of eliminating the Spanish question as a source of international friction'.[50] Now, under persistent Italian pressure during October, it was decided to interpret even a partial withdrawal of Italian infantry from Spain as meeting that revised condition.[51] The Cabinet agreed on 26 October that the Agreement should be brought into force within the following few weeks.[52] Chamberlain promptly received what seemed to him a worthwhile reward. His wish to visit Rome in January was communicated to the British Ambassador on 31 October and Lord Perth successfully broached the matter when the Agreement was formally brought into force on 16 November.[53]

Unease within the Foreign Office as to France's relations with Germany had already surfaced during the summer. Officials had wondered whether the Quai d'Orsay's reticence about a visit in July by a French general to Hitler betokened the visit's insignificance or the reverse. They had noted also a visit in August by senior officers of the French Air Force to their German counterparts, and a press report of Pierre-Etienne Flandin's arguments for a Franco-German rapprochement.[54] After the Munich crisis, the contrast between Hitler's cordiality towards the French government, as reported by Phipps, and his surliness towards Great Britain's leaders gave greater cause for concern while enhancing uncertainty as to what it all meant and what to do about it. When asking Oliver Harvey, his Private Secretary, to draft a letter to Phipps on lines they had been discussing, Halifax observed that it would be 'interesting to see whether there is any truth in certain indications that are reaching us to the effect that the French government are *ready to do a deal with Germany behind our backs*'. (Underlining by either Halifax or Harvey.) Yet when Harvey rendered this more diplomatically but still accurately as 'the French Government might be tempted in certain circumstances to conclude a direct agreement with Germany at our expense', Halifax modified it further to 'the French Government might be tempted by German intrigues to drift apart from H.M.G.' The suspected initiative was thereby attributed to Germany rather than France.[55] When Phipps sent news on 8 November of Germany's proposed agreement with France and of Bonnet's assurances that France's obligations to Great Britain and Belgium would be unaffected, Foreign Office opinion was divided. Strang saw no objection and thought that European détente would be brought appreciably closer if Germany offered agreements to all its neighbours. Cadogan was 'almost tempted to hope that there may be nothing Machiavellian in this move, if Herr Hitler's past performances had not accustomed one to suspect something of that kind'.[56]

Certainly the unease felt in London reflected only the wish for a parallel rapport with Germany. In trying to get into shape the letter to Phipps, Halifax stressed that a Franco-German rapprochement would be welcomed as long as what it involved was no more likely to be inimical to British interests than an Anglo-German rapprochement would be to those of France.[57] At Cabinet on 7 November, he made clear that he wanted to canvass actively for just such a rapprochement. In discussing an Admiralty proposal to lay down twenty escort vessels for convoy duty, about which Germany would have to be notified under the terms of the Naval Agreement, Halifax suggested that in the wider context of relations with Germany 'steps should be taken in the near future to prevent the Munich wax setting too hard before we had taken some further action towards implementing our policy of appeasement'. He thought that the German government might be asked for suggestions as to what could be discussed.[58] It is clear that in the first week of November the alarms experienced since March were thought by the Foreign Secretary to have been dispelled by the Munich Agreement, and that he sought the sort of relationship with Germany which was being forged by the French. Hitler's currently unpromising mood was not seen by Halifax, any more than by Chamberlain, as a reason for abandoning the policy of European appeasement.

3
The Challenge of Barbarism

By the first week in November, 1938, the British Government had reverted to the systematic defensive preparations combined with patient diplomacy which they had deemed appropriate before the recent crises. Within a month, between 11 November and 11 December, this policy had been once more thrown into confusion by developments which undermined the assumptions upon which it was based.

The first of these developments was the savage onslaught against German Jews and their property, organised by Goebbels and other leading Nazis, in the early hours of Thursday 10 November. There followed measures meant to exclude them altogether from the economic life of Germany. Witnessed by foreign diplomats, journalists and travellers, the *Kristallnacht* was unusual among atrocities in that the essential facts were published to the world within a few hours and were beyond the controversy and incredulity with which such events are often greeted. Nazi leaders themselves had every interest in the intimidating effects of publicity as part of their campaign to make life so intolerable for Jews as to drive them into exile or worse. G.E.R. Gedye, the *Daily Telegraph*'s correspondent in Central Europe, noted that an article on 23 November in the official organ of the S.S. claimed the object of the attacks on the Jews to have been so to impoverish them that they would be driven to crime and then 'to extirpate them with fire and sword' as criminals.[1]

Public debate in Great Britain about Hitler's Germany was transformed by this pogrom. Against the post-war background of communist and fascist regimes, the early years of Hitler's rule had been widely regarded as constituting an already familiar mixture of brutality and radical change. Now that three of the five Great Powers of Europe were dictatorships and French democracy was seen as vulnerable, regimes of this kind had apparently become a fact of international life that it was futile simply to deplore. The main concern was whether National Socialism would be so successful as to restore Germany's power and will to threaten its neighbours. Initially, distaste for the repressive measures was often tinged with respect for the evidence of economic recovery, and even the remilitarisation of the Rhineland had been treated with some degree of sympathy. It was the annexation of Austria and the threat to Czechoslovakia which brought about a general revulsion. Reports by foreign journalists – before their expulsion – of the violence inflicted on Jews and on political opponents in Vienna had a profound effect. Nor was the public mood of anger and alarm in the spring and summer of 1938 confined to events in Central Europe. It had already been fuelled by horrific reports of Japanese atrocities in China, continuing carnage in Spain, and recurrent slaughter within and beyond Russia's political and military establishment. This mounting and murderous disorder across Europe and Asia was seen by many to represent something more than the by-product of traditional power politics. The idea that Western civilisation itself was again in peril took hold among commentators on international affairs.

The view that Hitler's regime, in particular, was alien to Western civilisation had been urged upon ministers, officials and diplomats as early as the autumn of 1933 by Sir Maurice Hankey, Cabinet Secretary and Secretary to the Committee of Imperial Defence. In his evaluation of the new regime after a visit to Germany, he argued that Hitler's hatred of the Jews had already resulted in measures 'inconceivable in a civilised country'. The aim of Goebbels was to arouse 'fanatical and hysterical passions' and to suppress 'the bourgeois virtues of peace and order'. Since Hitler's advent to power, 'nationalism has become exacerbated into militarism'. As soon as he and his wife left Germany, they both 'had an astonishing sense of having come back to civilisation'.[2] At the same time, a wider public had been increasingly warned of threats to their civilisation from the new barbarism within Europe. In October 1933, Leonard Woolf had edited a collection of essays entitled *The Intelligent Man's Way to Prevent War*. The recent war was seen as the first big step on 'the road back to barbarism'; then, after a brief interval, 'the process of breakdown or break up of European civilization began again' with the suppression of liberty, barbarous persecution and the glorification of war in Italy and Germany. Not that the distinguished contributors, such as Norman Angell, Gilbert Murray, Viscount Cecil and Harold Laski had much to offer by way of a remedy apart from the spread of socialism or support for the League. In 1934, the first volume of Arnold J. Toynbee's *A Study of History* fuelled debate on the rise and fall of civilisations, and on whether Western civilisation could respond to the challenge it now faced.

By 1938, a sense of urgency had entered the debate. The *New Statesman*, for example, published a stream of articles and letters, which, however wide their disagreement as to the precise significance of current events, were mostly cast in just such apocalyptic terms. A leading article on 19 March 1938 had argued that no concessions would deflect the German and Italian governments from their goal of irresistible military power 'over the whole middle region of the Old World'. Lest conscience over the errors of 1919 should make cowards of us, moves should be made to rid Czechoslovakia of its Sudeten Germans, but that should be accompanied by unambiguous declarations of military support for both the Czechs and the French against Germany. 'If Western Civilisation means to make any stand, before all the strategical keys are in its enemies' hands, it must call a halt before Prague and Barcelona.' In the following issue on 26 March, John Maynard Keynes, who also wanted a reconstructed frontier for the country he already called Czecho-Slovakia, called similarly for a stand in defence of Western civilisation, even though he believed that 'appearing formidable' through 'the power of courageous bearing, the majesty of right action' would be sufficient to deter the enemy: 'the lion's roar is worth more than his power to spring.' He thought that Churchill realised this, while Chamberlain did not. He had no doubt as to what was at stake:

> We are learning to honour more than formerly the achievements of our predecessors and the Christian civilisation and fundamental laws of conduct which they established in a savage world. We are seeing and enduring events worse than which have not been seen and endured since man became himself.

On 19 October 1938, Victor Gollancz, founder of the Left Book Club, confessed to Leonard Woolf that recent events had undermined even his belief that dictatorship in the Soviet Union was justified as the only means of bringing about a socialist society. He was now convinced that liberal ideas such as tolerance and open-mindedness, freedom of thought and discussion had to be defended immediately and without any compromise from whatever direction the threat came. Otherwise, he foresaw 'the extinction of everything decent in humanity'. He asked Woolf to write for the Club a defence of Western civilisation; the result, enraging many members, was *Barbarians at the Gate* (1939).[3]

The organised onslaught against Jews in a major European capital came thus as the latest in sequence of appalling developments. It was the more readily interpreted as a barbaric challenge to Western civilisation in that it took place in circumstances of internal and external peace. There could be no pretence that it was some uncontrollable accompaniment of war or revolution. On 14 November there was only a brief discussion in the Commons as to where Germany's Jews might find refuge, as it was the week devoted to debating the King's Speech. Press denunciation was immediate. The Berlin correspondent of *The Times*, for example, reported (11 November)'scenes of systematic plunder and destruction which have seldom had their equal in a civilised country since the Middle Ages.' A leader commenting on the report observed: 'No foreign propagandist bent upon blackening Germany before the world could outdo the tale of burnings and beatings, of blackguardedly assaults upon defenceless and innocent people, which disgraced that country yesterday.' In one of numerous letters to the paper, Margot Oxford forecast that any future war would not be lost by Hitler's soldiers but won by 'moral, spiritual and material forces in which every nation of humanity and right feeling will join'. (11 November) A speech by Clement Attlee compared the waves of indignation at this 'appalling outrage of barbarism' with those in response to the Bulgarian and Armenian atrocities.[4] Detailing the 'orgy of destruction and terror' in his despatch to the Foreign Office, Ogilvie-Forbes undiplomatically described those who had 'let loose the forces of mediaeval barbarism' as 'the insensate gang at present in control of Nazi Germany'.[5] Letters to *The Times* stressed the impossibility now of any colonial restitution by which non-German peoples would be handed over to the present German regime, and a leading article on 16 November endorsed this view.

The weeklies had more time to ponder on the events, but their comments were essentially the same. Typical was a *Spectator* article (18 November) on 'The New Barbarism'. 'Never before in living memory, or for generations before that, has brute force divorced from every canon of morality been erected into a national policy on a scale comparable to this, and there are no precedents to determine the attitude to be adopted towards it.' Most normally minded people would expect the government 'to reduce to the minimum of strictly official relations all contact with a country whose rulers apply the methods of barbarism in the midst of a civilised continent.' Nor was this a fleeting reaction. *The Economist* observed on 24 December that 'the outbreak of revolting barbarism and calculated cruelty against the Jews has put the Nazis once and for all beyond the pale of modern civilisation.'

An example of how quickly attitudes could change can be found in successive editions of *Across the Frontiers* by Sir Philip Gibbs, famous on both sides of the Atlantic as a war correspondent and, subsequently, as a prolific commentator on international affairs. He was personally convinced that war could and should be avoided, but he tried to be detached about contemporary currents of opinion, especially in Great Britain and Germany because in 1913 he had been rashly reassuring about 'peace-mindedness' in Germany. In the late 1930s he sampled opinion much more carefully among major public figures, personal friends, casual acquaintances and total strangers. He realised that his own optimism about the prospects for European appeasement was less widely shared than he had hoped within Great Britain, and he attributed this above all to Nazi persecution of the Jews. In a chapter on 'The Problem of the Jews', written before the *Anschluss*, he was understanding of his liberally minded compatriots who regarded Nazi conduct 'as an attack on civilisation itself and upon all the liberties and victories of the mind gained by civilisation'. This did not convince him, however, that such an attack should be met by war, which he believed this time would destroy civilisation altogether. He called instead for a change of attitude in Germany and elsewhere towards Jews, and he tried to make the message more persuasive by casting it in jocular terms. The 'Jewish problem' could not be solved by killing them all or expelling them all as this might shock public opinion! 'Be reasonable in your anti-Semitism!', he pleaded; the Jews should be given a chance of keeping body and soul together.[6]

During the autumn of 1938, he prepared a new edition to take account of the *Anschluss* and the Czech crisis; in view of the intensified suffering inflicted on Jews in the course of these, he excised the ironic pleas altogether as tasteless. Having thus revised the chapter before the events of November, he then, to take account of them, added a passage in which his tone and attitude changed dramatically. Since the re-writing of this chapter, he observed, 'more frightful things have happened'. He wrote of 'the flame of indignation which swept England and the United States on account of this inhumanity'. What the Nazis had done had 'spoilt all the hopes of those who had been working for better relations between Germany and England for the sake of European peace'. He now described the Jewish situation in Germany as 'a test case of civilisation'. If we could not protect the Jews, if we allowed them to be hunted and degraded, 'then our civilisation is a mockery and deserves to perish'.[7]

This construing, by journalists and other writers, of Nazi behaviour at home and abroad as a threat to Western civilisation became established in public discourse and remained so until the ending of the regime. It was a principal justification for war against Germany, and the overthrow of Nazism, rather than of Germany, was a central war aim. Over-simplification was obviously involved. Tyranny, persecution and aggression had been recurrent features of Western – as of every other – civilisation; nor was there anything surprising about the refusal by a government to pay even lip-service to the new rules of international conduct, which had been optimistically devised in the aftermath of the Great War to eliminate these. What was seen at the time, however, as distinguishing Western civilisation above others was the persistent survival over 2500 years – despite long periods of institutional intolerance – of scientific enquiry into the natural world and rational debate about human behaviour, culminating in their almost universal vindication since the eighteenth century. The ambivalence of many on the Left towards Russian Communism and on the Right towards Italian Fascism was excused by the lip service paid by each regime to those traditions. Nazism was, by contrast, their declared enemy and was also the enemy of Judaism and Christianity, both of which had managed an accommodation with science and humanism. Journalists experience sooner than most any manifestation of tyranny, and they had been quick to assess the wider implications when they directly observed intolerance and irrationality, violently expressed by a Western government with the strongest army in Europe. It was not surprising that the November pogrom was immediately interpreted by so many of them as the most spectacular evidence to date of Nazism's hostility to Western civilisation.

Ministers likewise registered anger and alarm in the Foreign Policy Committee (FPC) on Monday 14 November and at Cabinet two days later, when the pogrom's implications for British policy were examined. The Committee had been summoned at short notice to consider recent intelligence reports of Hitler's hostile intentions towards Great Britain, and the attack on the Jews was simultaneously discussed as yet another aspect of the Nazi threat to the European order. On Sunday evening and for an hour before the FPC assembled at 6 p.m. on Monday, Cadogan had briefed Halifax about five reports from German sources which, if true, rendered nugatory the proposal for fresh steps towards appeasement, which the Foreign Secretary had made so optimistically in Cabinet just a week before.[8] In response to this double manifestation of Nazi malevolence, Halifax reverted to the mood which had seized him after the Godesberg meeting. He told the FPC that he no longer expected at the forthcoming conversations in Paris to discuss how best to follow up the Munich discussions. The happenings of the past few days, together with reports that Hitler now regretted a deal for which Chamberlain had got the credit, and that he no longer believed that Great Britain had been serious about going to war, had changed the situation. Halifax was, therefore, inclined to take seriously some disturbing reports from secret German sources, especially since four out of the five sources seemed to him to have provided generally accurate information in July and August, and since all five conveyed essentially the same message.

Halifax read to the Committee extracts from each report, all to the effect that Hitler and his more extreme advisers now believed that the British Empire was vulnerable to partition by Germany, Italy and Japan. The fifth report was derived from instructions given by Ribbentrop to an informant, and Halifax declared it to be quite certain that this particular information was correct. According to Ribbentrop, Hitler would promote the empire's disintegration by cultivating friendship with France at Great Britain's expense; by aggravating British difficulties in the Near East, while strengthening Germany's position in South-Eastern Europe; and by co-operating with Japan and Italy to undermine Great Britain's position in the Far East and in the Western Mediterranean. There was now no need to seek the return of colonies, which would fall to Germany anyway when the time was ripe. Nor need the Naval Agreement be abrogated; it could be allowed to run its course for the next two years as Germany had still to build to the maximum allowed under its terms. Halifax had reluctantly concluded from all this that there was now no point in resuming conversations with 'the crazy persons who had managed to secure control of the country'. The government's immediate objective must instead be 'to correct the false impression that we were decadent, spineless and could with impunity be kicked about'. Resolution and a show of strength might also encourage 'moderates' around Hitler at the expense of the 'extremists'. He had always tried to take a calm view, but the warnings could not be ignored. As an immediate measure he proposed a compulsory National Register, which would spark enthusiasm at home and create the right impression abroad. Aircraft production should be increased by new working practices.

The ensuing discussion centred more on the plight of the German Jews than on the secret reports. Ministers waxed indignant, but they floundered when they tried to find means of either helping the Jews or penalising Germany. Hoare, Simon and Halifax all stressed the danger of failing to act against Germany on behalf of the Jews. Hoare feared that the Commons and the country might get out of hand. Simon thought that doing nothing would confirm the Nazis in their view of British ministers as spineless and afraid. Halifax had been appraised of the anger in the United States at Great Britain's apparent passivity in face of the pogrom; Hitler might be reinforced in his belief that the democracies would never do anything. Yet the Committee were at a loss as to what could be done. Recalling the Evian Conference on Refugees would result only in verbal protest. America would not participate in economic sanctions. Even helping the Jews directly would become a much bigger problem, as a mass exodus could be expected of Germany's Jewish population, now greatly increased by its territorial acquisitions. Various possible destinations within the empire were to be considered, but, with an Arab revolt still in progress, Palestine could not be prominent among them. It was decided to ask Washington if part of Great Britain's migration quota could be assigned to German Jews. In practice, no obstacles were placed in the way of Jewish refugees from Nazism entering Great Britain.[9] Discussion of Halifax's proposals for anticipating German aggression was scarcely more productive, turning mostly on whether a National Register, or something similar, should be compulsory or voluntary. It was decided to consult Sir John Anderson, Lord Privy Seal, in charge of air raid precautions. The Prime Minister proposed to counter the predicted trend in German policy by broadcast propaganda and by trying to detach Mussolini from the German orbit.[10]

The Cabinet meeting on Wednesday, 16 November did little to advance matters. Chamberlain and Halifax reiterated that any approach to Germany in search of a general settlement was out of the question for the time being. The prospect of restoring colonies to Germany could no longer be aired, and circumspection had been urged on the pro-German South African defence minister, Oswald Pirow, during his forthcoming visit to Berlin. Halifax reported a considerable stiffening of the French attitude to the question. He dwelt on the powerful international repercussions of the pogrom, and on the blame being attached by American public opinion to British policy for failing to forestall it. The government should now accelerate defence preparations and, in its dealings with Germany, encourage moderate opinion at the expense of the extremists. Immediate action must be taken to help the Jews. What that should be remained as unclear as at the earlier meeting, despite the presence this time of the Cabinet's only Jewish member, Leslie Hore-Belisha, and of Walter Elliot, a close associate of Balfour's niece, Baffy Dugdale, in support of Zionism. All that emerged was the assigning of Halifax, Hoare, MacDonald and Winterton to frame a declaration of urgent *intent* to take action.[11]

During the discussion, Elliot had warned of the danger of another electoral campaign reminiscent of Gladstone's in Midlothian, so high was public expectation of government action to relieve the suffering and humiliation inflicted on German Jews. Whether the British public at large was so instantly incensed is unclear. Attitudes towards British Jews ranged widely. The results of by-elections held shortly before and after the pogrom can be variously interpreted.[12] Yet public interest in foreign affairs had been traditionally slow to ignite and had understandably lapsed once the immediate threat of war had been lifted by the Munich Agreement. Ministers could not afford to assume that these new press reports would have no impact. Lord Zetland, Secretary of State for India, had direct experience of popular reaction. Addressing a rally at Torquay on 18 November, he was impressed by the volume of applause he received on promising that the government would help the Jews.[13] As he sat down, he was handed the result of the Bridgwater by-election. Vernon Bartlett, running as an Independent candidate but with Labour and Liberal support, had won after a campaign attacking the government's policy towards Germany. Whether or not that explained the scale of the Conservative defeat, Zetland and his colleagues could not have dismissed the likelihood of the pogrom having undermined the popularity of appeasement, even had they been so minded.

The record of these two meetings shows that active pursuit of the goal of appeasement had been at least temporarily abandoned. The implications of this were anything but clear-cut. Co-operation with France was to be enhanced in face of German truculence. Relations with Mussolini were to be cultivated in the hope that he might persuade Hitler to look favourably on a general European settlement of what the latter denied were 'European' problems. Both processes were likely to be slow and of uncertain outcome, and neither could be expected to moderate Hitler's hostility towards either Great Britain or the Jews. Halifax realised this. When one of his colleagues suggested that a refusal to talk about Germany's colonies would be an effective form of pressure, he retorted that the refusal would have to last until either the German government mended their ways or they ceased to be Nazis.[14]

Sir Orme Sargent was disturbed by the inadequacy of this reaction. The Assistant Under-Secretary at the Foreign Office was irritated by ideas canvassed by Frank Ashton-Gwatkin and Strang at the end of that week. Ashton-Gwatkin's recent welcoming of the long-term prospect of German economic predominance in Central and South-Eastern Europe might be partly explained by his clandestine contacts with opponents of Nazism, whom he expected to be managing that process after their overthrow of Hitler. On 19 November, taking his cue from Karl Goerdeler, he urged the importance of conducting policy towards Germany in such a way as to help, or at least not to hinder, the German opposition. Time, he believed, was not on Hitler's side, because the German economic structure would not be able to stand the strain much longer. The Nazi regime was 'desperately hard-up' after the extraordinary expenditure of the past year; very high taxation and the scale of the fines levied on the Jewish population signified its difficulties. Hitler still believed, however, that the Western democracies were too weak to resist his demands and that a still more menacing attitude would bring the rapid results he needed. Ashton-Gwatkin argued, presumably unaware of the decisions earlier in the week, that a further concession to the Nazis now would strengthen the power of the extremists, while any sign of a determination to resist them would correspondingly weaken their hold. He saw the first three months of 1939 as critical on this analysis. Strang's minute of the same day agreed that concessions were currently inappropriate, the more so in that public recognition of Germany's predominant role in Central and South-Eastern Europe had put Great Britain in a strong moral position. By this he meant, presumably, that criticism of German policy in other respects would appear reasonable to the rest of the world and to non-Nazi opinion within Germany. He went on to define what he saw as obvious British policy now that the spirit of Munich had faded away. 'If Germany goes further in Europe, she brands herself as aggressive and expansionist. We may not be able to arrest her progress in Central and Eastern Europe: but we ought not to yield anything that it is within our power to withhold from her.'

On Monday 21 November, Sargent derided the optimism of Ashton-Gwatkin and the vagueness of Strang. He deplored reliance on yet another prophecy that the German economy would be unable to stand the strain much longer, and pointed out that what had strengthened the extremists was spectacular Nazi successes rather than British concessions. There was now probably even less chance of preventing such successes than in the past. He assumed that it was colonies which Strang wanted to withhold from Germany lest the extremists be strengthened; since these would be central to any general understanding with Germany, did this mean that appeasement was to be abandoned simply 'in vague hope that if instead we continue to sulk and quarrel with Germany, she will suffer more than we shall in consequent insecurity and irritation?' Yet Sargent did not suggest the means by which Hitler's run of successes might be halted, presumably because he could see none available as circumstances stood.

Neither could Cadogan or Halifax, who joined in the 'minute conversation'. Cadogan (21 November) agreed with Strang. He insisted that the government had not abandoned appeasement, though German actions, 'deliberately or not', had made it currently impossible. He suggested that there had always been two hopes in pursuing the policy, namely that it would either succeed or that, if Germany rebuffed it, there would be the tactical advantage of putting Germany in the wrong and Great Britain in the right, 'a position we have not always occupied'. Halifax (22 November) defined 'our line for the present' as being no less anxious than before for friendly relations but that the absence of reciprocity had made for difficulties which had been enhanced by recent events. If the question of colonies came up, it should be made clear to the German government that discussion was quite impossible 'in the present atmosphere which they had created'. Meanwhile, 'press on with rearming'.[15]

It also meant pressing on with the well-established policy of developing ever closer relations with those maritime states crucial to the security of Great Britain and its imperial communications. One aspect of that policy was currently under review. On 17 November, at a meeting of the Committee of Imperial Defence, Halifax renewed his argument, countered by Stanley for the Board of Trade, that arms should be supplied free to any such states unable to afford them. He was supported by Hoare, who pointed to Germany's success in 'digging herself in' by making countries dependent on the supply of German spare parts for their armaments; not to compete would be to accept German domination in that sphere. Hore-Belisha agreed that the policy was needed to 'press our strategic influence in the world'. Present was the Australian High Commissioner, Stanley Bruce, who argued that the detrimental effects to Great Britain of the German arms drive would also affect the Dominions. A decision was postponed, but circumstances were giving Halifax the better of the argument.[16] Even if made more uniformly successful by such means, this policy of securing much of the periphery would, of course, still leave Hitler ample room for those further spectacular successes which Sargent expected to boost his regime's prestige within Germany, but it might be expected to contain German expansion within that perimeter. Over the next three weeks, however, further developments undermined both the prospect of making those states a barrier, in the sense of being independent of German control, and the hope of an early reversion to active appeasement, even if some rescue plan for the Jews could be devised.

This postulated 'barrier' of the Low Countries, France, Portugal, Greece, Turkey, Iraq, Egypt and, perhaps, Saudi Arabia would always be uncertain and precarious. Spain and Italy were unlikely additions. The vulnerability of Holland and Belgium was obvious. Great Britain's influence in Saudi Arabia and its treaty rights in Iraq and Egypt were seen to be at risk from Arab nationalism, exacerbated by events in Palestine, by

Italian radio propaganda and by German intrigues. On 28 October, the British Ambassador at Ankara, Sir Percy Loraine, had reported assurances by the Foreign Minister, Tevfik Aras, of Turkish aid for Egypt and Iraq if the neutrality of either was violated by Great Britain's enemies. The nature of the aid was unspecified. Kemal Ataturk's cordial personal relations with Loraine had undoubted diplomatic value, but the Turkish ruler, who died on 10 November, had been determined to avoid any commitments likely to involve war, and his successors followed his advice.[17] The recent strains in the old alliance with Portugal had eased, but Greece wanted a more definite alliance than Great Britain was ready to concede. An annual purchase of £500,000 of tobacco would have been at least enough to consolidate relations, but consumer resistance to Balkan tobacco meant an adamant refusal by British companies to buy it. Halifax believed that Greece would 'fall into the German maw' without such a deal, but he failed to convince the FPC on 21 November that political pressure should be applied to the Imperial Tobacco Company. Chamberlain, Simon, MacDonald and Stanley forecast American opposition even if the Company did give way. Such an arrangement would breach the spirit of the Anglo-American Trade Agreement, signed only a few days earlier after hard bargaining on, among other matters, a tobacco formula.[18] Although Chamberlain had high hopes of Mussolini and although the civil war in Spain was still unresolved, the likelihood of Italian and Spanish alignment with Germany in any war had to be faced.

In these circumstances, Great Britain was more than ever in need of close co-operation with France. Aware of divisions within French governing circles on how best to cope with the enhanced power of Germany, the British leaders arranged a visit to Paris and discussed matters with Daladier and Bonnet on Thursday, 24 November. This was a meeting of allies with shared problems and aims. Each government faced threats to the homeland, to territories and interests in the Mediterranean and the Middle East, and to its Asian empire. The threats came from the same three Powers, namely Germany, Italy and Japan, and the outcome of the Spanish Civil War might bring a fresh threat to them both. Each government sought to reduce the number of its enemies and to improve its prospects of success in any war. Each realised that German predominance in Eastern Europe could no longer be challenged, but each hoped to limit the consequences by alliance with Turkey and by fortifying traditional British and French influences in the Balkans. In the wake of the Munich crisis, however, confidence as to the diplomatic and military prospects was at a low ebb in Paris and

London alike, and irritation at the other's shortcomings in both spheres was correspondingly high. The one-day meeting did little more than clarify the areas of disagreement, but neither did it damage a relationship each knew to be essential.

In three negative respects they did find it easy to agree. They lamented together their ineffectiveness in trying to help Germany's Jews, to end the civil war in Spain and to support China against Japanese aggression. They agreed also that their agents in the Middle East ought to desist from rivalry and combine instead to resist German and Italian penetration of the region. More importantly, Daladier and Bonnet reassured the British on three matters which had caused them unease. In the first place, the text of the forthcoming Franco-German declaration was produced and Chamberlain, disregarding recent events in Germany, welcomed its content as 'another step towards appeasement in Europe'. Secondly, Daladier reaffirmed that France would go to Great Britain's assistance if the latter were attacked by Germany, and was ready for this to be stated again publicly at the earliest opportunity if Chamberlain so wished. Thirdly, the British were assured that France's commitment to the Soviet Union would not involve war if German aggression was confined, as then expected, to subversive activities in the Ukraine.

It was the nature of the assistance expected by each government of the other during the initial defensive phase, anticipated in a war against Germany, which was the principal area of dispute. Daladier pictured this opening phase as one of relative immobility on the ground because of the defensive strength of both sides, but he stressed the importance in this context of Great Britain committing larger motorised and more rapidly deployed ground forces to north-eastern France against which, he assumed, the initial German attack would be launched. Meanwhile, French forces might strike at the territory of the weaker Axis partner. Chamberlain, by contrast, assumed that Italy would remain neutral until the course of the war became clear, and he did not take it for granted that Germany would attack France first. The vulnerability to air attack of London and major British industrial centres was such that German bombers might well initiate a war against Great Britain alone. Until sufficient anti-aircraft guns had been produced to meet this threat, the British could not provide necessary artillery for any additional divisions on the Continent. Daladier questioned the practicability of any air defence and argued for concentration on building bomber forces sufficient to deter both Germany and Italy from fighting at all. Chamberlain insisted that air raids could be effectively disrupted, and he denied that Great Britain was neglecting bomber production. He challenged French estimates of their own future output of aircraft and lectured Daladier on the British experience. The debate was predictably inconclusive and its continuation left to the experts.

As well as their open discord on the terms of a Czech guarantee, there was an undercurrent of tension whenever the discussion touched upon relations with Italy. Although the British understood from their Ambassador that Bonnet himself was inclined to conciliation,[19] there was no sign of this at the meeting. The French made it clear that they expected full support from Great Britain in their resisting Italian demands for representation on the Board of the Suez Canal Company, and they bitterly accused Mussolini of making matters worse over Spain. In face of this, Chamberlain cautiously expressed his hope of compromise in future dealings with Mussolini, but he gave the French ministers no hint of his forthcoming visit to Rome in search of it.[20]

This lapse from courtesy was especially unfortunate because the press got wind of the visit only two days later, on Saturday 26 November.[21] French suspicion quickly acquired fresh importance on the following Wednesday, 30 November, when there was an officially orchestrated demonstration in the Italian Chamber, with deputies and spectators clamouring for the acquisition of Tunis, Corsica and other French possessions. The French government sought British diplomatic support for its protests. Chamberlain himself was annoyed with Mussolini for thus spoiling the prospects of his own diplomatic initiative. Halifax promptly authorised appropriate representations to Ciano, probably delivered with sympathetic reserve by Lord Perth, who tried to convince the Foreign Office that the demonstration was merely an attempt to strengthen Italy's bargaining power. Halifax realised that an indefinite period of tension between Italy and France had been initiated by Mussolini and that more than formal backing from Great Britain would be expected by the French government. This became all the more necessary after Ribbentrop's visit to Paris on the following Tuesday, 6 December, to sign a Franco-German Declaration. Bonnet hinted that there now seemed no question of Germany supporting any Italian claims.[22]

This ominous episode in Rome came at a point when it was becoming especially difficult to read the diplomatic situation. During the three weeks since the pogrom, Germany had shown growing hostility towards Great Britain, but was friendlier towards France, while its Axis partner was moving in the opposite direction: an Italian rapprochement with Great Britain was followed by a show of antagonism towards France. The Franco-British relationship, crucial to their defences in a conflict with either or both of the Axis Powers, had been showing signs of strain during and since the Czech crisis, and the conversations of 24 November left many points of difference unresolved. All this made for confusion at a time when Great Britain had temporarily given up hope of appeasement and was concentrating on the difficult enough task of reinforcing its diplomatic position among the other maritime states.

Two other developments during the second half of November did have more encouraging implications for Great Britain and France, but what they would actually amount to was not at all clear. In the first place, there was a secret promise of practical support from the other side of the Atlantic if attempts to contain Hitler landed the British Government in war. The message from President Roosevelt was conveyed by a trusted Scottish friend of his, Arthur Murray, as even the British Ambassador in Washington was not to know of it. When visiting the United States in October 1938, Murray was told to assure Chamberlain that American neutrality need not stand in the way of military aid. Roosevelt would do all he could to see that Chamberlain had 'the industrial resources of the American nation behind him in the event of war with the dictatorships'. The President went into detail on the ways in which American supplies would be able to ensure air superiority over Germany and Italy. Though necessarily secret for diplomatic and domestic reasons, the promise could be hinted at in speeches by a formula which Roosevelt supplied, namely that 'Great Britain, in the event of war, could rely upon obtaining raw materials from the democracies of the world'. Halifax got the gist of what Roosevelt had said in a letter from Murray just before the conversations in Paris, and he passed this on to Chamberlain. Halifax met Murray at the Foreign Office on Tuesday, 29 November. Chamberlain talked with him at the Commons on Thursday 15 December.[23] Roosevelt's commitment, personal and private though it still had to be, was at least one reassuring factor which Halifax could set against mounting German enmity and a nagging worry about France.

Secondly, but more ambiguously, arguments for a more confident stance might be derived from renewed contact with German opponents of Nazism. Some had been discouraged by their failure to convince British leaders that facing down Hitler over the Sudeten crisis would have occasioned his removal from power, but Goerdeler and associates of his, especially in military intelligence and in the Foreign Ministry, had persisted.[24] During October and November, Ashton-Gwatkin continued to receive reports of planned aggression by the Nazi leadership and of an impending financial crisis arising out of German preparations for war. Towards the end of November, he asked Arthur Young, the

British business man used by Goerdeler as a secret channel of communication, to clarify the foreign policy to be expected of a post-Nazi government, especially in its relationship with Great Britain. Goerdeler obliged with a lengthy exposition, which reached Ashton-Gwatkin on 6 December. This was followed on 10 December by a visit to the Foreign Office by Goerdeler's associate, Reinhold Schairer, who held out the prospect of a coup by German generals before the end of the month if there was a favourable response to Goerdeler's programme.[25]

These communications were taken seriously in the Foreign Office, but not in the way intended by Goerdeler. His prescient vision of a post-Nazi Germany co-operating with Great Britain, France and the United States to control the international order and to undermine the Soviet Union by means short of war arrested the Foreign Office's attention much less than the priority he gave to British support for action by an incoming German government to abolish the Polish Corridor. Given that Polish resistance to the temporarily more moderate Nazi aim of a corridor across the Corridor was expected to implacable,[26] Goerdeler was seeking British acquiescence to forcible territorial change on a scale even greater than that conceded at Munich, and almost certainly involving war. Prior agreement to this reincorporation of the Corridor into Germany, together with massive financial aid, an immediate transfer of colonial territory and an immediate end to rearmament everywhere were conditions which Goerdeler believed, no doubt realistically, to be necessary if those capable of removing Hitler were to see the coup as worth the risks involved and as guaranteeing their prestige and popularity with the German people.[27] Unrealistically, he assumed that the British would find these conditions a reasonable price to agree in advance for a merely hypothetical change of regime in Berlin.

They did not. Cadogan failed to detect 'any positive indication that Dr. Goerdeler and his associates can do anything effective for the overthrow of the present regime'. To Sargent, Goerdeler appeared to be arguing 'that we should refuse everything to Hitler personally because he is out to destroy Christianity and capitalism, but that we should at the same time be ready to give everything that Hitler is asking to any future German government which overthrows him, not because such a German government would necessarily be more friendly disposed towards Great Britain – Dr. Goerdeler has never promised that – but because from the internal point of view it would socially and politically be a conservative government under the control of the Army.' He suggested that a 'straightforward and efficient military dictatorship might be even more dangerous'.[28] Given this way of thinking, a favourable reaction to Goerdeler's proposals would not have been likely even if ministers and officials had imagined and thought inevitable the disasters of 1940–42. The full consequences of a Nazi conquest of Europe were still unimagined by them, and they saw Hitler's regime as vulnerable to economic collapse. They saw no reason to abandon their goal of a Europe in which territorial and other disputes would all be resolved by peaceful negotiation, even if it had to be of the dubious kind to which they had resorted at Munich.

This was not a vague and pious aspiration. British ministers and officials alike were entirely serious about it, however varied their ideas as to how it could be achieved and however bogus the compromises and formulae by which they might square their consciences when falling short of that achievement. The use of force by Germany against another sovereign state could not be condoned in advance, whoever was in power in Berlin and whatever excuses a British Government might subsequently give for failing to resist it. Hence, an otherwise unlikely unanimity between Chamberlain, Halifax, Vansittart, Cadogan, Sargent and Strang in offering no encouragement to Goerdeler's proposals.[29] They were, nevertheless, encouraged by them. The fact that such approaches had been made, both during and since the Munich crisis, was taken, especially by Halifax, as evidence of serious dissent within the Nazi regime, which might be promoted and exploited in other ways than those proposed by Goerdeler and his associates. British spurning of Nazism's opponents during and after the Munich crisis has sometimes been represented as a missed opportunity,[30] but only a desperate or reckless government would have based its policy towards another Great Power on the chance success of a *coup d'état.*

While some reassurance could be found in what both Roosevelt and Goerdeler had to say, the main trend of events continued to alarm and confuse. The Franco-German Declaration looked like being put to an immediate test when, on the day after its signature, questions about the future of Memel were raised in Paris by the British Foreign Office. By the Treaty of Versailles, the seaport of Memel and its hinterland had been detached from Germany; the victor Powers were to decide its future once political realities had become clearer in a still turbulent Eastern Europe. It was still undecided in 1923, when Lithuanian forces seized the territory. Sovereignty was then formally granted to Lithuania, but by the Memel Convention of 1924, negotiated by Great Britain, France, Italy and Japan, Lithuania agreed to the region's autonomy. Within ten years, Lithuania's hold on its only port had become precarious in face of a resurgent Germany. Elections to the

Memel Landtag, due on 11 December, were expected to increase its already overwhelming majority of German nationalists calling for reunion with Germany. That, however, would mean a further revision of the Versailles Treaty and would be inconsistent with the Memel Convention. Begging for secrecy, the Lithuanian government sounded out Great Britain and France, signatories to both, as to their possible diplomatic support.[31] This was just the sort of problem which Chamberlain had been convinced would be a matter for international consultation, as provided for in the Anglo-German Declaration of 30 September 1938 and, now, in the Franco-German Declaration.

Treaty revision on account of changed circumstances was a familiar enough diplomatic exercise. Major territorial settlements in Europe had not normally remained intact for more than a decade or so, and that of 1919 had already proved no exception. In this case, the German government could have cynically invoked the principles of self-determination and democracy; those Great Powers which had signed the Memel Convention could have arranged, with embarrassment or indifference, some compensation for a helpless Lithuania; and another step towards ensuring the normality of peaceful change within the European order would, on the face of it, have been taken. From the British standpoint, indeed, it was crucial that any territorial revision should appear to result from peaceful discussion and not from the threat or use of force. That the outcome of the discussion would have simply reflected the military superiority of the successful claimant mattered less. An unequal distribution of power was a plain fact of international life; tacit acknowledgment as to where superiority lay in any particular situation was implicit in most diplomatic activity. Admittedly, any uncertainty as to where it lay or what it could command was likely to be resolved by war or the threat of war, but it did not have to be demonstrated by war when the inequality of the contending parties was obvious and when, as in this case, Lithuania had no powerful allies to redress the balance. It was up to the signatories of these international agreements about Memel, now under challenge, to insist that the diplomatic decencies be preserved and that any changes would appear to have been peacefully negotiated within the international system. It looked like being the first test of whether, at Munich, Hitler had been won over to such procedures, as Chamberlain continued to believe.

Thus when, on the afternoon of Wednesday, 7 December, Bronius Balutis, the Lithuanian Minister at London, explained his Government's fears, he evoked a ready response. He told Collier, Head of the Northern Department at the Foreign Office, that Bonnet had already been approached and was ready to raise the matter while Ribbentrop was still in Paris, as long as the British Government agreed. Ribbentrop was due to leave Paris the following morning. Reports reaching the Foreign Office from Kovno tended to confirm what Balutis had reported. Collier promptly got Halifax's authorisation to instruct Phipps by telephone that he was to assure Bonnet of British support.[32] Phipps discovered, however, that Bonnet had given no such undertaking and had no intention of tackling Ribbentrop about Memel. France would make instead a formal representation through its Embassy in Berlin.[33] As this could be reasonably interpreted as no more than a wish on Bonnet's part not to spoil the atmosphere of a successful visit, Halifax went on to instruct Ogilvie-Forbes on Saturday 10 December to concert with Coulondre, the new French Ambassador, to make identic representations by which each government would base its call for consultation on the Declaration it had signed with Germany.

Halifax realised, as his telegram told Ogilvie-Forbes, that 'if German government agree to discussions at all, they may demand cession of Memel. In that case Lithuanian government would probably submit under protest, but His Majesty's Government and French government could try to secure that no further demands are made on them.' He assumed that Bonnet would find acceptable his proposed approach, namely to trust that the German government would use their influence with the Memellanders to ensure respect for the Memel Statute, which regulated its autonomy, and that since 'from their respective standpoints German government and His Majesty's Government cannot fail to be interested in the situation in Memel', to hope that, 'having regard to Chamberlain–Hitler declaration, German Government will be prepared to discuss with His Majesty's Government any grievance which they may have against Lithuanian Government in this connexion'.[34] Thereby Halifax could demonstrate whether Hitler did or did not interpret the Munich Declaration in the same way as Chamberlain had done.

Phipps briefly reported French agreement.[35] So Halifax was taken aback when he learned that Bonnet had told Coulondre that, in concerting with Ogilvie-Forbes, he was to omit any reference to the Franco-German Declaration and to express only a vague readiness to consult with Germany for any purpose which would appear useful. Coulondre wanted to mention Memel 'quite casually' among other subjects. He argued that the Paris and Munich Declarations should be invoked only when there was in prospect 'a concrete and successful result'. In the case of Memel, there was the certainty of a rebuff.[36] From Halifax's point of view, this would defeat one underlying purpose of the *démarche*, which was to test the efficacy of both Declarations. He told Ogilvie-Forbes (12 December) that he did not understand the reasons for Coulondre's instructions and that he preferred to maintain the British text in what he still expected to be similar and simultaneous representations.[37] His telegram arrived too late. Finding Coulondre adamant and assuming that the greater importance lay with making the representations as nearly identical as possible, Ogilvie-Forbes had gone ahead, dropping the reference to the Munich Declaration and mentioning only the Memel Convention. Even so, Coulondre was at pains to play down the move. 'This morning at the last moment', reported Ogilvie-Forbes, 'he sent his Counsellor to me with a message to the effect that he saw objection even to a *note verbale* and preferred an *aide-memoire* without any heading. I saw his text which was addressed "Office of Ministry of Foreign Affairs".'[38] Bonnet justified the French attitude by pointing to the likely need to use the Declarations in the near future on more important issues such as the Ukraine.[39]

As well as using a lesser category of communication, Coulondre was significantly briefer and vaguer than Ogilvie-Forbes, expressing confidence in the German government's intentions rather than reminding them of their obligations.[40] He accompanied his written communication with oral enquiries about Lithuanian failures to respect the Statute, scarcely necessary in view of the loud and repeated German complaints on that score but in keeping with the tone of dutiful detachment.[41] By contrast, Ogilvie-Forbes expressed British interest in the whole *status quo*, not merely observance of the Statute, a distinction noted uneasily by German officials. Not that the distinction bothered the Nazi leadership; Ribbentrop made it clear to both governments that no representation at all was acceptable about Memel, which was none of their business.[42] It was, of course, but since to French indifference had to be added that of the other signatories, Italy and Japan, Halifax dropped the matter. The German attitude was ominous, but so might be that of Bonnet.

By 11 December Sargent's complaint that no alternative to appeasement had been found was still valid. Marked German hostility to Great Britain, an apparent Franco-German rapprochement, undoubted Franco-Italian antagonism, evidence of German contempt for the Munich Declaration, and public hostility at home to further deals with Hitler made it difficult to follow a clear course in relation to the major European Powers. Even the hopeful signs were of no present help. Contacts with Hitler's opponents inside Germany were welcome, but his overthrow remained a remote possibility and his likely successors did not appear to share British ideas of appeasement. Roosevelt's assurances were of supplies to help Great Britain fight a war which it was the object of British diplomacy to prevent, and the public hints which he authorised would be of uncertain diplomatic weight. The Memel episode illustrated British diplomatic impotence, fortunately in a low key.

4
The Prospect of War

Between 12 December 1938 and 6 February 1939 intensive discussions among ministers and their advisers brought some clarification to British policy in respect of Germany, France and Italy. Rumours of imminent German aggression were largely responsible. Urgent answers were needed to two hypothetical questions, the kind which politicians publicly disclaim any obligation to answer. The hypothesis was that the rumours were true and that Hitler intended shortly to attack Great Britain or another state in Western Europe. The first question was how best diplomatically to avert this if he did so intend; the second was whether the sort of war for which preparations had long been underway would still be appropriate if he was not so deterred.

The rumours were taken seriously because, during the past month, ministers and officials had come to accept as fact the view that Hitler was an unpredictable leader, unrestrained by normal diplomatic considerations and liable to launch sudden and violent attacks on those he regarded as his enemies at home or abroad. Since they had also actual evidence of Hitler's current hostility towards Chamberlain and his colleagues, they had reluctantly conceded that appeasement, in relation to Germany, must temporarily become an ultimate goal rather than a present policy. At the same time, they refused to believe that Hitler was immune to popular opinion in Germany and they hoped, too, that he might be influenced more by those among his entourage they dubbed 'moderate' than by the 'extremists'. They still found it difficult to believe that the regime's autarky could endure much longer without a major economic crisis. By dint of broadcast propaganda directed at the German people, exchanges of view at a high level with 'moderates', and patient negotiations with German business leaders, they hoped to give Hitler reason to hesitate before plunging into war. They hoped also that Mussolini could be persuaded, during the visit by Chamberlain and Halifax to Rome, to exert his supposed influence on Hitler in the direction of renewed appeasement. Whatever the result of all this, they needed to be sure of France's continued diplomatic and military collaboration, though there was disagreement within Cabinet as to whether the price of this would be a substantially greater commitment of British troops to the Continent. It was with all this in mind that British policy-makers dealt with disturbing news and rumours during December and January.

The disturbing exchanges with Berlin and Paris over Memel coincided with an equally disturbing communication from the German government about their naval plans. By the terms of their Naval Agreement of June 1935, Great Britain had acknowledged Germany's right to a submarine tonnage equal to that of the British Commonwealth, while the German government had agreed to a limit, in practice, of 45per cent of that entitlement unless changed circumstances directed otherwise. If circumstances did so change, notice would be given and friendly discussion of the matter would precede Germany's exercising of its right. On Monday 12 December, the Foreign Office received due notification that a new situation had arisen and that dropping this self-imposed restriction was among changes to be implemented by the German Navy. Developments over recent months, it was said, had made increased protection of Germany's maritime communications necessary in case of 'warlike complications'.[1] Given that the gestation of such a programme would be prolonged and that secrecy in matters of rearmament was the norm, Hitler's untypical and unnecessarily early concern for diplomatic propriety suggested his readiness to budget for war with the British if they tried to frustrate his ambitions. Halifax and his colleagues resigned themselves to the futility of 'friendly discussions'.

It was on this same Monday that Halifax learned of Bonnet's perhaps equally ominous reluctance to invoke the Franco-German Declaration in the matter of Memel. At 1.15 p.m. he had stressed to Ogilvie-Forbes by telegram the importance of reminding the German government of its obligations to both Great Britain and France in such a matter.[2] He was still waiting to hear what had happened when, in the Commons, Chamberlain gave a notably guarded response to a question about British obligations to France. This was to upset Bonnet as much as the latter's attitude over Memel disturbed Halifax when he learned of it from Ogilvie-Forbes at 5.20 p.m.[3]

The Prime Minister had been asked by an Opposition M.P., John Morgan, 'whether any treaty, pact, or agreed understanding exists which, in the event of Italy embarking on warlike operations against

France or her possessions, would specifically require Great Britain to render military aid to France'. Chamberlain replied with strict accuracy that no such specific requirement existed in any treaty or pact with France. The answer was ambiguous. It was arguably more discomfiting to Italy than to France in that it left open the question as to whether there was an 'agreed understanding', but it was so baldly and neutrally expressed as to be disconcerting to a threatened ally. Nor in his additional responses did Chamberlain elaborate in a manner explicitly supportive of France. Morgan enquired sarcastically whether his answer meant he would be freer when in Rome 'to bargain away French interests to advance our own', and another Labour M.P., R.W. Sorensen, wanted to know if Mussolini had been made aware of how adversely the anti-French demonstrations would affect his forthcoming conversations with British ministers. Lt. Commander Fletcher called for a protest at claims against France which violated the Anglo-Italian Agreement. The Prime Minister merely repeated remarks he had made a week earlier that, unless the Italian government corrected the impression made by the demonstrators, it would be to the detriment of further collaboration between 'the four Munich Powers'. He did not take the obvious opportunity during these exchanges to express any support for France.[4] Yet in the morning he had shown his awareness of the problem by arranging for Ciano and Mussolini to be warned that they were putting his visit to Rome at risk.[5]

On Tuesday morning, therefore, Bonnet asked that Chamberlain should clarify matters in a speech he was to make that evening at the jubilee dinner of the Foreign Press Association. He told the British Ambassador that 'in the present unreasonable state of Italian feeling', Chamberlain's reply in the Commons might be magnified and give unjustified encouragement to the extremists. If the Prime Minister would refer in his speech to the *status quo* clause in the Anglo-Italian Agreement, it would have 'a very healthy effect'.[6] Corbin saw Halifax, also on 13 December, and his complaint was franker still. He pointed to the Italian government's 'constant efforts to represent England as not disapproving of the agitation'; they would see to it that Chamberlain's remarks would be distorted to that end in the Italian press. He stressed the value of anything that the British Government could say which would be 'incapable of misrepresentation'. France could cope with Italy, 'but the matter might easily become one of rather wider significance'.[7] He did not need to elaborate on that significance at a time when Germany's relations with France were improving and its relations with Great Britain were deteriorating.

There had been Foreign Office concern about Chamberlain's FPA speech on general grounds before these expressions of a specific French anxiety were received. Cadogan had been consulted about some parts of it but had not been able to borrow a copy of the final version until the evening of Monday 12 December. 'Very feeble and bad' was the comment he recorded in his diary and early the following morning he got Halifax to phone No.10 with a view to revising it. To their irritation, the speech had already by then been circulated in various translations. When Bonnet's request reached the Foreign Office at 12.15 p.m., Chamberlain refused to change the text, arguing that a further circulation of additional sentences would, as Halifax apologetically informed the French, 'call undue attention to the matter'.[8] Halifax was only too aware of how much attention the French government considered was due.

Chamberlain miscalculated in preparing his speech to the FPA, although he did make an unequivocal reference to relations with France. He defended his policy (though he did not once use the term 'appeasement'), lauded its achievements and proclaimed his intention to persist with it.[9] The majority of the assembled journalists did not, however, respond in the way he had anticipated. By the volume and length of their applause at particular sentences, they made their own views clear. The absence of German press representatives, who had learned that Chamberlain was to protest in passing at a recent insult to Baldwin, facilitated this. References to the Munich Agreement, the Anglo-German Declaration and the Franco-German Declaration were received in silence, to the Anglo-Italian Agreement with sporadic clapping, to the Anglo-American Trade Agreement with loud applause and to relations with France – 'so close as to pass beyond mere legal obligations, since they are founded on identity of interest' – with 'a wild ovation lasting several minutes'. According to his National Labour Minister, De La Warr, 'it was almost a vote of censure on the P.M.'s policy.'[10] Presumably in reaction to this experience, Chamberlain surprised the Foreign Office by asking that Rex Leeper, whose handling of the press through its News Department he had so often resented, should draft his next speech.[11]

On the following day, Wednesday 14 December, the Cabinet discussed a major proposal on propaganda, which both Chamberlain and Halifax enthusiastically supported. It was explained in a Foreign Office memorandum of 8 December. Like the programmes for rearmament and civil defence, it was a considered response to the general threat posed by Hitler's policy, and meant to be sustained indefinitely; it was not hastily devised to counter a particular act. Unlike rearmament and civil defence, it would be most effective if heavily disguised.

According to the memorandum, German recognition of the role played by British propaganda in breaking down German resistance during the last war would explain current Nazi expenditure of probably £5 million per annum on propaganda. They were right, moreover, to fear British counter-propaganda now. 'If Europe may have to choose between a *Pax Germanica* and a *Pax Britannica*, the issue may to some extent – and perhaps to a considerable extent – be determined by the success of British propaganda not only in the countries surrounding Germany, but in Germany itself.' Propaganda should be funded, therefore, 'in no niggardly fashion'. The usual cultural and educational propaganda of the British Council would take too long to bring about results on the scale required, so there must be short-term measures to match the pace of events. Broadcasting directly to the German people was of the highest importance, supplemented by personal business contacts and the distribution of literature within Germany about Great Britain. In each case, the propaganda would have to be unobtrusive and unprovocative, simply informing Germans about Great Britain and the British outlook without any criticism of German affairs.

Existing ten-minute news bulletins in German, prepared by the BBC in association with the Foreign Office, were not jammed and might soon be made longer. The new Director-General of the BBC, Frederick Ogilvie, wanted reciprocal agreements with Germany among other countries; while this would be the easiest way of communicating with the German public, it would mean getting Goebbels and his spokesmen to abstain, on their part, from using material such as anti-Jewish diatribes, offensive to British listeners. A less direct but far more hopeful means of reaching German listeners would be by buying time for programmes in German to be broadcast from radio stations at Luxembourg, Strasbourg and Liechtenstein. The Foreign Office had assured Halifax that this could be done. The programmes would be sponsored in the normal way by a travel agency or some other commercial firm, and a general news review would be inserted among other items. The material used would require advance approval from the Foreign Office, but the participation by the British Government could be effectively concealed. The estimated cost of six programmes a week was £6000.

As to using British business in the work of propaganda, Sir Charles Granville Gibson of the Associated Chambers of Commerce and Peter Bennett of the Federation of British Industries should be asked to impress on their representatives the national importance of what they said to their German contacts. A new monthly publication was suggested, summarising British achievements with extracts, photos and short articles. This could be shown by commercial representatives to German business men, supplementing a planned series of pamphlets by the British Council. Establishing branch offices in Berlin and the provinces through an extra grant to the Travel Association would be another means of distributing tourist literature and general information about Britain. The German government already had similar facilities in London. Financing all these proposals was an urgent matter. They were 'an important item in our general defence programme.'[12]

At Cabinet, Halifax reminded his colleagues of the Prime Minister's suggestion at a meeting of the Foreign Policy Committee on 14 November that greater use should be made of the Luxembourg broadcasting station in getting across the British viewpoint to the German public. The measures now being proposed would cost about £50,000 p.a., to be contrasted with the annual spending on propaganda by France of £1million, by Italy of £1.5 million and by Germany of £5 million. Yet the importance and urgency of these relatively inexpensive and unostentatious forms of propaganda should not be underrated as 'the issue of peace and war might well turn on the extent to which we could make the British point of view known'. Chamberlain reiterated his enthusiasm for Radio Luxembourg, which was in range of most German radio sets and which had the previous night specially relayed his speech to the Foreign Press Association. Simon doubted whether the government's involvement could be secret if money had to be voted. There was some concern expressed by critics of the Foreign Office News Department and of Lord Lloyd's role at the British Council, but Halifax defended both and insisted that the operation must be directed by the Foreign Office. It was left to the Treasury and the Foreign Office to work out the details in time for the following week's Cabinet.[13] Nothing was said, or at any rate recorded, of the clandestine control exercised by the British Government over the ostensibly private Radio Luxembourg, nor of manifestly obsolete international commitments to abstain from trying to influence populations abroad by radio.[14] Thus two days after Hitler had found an uncharacteristic show of diplomatic propriety convenient in rendering nugatory his naval agreement with Great Britain, British ministers displayed an encouraging readiness to discard scruples in countering an unscrupulous opponent.

After this interval on Wednesday of optimism and unanimity, unease and controversy returned at successive meetings of the Committee of Imperial Defence (CID) on Thursday and Friday. At its 341st meeting on Thursday, 15 December, the CID had before them a paper by Hore-Belisha on the Army's state of preparedness in relation to its role. This phrasing was carefully chosen. After much argument, referral and revision within the War Office, Hore-Belisha had insisted that the emphasis should be placed upon improving the Army's preparedness rather on trying yet again to redefine its role, a matter recurrently debated over the previous five years. The possibility of renewed war with Germany had been faced by the autumn of 1933, and in February 1934 a Defence Requirements Committee had recommended that an expeditionary force should be made available to prevent conquest of the Low Countries and their use by Germany as a base from which to bomb Great Britain. As politicians anticipated as much public hostility to the prospect of a renewed mass slaughter of troops across the Channel as to the expected mass slaughter of civilians by bombing, there was little enthusiasm among their ranks for this plan. Chamberlain led the opposition to a continental role for the Army, arguing for priority to air defence by the RAF's fighters and the Army's AA guns. He succeeded. It had been agreed that, in a future war against Germany, Great Britain would concentrate on the use of air and sea power, especially in the enforcement of a blockade. Apart from the defence of the British Isles, the Army's role would be to protect British interests and territories overseas, notably in the Middle East.[15]

Decisions to this effect had been reached by the time of the Anschluss. Although the policy remained unchanged by this and by the events which culminated in the Munich Conference, the firmness with which the government pursued it had been undermined. In conversations with French leaders on 28 April 1938, the possibility of troops being sent to France in the event of a German attack was no longer denied outright. Halifax had said rather that no more than two divisions could be assigned to support France, while Chamberlain warned that none might be sent at all.[16] The apparent imminence of war towards the end of September and the brevity of the Munich rapprochement with Germany gave rise to some unease and uncertainty as to whether the Army could avoid a continental role or even set a limit to its extent. This view was not, however, shared by most of the Cabinet. Hence Hore-Belisha's decision to argue at the CID meeting simply that expenditure on the Army was insufficient for it to enact an effective role anywhere outside the United Kingdom.

At Thursday's meeting, discussion of this item was, for the most part, on predictable lines. Hore-Belisha dwelt on the argument central to his memorandum, namely that the divisions available to be despatched abroad were equipped only for defensive warfare and that there were no adequately equipped reserves which could reinforce them. The position was made worse by the continued crisis in Palestine, where the needs of eighteen infantry battalions had to be met by the transfer of equipment from the Field Force. The General Staff had made it clear to him that, in the event of war, the Army would not be able to discharge effectively the responsibilities expected of it by the government. There was a largely cool response among the politicians to this inherently reasonable argument, perhaps because Hore-Belisha's disclaiming of any intention to change the Army's role was not believed. Inskip, who chaired the meeting in Chamberlain's absence, said that the 'gaps' Committee, set up after Munich to consider what parts of the defence programme should now be accelerated, had decided that Hore-Belisha's proposals involved changes in principle which CID should examine only when there was a full attendance and when the Prime Minister was in the chair. Hore-Belisha admitted to having overlooked this provision. It made little difference, as Chamberlain's predictable scepticism was represented by Hoare, who stressed that the Army's principal role remained the Air Defence of Great Britain, for which additional expenditure had been granted since Munich, and by Simon, who complained of short notice and of the formidable cost, as well as observing that in November similar proposals had been advanced explicitly with a view to changing the Army's role. Instead of meeting Hore-Belisha's request that his proposals should be referred straight to Cabinet the following week, the CID referred them to the Chiefs of Staff (COS).

Hore-Belisha had received unexpected support at the meeting from Halifax, which was to assume great significance, but at the time undermined the War Minister's claim that no change of role for the Field Force was envisaged. Halifax, conceding the priority which had to be given to air defence, recalled having to withstand very strong French pressure during the Paris conversations in November for 'a contribution by Great Britain on land'. Like Hore-Belisha, he had pointed to Great Britain's lack of a field Army fully equipped for war, but both the British Ambassador and his Military Attaché had assured him that the French 'would return to the charge on this subject'. Halifax disclaimed any wish to see a large British Army involved on the Continent, but 'a time might come when the French would cease to be enthusiastic about their relations with Great Britain if they were left with the impression that it was they who must bear the brunt of the fighting and slaughter on land.' When Hoare retorted that 'whatever the French might think, their interests were so bound up with ours that they could not afford to stand aloof from us', Halifax became more explicit in his warning. He had discerned 'some slight danger that, if Germany attempted to come to an agreement with France for her to stand aside while Germany attacked us, they might be tempted to accept the German request if attention was not paid to requests for assistance on land'.[17]

Halifax's intervention was vague and, in part, misleading. French generals did, of course, want as many British troops as possible to help them resist any initial German offensive through the Low Countries and, in the long run, a large conscript Army from Great Britain as essential to a joint offensive to defeat Germany. Major-General Pownall, Director of Military Operations and Intelligence at the War Office, had urged Colonel Fraser, Military Attaché at the British Embassy in Paris, to hint that the matter should be raised with Chamberlain and Halifax, at least with regard to the initial commitment of troops,[18] but any representations he may have made were not used by Daladier and Bonnet at the Paris conversations on 24 November. With a politician's grasp of what might actually be realised, Daladier had not asked for a larger Army than the British had already half-promised, only that it should arrive more quickly and that it should be fully mechanised for a counter-attack. This appears to have been in keeping with current French military expectations as to the initial stages of a war. For example, General Prételat had reported to his superiors on 23 June 1938 his estimate, after a map exercise, that German forces making a surprise attack through the Ardennes could reach the Meuse within 60 hours of crossing the Rhine. He was denied the extra division which he claimed would be needed to forestall this, as it was thought that such an advance would take a day longer than Prételat had calculated, giving the French ample time to get enough troops into defensive positions.[19]

The French government had far more immediate worries about British policy than those hinted at by Halifax, namely Chamberlain's apparent reluctance to give a full public commitment to fight if France was attacked, and his suspected inclination to make some sort of deal with Mussolini at the forthcoming conversations in Rome, a deal in pursuit of which he might expect concessions from France which Daladier had no intention of making. Halifax realised that these concerns had urgently to be addressed, and a more precise commitment to a better armed expeditionary force of the size the French expected would provide some reassurance. It made sense for him to back Hore-Belisha to that extent. His further vague hint that, without a much larger commitment of land forces, France might choose to remain neutral in the event of Germany attacking Great Britain alone was more questionable. Faced already with belligerent Italian claims and the prospect of a war on two fronts if the recent agreement with Germany proved no more substantial than the parallel Anglo-German declaration at Munich, it would take more than the handful of French ministers, believed by the Foreign Office to be vulnerable to German blackmail, to convince Daladier and his Service chiefs to abandon their only powerful ally, whose defeat would leave them isolated against both Axis Powers. It was unsurprising that Hore-Belisha was keener to re-emphasise the modest nature of his proposals than to welcome Halifax's apparent advocacy of a major change in military policy.

Yet, on the same day, Ivone Kirkpatrick, First Secretary at the British Embassy in Berlin, arrived in London to take up new duties at the Foreign Office and brought with him a story of a plan to attack Great Britain alone which lent some substance to Halifax's anxiety. He told Cadogan that Hitler, still furious with Chamberlain and with Great Britain generally, had ordered plans to be drawn up within three weeks affording him the option of an air attack on London in March 1939. The pilots would take off from civilian aerodromes so as to ensure surprise. His source was a German friend, a former high official in contact with German generals and with members of Hitler's entourage.[20] Cadogan passed this on to Halifax, who saw Chamberlain about it at 7 p.m. The outcome of these consultations was the reassembling of the CID the following morning, Friday 16 December. Halifax pointed out that such a plan would be in keeping with intelligence reports that Hitler was unbalanced and that those closest to him were suffering from 'swollen head'. Hopefully, the report was ill-founded, but precautions were essential and urgent. At the same time, they should be inconspicuous lest Hitler be moved to bring forward the date. All government Departments should try to accelerate their preparations, and the TUC should be confidentially informed of the position. The Air Ministry should organise practice exercises and black-outs in London, and Anderson might set the unemployed digging trenches under the guise of providing employment.

Chamberlain's approach to the problem was more complicated. He accepted that the evidence of an impending German attack had to be taken seriously, and he reinforced it. He had heard similar reports from other sources of such a possibility, if not of a definite plan. Furthermore, Schacht, who was on a visit to London to organise the emigration of German Jews, had told him the previous day, 'in an extraordinarily frank conversation', that Hitler would be up to some mischief in the East in the next month or so, and that he despised the British as powerless. The French government also regarded March as the dangerous time, while it was significant that German and Austrian domestic servants were being recalled to the Reich. It was essential to be prepared; that was why he had called the meeting. He assumed from what Schacht had said that Hitler's ambitions lay essentially in the East, and that the point of a surprise attack on London would be to discourage any British intervention. This would involve, he believed, first picking a quarrel with Great Britain as a pretext. That might be afforded by signs of an attempt to thwart his ambitions. Chamberlain, however, 'could not see that there was any need for us to be mixed up in any Eastern quarrel, and, therefore, thought it unlikely that this surprise attack would materialise'. He doubted whether the fresh powers they had been discussing would bring results before March, yet taking them might be the very sign Hitler needed to justify an attack. Preparations were certainly necessary, but they should be unostentatious. Thus, Chamberlain shared Halifax's apprehension about the danger and his wish to take precautions, but he wanted primarily to avoid provocation. Halifax hoped to deter Hitler altogether, or, as a longer shot, to alarm those in Germany opposed to war with the West to the point of overthrowing him.[21]

It is not clear what Chamberlain had in mind when he referred to an 'Eastern quarrel' in which there was no need for Great Britain to be involved. Since it was a fixed point in his thinking after Munich that Hitler would keep his word over consulting Chamberlain on further territorial changes, it is difficult to see what 'mischief' by Hitler in the East would not, in the Prime Minister's eyes, concern Great Britain. The possible German moves about which there was most guessing at this time would be directed against Memel, Danzig or the Ukraine. Of these, Memel was that most likely to have been in Chamberlain's mind, on account of what had happened a few days earlier. Its status was certainly of international concern, but the elections on the previous Sunday had underlined the case for transfer by self-determination, which Lithuania would be in no position to contest. The abortive diplomatic activity preceding them had indicated that any ensuing German intervention would be met, at the most, by a formal plea from Great Britain and France for a show of diplomatic propriety in the process. This would be a very low-key exchange, even if Hitler made an unnecessary show of military force, and scarcely a situation in which he would provoke a major war by bombing London. This may explain Chamberlain's casual attitude to 'mischief' in the East. If he was expecting Hitler to risk war with Poland by action against Danzig, or with the Soviet Union and Poland by promoting Ukrainian separatism, he would scarcely have been so sanguine. Either move would have meant upheaval on such a scale as to have made nonsense, in Chamberlain's eyes, if not those of Hitler, of the Munich declaration on which he continued to set such store.

The cautious reception of Kirkpatrick's report was justified as the story was false, but its tenor was, in any case, so in keeping with developments over the past week that it did no more than reinforce an appropriate mood of unease and foreboding. Added point to the discussion was provided by a CID memorandum of the same date[22] on how to deal with the anticipated destruction, during the first year of a war, of half a million houses and with substantial damage to one or two million others. During the first week 6000 tons of bombs were expected and 7000 tons of bombs over the following fortnight. There was no firm basis for the impression that some fateful move would be made by Hitler in March, but it gave a sense of urgency to men trying simultaneously to prevent and to prepare for such a war.

On the following Monday, 19 December, the Commons debated an Opposition motion expressing no confidence in the Government's foreign policy. Hugh Dalton's wide-ranging attack dwelt on the lack of any effective policy in the Far East, on the dangers posed by Hitler's exploitation of the Munich settlement, on the failure to protect British shipping caught up in the Spanish Civil War and on widespread apprehension as to the kind of concessions which Chamberlain and Halifax might make during their January visit to Rome. With wishful thinking they would one day share, he recommended bringing together France, the Soviet Union, Poland, Roumania, Yugoslavia, Greece and Turkey to resist any further dislocation by Germany of Eastern Europe. Chamberlain replied with the speech for which Leeper had supplied the draft. It was appropriately more sombre than the speech he had delivered to the FPA the previous Tuesday. Although he insisted that there had been no alternative to the course pursued over the past 18 months and that Dalton's policy would have involved simultaneous war with Germany, Italy and Japan, he was notably less complacent about the past and less optimistic about the future. He thus defended his attempts at peaceful revision of the Versailles settlement simply as the only alternative to war, and he conceded that he had yet to see any sign that the German leadership shared his vision of peaceful change. He reassured the House that the conversations in Rome would be confined to an exchange of views.[23]

What views were to be expressed on the British side of this exchange was a matter for dispute when Cabinet met two days later. This was because Halifax feared that Chamberlain might concede so much in persuading Mussolini to exercise a moderating influence on Hitler as to arouse French suspicion and resentment. Halifax's own position was clear and simple. 'We should make no concession to Signor Mussolini unless he would help us to obtain the *détente* which it was the object of our policy to obtain.' His stated formula for the conversations was 'nothing for nothing'. Chamberlain's intentions were neither simple nor clear, despite his matching Halifax's phrase with that of 'something for something'. The 'something' which he seemed ready to offer Mussolini was quite at odds with the priority which Halifax wished to give to fortifying relations with France. To secure Mussolini's good offices at Berlin in forestalling a 'mad dog' act by Hitler, the Prime Minister was prepared at least to hint that Great Britain's attitude to the Franco-Italian dispute might not be exclusively pro-French. While ruling out the possibility of territorial concessions, he thought he could reasonably agree to discuss questions raised about the Djibuti railway or the Suez Canal, and he might say that Great Britain would not discourage France from discussing Tunis with Italy provided that Mussolini joined them in appealing for an armistice in Spain. Chamberlain seems to have found no echo in Cabinet for his approach to the conversations. Unease was expressed at the danger of offering concessions merely for an appeal about Spain which might come to nothing. Halifax knew from Corbin that France might eventually bargain away some minor non-territorial matters, but would obviously resent a premature and unsought initiative by their ally. He stressed the impossibility of territorial concessions and the need to profess ignorance as to other issues between France and Italy. Chamberlain offered his colleagues no reassurance. He promised only that he would not go beyond the – highly equivocal – line that he would not encourage the French to refuse to discuss such matters.

Relations with Germany, by contrast, did not occasion much debate at this meeting. The fact of German enmity was no longer questioned and the limited means available to counter it had been agreed. Those involving indirect attempts to undermine the regime and to encourage those opposed to it received attention. There was further endorsement for broadcast propaganda to subvert Nazism, and Halifax again assured his colleagues that the Government's involvement could be concealed. Runciman had heard that the Liechtenstein broadcasting station was for sale, and the importance of its not going to the German government was agreed. Schacht's visit to London was discussed, Chamberlain referring to his current hostility to the Nazi regime, his welcome plea for trade talks and deals, and the less welcome aspects of his scheme for Jewish emigration. The President of the Board of Trade spoke of his own likely visit to Berlin. Halifax was encouraged by reports of the regime's serious economic difficulties. All this related to a settled policy.

The current uncertainty as to how relations with France and Italy should be developed at a time of possible conflict between them was heightened by a problem to which there seemed no immediate remedy, that of Palestine. Halifax had circulated to his colleagues a letter from the British Ambassador at Cairo, Sir Miles Lampson, warning of the dire consequences of Arab hostility if Great Britain was involved in a European war. At the forthcoming conference on Palestine, Lampson claimed, 'you will be obliged to call off [Jewish] immigration if you want to keep the friendship of the Arab world.' Although Halifax thought the Ambassador a shade pessimistic, he accepted that the negotiations would, indeed, have to be conducted so as to ensure Arab friendship. The strategic consequences of losing it were confirmed by Kingsley Wood and Inskip. A hostile Arab world would make Great Britain's military position in the Middle East untenable, involving the loss of land, sea and air communications to the Far East. COS planning for a war with Italy had so far assumed that Iraq and Egypt would side with Great Britain and that Saudi Arabia would, at least, not be hostile. If the Arab world united against Great Britain, all plans would have to be recast.[24]

The implications of Arab hostility during an Italo-British conflict were discussed the same day, Wednesday, 26 December, by the Chiefs of Staff. The Foreign Office had asked the Joint Planning Committee about the strategic implications of any deal for a mutual reduction of forces in the Mediterranean which Italy might put forward. They instanced the dismantling of Malta's defences and its abandonment as a fortress if the Italians did the same at an island of theirs, such as Leros in the Dodecanese or Pantelleria between Sicily and Tunis; or an undertaking not to fortify Cyprus, nor to use it as a naval or air base, in return for some comparable restraint by Italy. The Deputy Chiefs of Staff on the Joint Planning Committee considered it unthinkable that Malta, invaluable as the main Mediterranean operating base, with facilities to maintain a fleet, should be used as a bargaining counter. Nothing that Italy could offer would compensate for its loss, which would also diminish British influence on Turkey and Greece, whose support would be important in any Mediterranean conflict. On the other hand, the fortification of Cyprus and its development as a base had so far been regarded as too costly to be worth while, so that an Italian concession in return for not doing so would be worth considering. The COS, however, rejected this advice about Cyprus as strongly as they backed the view of Malta as a non-negotiable asset. The deterioration of relations with the Arab world was the reason, rendering uncertain the potential value of Alexandria, Port Said and Haifa as bases. Assessments about Cyprus had to be revised: with relatively modest expenditure Famagusta could be made to accommodate a considerable fleet, while air attacks could be mounted on Italian bases in the eastern Mediterranean.[25]

When the Chiefs of Staff moved on to the other question on their agenda, there was no such unanimity. Hore-Belisha's memorandum on making the Army better equipped for its role had been referred to them after the difficulties encountered at CID on the previous Wednesday. Backhouse and Gort had been present at that meeting, and Newall would have been briefed about it by his deputy Peirse. They were, therefore, aware that the eminently reasonable case made by the War Minister that without more resources the Army would not be able to fight effectively anywhere overseas had aroused suspicion that 'overseas' would, in practice, mean France and an indefinite commitment to continental war. They were also aware that Halifax now feared for the French alliance without a greater commitment of that kind. At first, it looked as though the COS would temporise rather than clash over Hore-Belisha's deliberately ambiguous formula. In the chair, Newall expressed uncertainty as to how they should proceed, and wanted more time to consider. As Secretary, Ismay assured him that only a preliminary survey of the problem was expected of them before Christmas. Gort briefly restated the case as made by Hore-Belisha, and stressed that he was not seeking to equip an Army on a continental scale.

The atmosphere of calm appraisal was disturbed by Admiral Backhouse, who insisted on clarity as to just what the Army was expected to do. He shared Halifax's concern that without an assurance, cast in definite terms, about assistance on land, France might shun the prospect of an unequal struggle and leave Great Britain to face Germany alone. At the same time, he drew attention both to the difficulty of limiting the extent of the commitment once made and to the necessity of so limiting it. Problems of manpower and production would make it impossible to maintain all three Services at the highest level of strength. On the face of it, this was merely supportive of Hore-Belisha's proposals, but the Chief of Naval Staff's (CNS) implication that it was the Army which could not be so maintained tempted Gort to be more outspoken. He began by quoting Kitchener on the impossibility of a great country waging a 'little war'. War with Germany would be a life and death struggle, and he questioned whether Great Britain could survive it if the opening operations led to German conquest of the Low Countries and the Channel ports, and the establishment there of air and submarine bases. With a promise of adequate and early support, the French might switch, say, ten divisions to the defence of Belgium, perhaps enough to turn the scale and save the Channel ports. Without it, they might simply concentrate on saving their own fortified frontiers.

Backhouse became more specific about the limits which he would place on such a commitment. Acknowledging the danger to overseas supplies which would be posed by submarine bases, especially if German control of the coast extended as far west as Le Havre, he thought it essential to contain the German coastal advance at about the same line as in 1914. Newall, however, was not convinced that loss of the Channel ports would be fatal; supplies could be diverted to western and northern ports. He challenged the wisdom of sending four divisions to France at the onset of war. It might lead to unlimited land warfare, which the country would not accept. This provoked Gort into an incautious response: however great the desire to limit the British contribution on land, stern necessity might force the government to undertake heavy commitments on the Continent.

Ismay hastened to intervene and to suggest what might be common ground; in effect, he tried to balance Hore-Belisha's proposals against the interests and requirements of the other two Services. The Navy and the RAF must retain priority over the Army, but there was no doubt that French leaders had interpreted recent exchanges as meaning that a Field Force of some kind would definitely be sent to across the Channel in the event of war. Only a categorical denial would now convince them otherwise. If there was even a possibility of such a force being despatched, it must be adequately equipped and, if Belgium was to be saved, more detailed plans for its use would have to be devised than had so far been authorised in Staff conversations. At the same time, the Field Force might be more profitably deployed elsewhere; it might be needed to help to knock out Italy or to assist in the defence of Lisbon. He recalled famous instances when, through seapower, British armies had achieved results out of all proportion to their size.

Ismay's bid for consensus failed. Gort chafed at the idea of even considering other theatres of war until a German offensive had been brought to a standstill. Newall rejected Hore-Belisha's proposal to equip Territorial Army (TA) divisions for war as opening the way to unlimited expansion of land warfare. Gort was so roused by the prospect of the Field Force being thus deprived of relief and reinforcements that he tackled head-on the spectre of heavy casualties, which had so influenced the thinking of British governments since 1918. He claimed that undue stress had been laid on the devastating effects of battle in the last war. It was always stated that we had been bled white at the Somme and Passchendaele, but the French never forgot that 1,350,000 of their men had been killed as against 824,000 British troops. When Backhouse suggested a definite ceiling on the number of troops to be maintained on the Continent of, say, 100,000, Gort refused to entertain such a suggestion. Events might so develop that, unless we were prepared to take a greater share on land as the war proceeded, we might be forced to sue for peace. Gort had come a long way from his opening disclaimer of seeking to equip an Army on a continental scale.

In face of this, Backhouse retorted that, during a war, the Navy and the RAF, to which priority had been given, would have to be expanded, as would the merchant fleet. There would not be the manpower to maintain additionally a large conscript Army and to provide it with munitions and equipment. The Army should be properly equipped to meet its existing commitments for ADGB, coastal and imperial defence as well as possible obligations to France, but it was not possible in peacetime to provide and equip an Army of more than a certain strength, governed by what size of voluntary Army could be raised. Unlimited expansion would mean reserve equipment and additional munitions factories, which no one was proposing. Gort was right to say that the course of a war was unpredictable, but 'we had to work to the standard of strength in peace which we could be sure of maintaining'. The meeting ended, as expected, without agreement, but also with more acrimony than might have been expected given Backhouse's readiness to accept Hore-Belisha's proposals. Cabinet opponents of them would have been confirmed in their suspicions.[26]

On the following day, Thursday, 22 December, the CID faced an apparently more urgent question of how to cope with an air attack on Great Britain alone. Halifax and Newall looked for confirmation that, if this happened, France would still allow British use of French airfields against Germany.[27] Kirkpatrick's story had thus further complicated the debate as to how a war against Germany could and should be fought, since it could be cited both in support of closer military collaboration with France and of greater concentration on home defence. Chamberlain himself had remained reluctant to divert resources away from the direct defence of the United Kingdom and the empire, and he had cause to be concerned at Halifax's wish to commit larger British forces to the Continent. On this same Thursday, he made a move towards reinforcing his case in Cabinet and at meetings of the CID and the COS. He wrote a personal and secret letter to Lord Chatfield, the former Chief of Naval Staff, provisionally inviting him to replace Inskip as Minister for the Co-ordination of Defence.

The timing of his letter may have been partly influenced by a much publicised 'revolt' of three junior ministers, who wanted rid of

Hore-Belisha, Inskip, Runciman and Winterton from the Cabinet. Chamberlain was scarcely of the temperament to be dictated to by under-secretaries, who subsided as quickly as they had surfaced, but the accompanying press speculation about Cabinet changes in the New Year conveniently prepared his colleagues for a move to counter questioning of his position as regards France and Italy. Before his retirement as CNS in August, Chatfield had been a consistent advocate of 'limited liability' on the Continent, and could be expected to deploy his expertise and authority in support of it now. Chatfield was currently in India, presiding over a review of its defences, but his task was due for completion in January. In his letter, Chamberlain misleadingly depicted Inskip as anxious for relief and told Chatfield to expect a terse telegram: either 'Carry on', if the proposal had been dropped, or 'Confirm' if he wanted Chatfield back immediately to take over the post.[28]

Developments during the previous twelve days had reinforced a now settled view of how to interpret and react to Nazi policy, but had heightened uncertainty as to how relations with France and Italy should be developed. Events during the first month of 1939 in respect of all three Powers would confirm Halifax in his determination to reassure France and Chamberlain in his decision to bring Chatfield into the Cabinet.

5
Resolving to Resist

'It seems to me', wrote Cadogan on the last day of the year, 'that, unless there is revolution in Germany, we must flounder into war. And the former hope is slender indeed'.[1] Yet this sense of drift soon faded. Before the end of the month, he shared in a growing mood of diplomatic resolution, despite grim warnings from the Treasury and the Chiefs of Staff as to the implications of carrying such resolution to the point of war. By 24 January, he had become dismissive even of aerial bombardment; it no longer had 'such terrors for us as it had in September. It is frightful, but it could only succeed if it brought a decision. I don't believe it will, and I think we should meet and survive it.'[2]

Conviction that Hitler would soon order some further dramatic move had been accompanied by complete uncertainty as to what it would be. The forecast of bombs on London could not be confirmed, but the inflexibility displayed by Germany's naval negotiators at the end of December had been hard enough evidence of Hitler's hostility. A mild suggestion that the large increase in the number of German submarines might come as less of a shock to British public opinion if signalled by annual announcements as construction proceeded, rather than by proclaiming the whole programme in advance, was rejected out of hand after the German admirals had consulted their political masters. Presumably the programme was meant to shock.[3] The rumoured air attack on London had, therefore, to be taken seriously, even though a more logical sequel to the annexation of the Sudetenland would be the incorporation of one or other of the neighbouring German communities currently in Memel, Danzig and Poland. The recent episode involving Memel had made it clear that Lithuania was resigned to its loss and would offer no resistance. It was just possible that a deal over Danzig might emerge from talks between Hitler and Beck, held on 5 January, and British readiness to endorse any agreed arrangement over its international status had already been conveyed to the Polish government.[4] Some Polish concessions to Germany over access across the Corridor were also thought possible, though only war could bring Poland's near three-quarters of a million Germans into the Third Reich. Alternatively, Hitler might give priority to gaining control of resources essential to a major war, perhaps by a move against Roumania for its oil, or in the direction of the Ukraine.

Given their impression that Hitler made sudden intuitive decisions with little or no regard for the expertise of advisers, the Foreign Office could only hope that signs of something having been decided would be observed by their Berlin Embassy, and the ways of interpreting those signs narrowed down. Colonel Mason-MacFarlane, the Military Attaché, had drawn only two certainties from a mass of rumour and speculation in Berlin, namely that preparations were in train for military action at an early date, and that it would not be such as to entail a long war. Its imminence was thought due to the country's economic and financial difficulties; discontent would be diverted by a new and rapidly executed foreign adventure. It was unlikely to be the taking of Memel, as that would not require serious military action. At the other extreme, it might be an attempt to make Great Britain crack under a sudden bombing offensive; although Mason-MacFarlane rated the odds against any attack in the West as ten to one, he covered himself by warning that such a catastrophic possibility should not be dismissed. He himself was incautiously dismissive of the military occupation of Czechoslovakia as the answer, referring obscurely to 'the weight of evidence and recent developments'. He expressed his own guess with due caution. 'As regards designs against the Ukraine and/or Poland there is no direct military evidence to confirm this possibility. On the other hand, there is *much evidence consistent therewith, and none to refute it.*'[5]

Ogilvie-Forbes, Charge d'Affaires during Henderson's prolonged sick-leave, supported both this general assessment and its particular stress on a strike to the East. 'There is only one direction in which Herr Hitler with comparative ease could possess himself of many of the raw materials lacking to Germany, and that is in the East, and consequently the agricultural and mineral resources of the Ukraine and even of Roumanian territory are the subject of much talk. It is in that direction that Germany appears most likely to break out.'[6] Predicting a conquest of the Ukraine was not seen by either as inconsistent with their accompanying assumption that the action must be brief. Mason-MacFarlane made only the reservation that there would be no intervention by the

Western Powers: Hitler 'is probably – and in my opinion rightly – convinced that he is strong enough to deal with Poland and any opposition to be anticipated from Russia, provided his objective in the Ukraine is a limited one.'[7] An unsigned War Office memorandum of 7 January also expected Hitler's next major goal to be the Ukraine, but ruled it out for the present because of Russia's defensive strength and the risk of Western intervention in the protracted war which would ensue. Germany's economic and military position was not at present such as 'to risk a war except with the certainty of a quick success and relying only on her own resources'.[8] None of the three expected Hitler to diverge from his own plans by helping Italy against France.

Ogilvie-Forbes offered advice on how to avoid a European war in these circumstances. If Hitler was determined to create a system of Central European vassal states, whether by diplomacy or war, Great Britain could at least keep out of any such war by timely recognition of its powerlessness to guarantee the *status quo* in that region. This was, of course, in line with the policy laid down by Halifax since the beginning of November. Nor was there anything new in Ogilvie-Forbes's other suggestion of cultivating good relations with Göring and the Nazi 'moderates', who might come to exert greater influence over Hitler than they currently enjoyed. He did, however, qualify this with a warning against the view apparently 'still current in authoritative circles in London' that, in the event of war, Great Britain would have 'the power to provoke internal revolt'.[9] In effect, these assessments tended to relieve apprehension of an imminent onslaught against the West and to validate Halifax's concentration on ensuring that this greater Germany did not control maritime states strategically vital to Great Britain. On the other hand, they held out no hope at all for Chamberlain's policy of territorial change through peaceful negotiation alone, nor for Halifax's expectation of resistance to war from within Germany.

Reaction in the Foreign Office to these despatches, received during the first week of January, was mixed. This was partly due to differing interpretations of their uncertainty, with Vansittart, for example, (5 and 10 January) seizing on Mason-MacFarlane's unwillingness to rule out altogether an attack on the West as reinforcement for his own expectation of it. More significant were disagreements as to whether relative insouciance about German expansion to the East was still appropriate. Although Frank Roberts, in the Central Department, thought that the French government's lukewarmness about its residual obligations there gave the British more freedom of choice, he questioned Ogilvie-Forbes's assumption as to what that choice should be. He suggested that 'a show of resolution and a clear indication that we are not prepared to purchase a short-lived peace at the expense either of our own possessions or of other people's possessions in Central and Eastern Europe will prove more effective with Herr Hitler and with the 'moderates' under Göring than overtures to the latter or public disclaimers of interest in Central and Eastern Europe.' Cultivating good relations with Göring might be, in any case, a dangerous waste of time, since Hitler alone decided policy. (9 January)

Vansittart agreed with Roberts on the need for a show of resolution, and thought that France's lukewarmness would turn out to have been short-sighted. The British Government might be in no position to guarantee the *status quo* in Eastern Europe, 'but it is surely to our interest that states threatened by German expansion should show the maximum of resistance and that all available deterrents should be put in the path of German action.' The most effective deterrent would be to instil in the German government 'the fear of being involved in a general war'. German resentment of British and French interest in Eastern Europe, an interest which Ogilvie-Forbes had deemed futile, was actually an encouraging indicator of that fear and 'might well cause the Germans to hesitate as well as to encourage the Poles, for example, not to accede readily to German demands'. The somewhat contradictory advice from the Embassy about approaches to Göring and his entourage in this context need not rule them out. (11 January)

Sargent, by contrast, agreed with Ogilvie-Forbes in facing up to the fact that Great Britain could not guarantee the *status quo* of Central and Eastern Europe. 'Up to the crisis of last September we had a choice of policies as regards Central and Eastern Europe, but since the collapse of Czechoslovakia, we are bound to accept the fact that Germany has become the dominant Power in this part of Europe and that we and the French are no longer in a position to challenge it. Spasmodic and ineffectual attempts to interfere in the course of events in Central and Eastern Europe are only likely to arouse the resentment of Germany, with all the incalculable consequences of such resentment, without achieving the creation of a new bulwark capable of resisting German expansion.' This did not mean abandoning the defence of British commercial interests in the region and, thereby, helping the governments there to maintain their economic independence, but 'when it comes to the purely political problem, the most we can do is to decide in our own minds along which line we are prepared to stand in resisting Germany's hegemony, and I suspect that if and when we face this issue it will be found the furthest line which we will be able to draw is one which will exclude nothing more than Turkey and Greece from German domination.' He found the other recommendation by Ogilvie-Forbes 'more problematical', not wishing 'to give the impression that we are running after Field-Marshall Göring', but he favoured 'responding to any advances which he might make to us at any time' and expected such occasions to occur in the near future. (12 January) He was presumably relieved that some definite alternatives to appeasement had finally emerged. He did not anticipate how extensively the line of resistance was soon to be drawn.

Cadogan agreed with Sargent. He went rather further on one point. Despite Ogilvie-Forbes's warning against looking for internal revolt in the event of war, he believed 'that should not deter us from doing everything we possibly can to encourage dissidents in Germany'. (16 January) This, however, did not signify any sharp difference of opinion. Ministers and officials alike, in one way or another, aimed to influence attitudes within Germany, presumably in the hope that, even if Hitler was immune to outside pressure in making his decisions, he could scarcely avoid taking into account changes in the popular mood and the views circulating among those who ran the armed forces and industry. Chamberlain and Halifax agreed in seeking to influence the German masses by wireless propaganda, and the business classes by direct contacts; Cabinet colleagues shared their enthusiasm. Within the Central Department of the Foreign Ofice a sceptical note was struck by Roberts. From Wheeler-Bennett's recent book on the Brest–Litovsk settlement he drew the lesson that only in the face of a major disaster would the German people 'succumb to any form of internal or external propaganda'.[10] (9 January) Most of his colleagues, however, believed that at least some of the people near to the top in Germany were susceptible to semi-formal approaches from London.

The really sharp difference of opinion, to be resolved so quickly and dramatically ten weeks later, related to the dilemma of September last. If it was British policy to demand that territorial changes in Europe should be implemented peacefully and by agreement among the Great Powers, should Great Britain fight for this principle even if the changes did not directly threaten its own national or imperial security? Halifax currently thought not. The Foreign Office was divided. Chamberlain had not confronted the issue since Munich.

The immediate difference of opinion between Chamberlain and Halifax as to how far risks should be taken with the French alliance in order to improve relations with Mussolini was effortlessly resolved by the dictator's manifest indifference to British overtures during the Rome visit. After a stopover in Paris to repeat their assurances to the French,[11] the British party arrived in Rome in the late afternoon of Wednesday, 11 January. The first formal conversation between Mussolini and Chamberlain followed almost immediately, the second taking place on Thursday afternoon. Ciano acted as interpreter. Halifax was present largely as an observer, as Chamberlain had intended, but he did have a conversation with Ciano on Thursday morning. At lunchtime that day Cadogan spoke informally and very generally with Mussolini, using French. Nothing came of all this beyond an exchange of familiar diplomatic standpoints, in which the subject of Italo-French relations was studiously avoided. Chamberlain's secret contacts with the Italian Embassy in London had led him to exaggerate Mussolini's readiness to urge a change of policy on Hitler.[12] Cadogan advised the Prime Minister to persist in this and at least to leave behind the idea that there would be a 'blow-up' if Hitler was not restrained. After dinner on Friday, 13 January, Chamberlain told Mussolini that the latter's assurances as to Hitler's intentions and defensive policies had not convinced him. He warned of 'terrible tragedy if aggressive action were taken under a misapprehension as to what lengths the democracies might be prepared to go'; the German Press purported to be contemptuous of the fighting qualities of the democracies and to believe that they would never go to war. This merely led to an irritable exchange between the two men about the nature of press freedom.[13]

The Rome visit had changed nothing. Neither Chamberlain's expectations nor Halifax's apprehensions were realised. Mussolini's tendency to deride the British leaders, to whose secrets he was privy through a spy in their Embassy, was simply reinforced by meeting them. Above all, Italy remained as dangerous a factor as ever in British strategical calculations, both as a military partner of Hitler and of Franco and as a disruptive force generally in Mediterranean politics. Italian forces in Libya and East Africa could threaten directly the neighbouring possessions of France and Great Britain, and the latter's ally Egypt. Italian propaganda undermined British prestige among the peoples and rulers of the Middle East, intensifying especially the acute military and political difficulties in Palestine. So, although Italy was still the least of the Great Powers, Mussolini could offer, as could the rulers of Japan, direct threats to the British and French empires in ways not open to the more powerful Germany. Relations with Italy were, therefore, a matter of acute sensitivity for policy-makers in Paris and London alike.

The extent of this had been illustrated in recent weeks by a curious act of censorship on the part of Whitehall. In August 1938, Sir Richard

Maconachie, Director of Talks at the BBC, had let Ismay know that a forthcoming series of broadcasts on the Mediterranean would include a talk on its strategical aspect. He sought the CID's involvement in arranging this talk, scheduled for 1 December.[14] This was not unexpected; Maconachie, a former diplomat, had been appointed in 1936 on the assumption, apparently, that he would make broadcast talks less controversial.[15] After consulting the Chiefs of Staff and the Foreign Office, Ismay listed three conditions under which the Service departments would co-operate. The first, that the speaker should be acceptable to them, created no difficulty for Maconachie, as their suggestion of the scholarly Admiral Sir Herbert Richmond could not be bettered; it was even a welcome surprise given Richmond's past tangles with the naval establishment and his views on the limitations of air power. Nor did their proviso that the absence of official backing should be stressed, even though it was being sought. The third condition, however, was challenged by Maconachie, who saw the exclusion of 'anything that was likely to be misinterpreted by, or distasteful to, any other Power' as likely 'to muzzle us altogether'. He thought it enough that the Foreign Office should see the script beforehand to check that there was nothing to embarrass the government in their conduct of foreign affairs. Richmond, too, was less than compliant. He spurned the proferred help and sent his script, including the questions and comments of the interlocutor, E.H. Carr, straight to the BBC without consulting the Services. It arrived only a fortnight before the talk was due to be broadcast.[16]

The script was examined by the Joint Planning Committee (JPC) on 21 November and, two days later, Bridges, the Cabinet Secretary, chaired a meeting of Maconachie, Lt. Col. Leslie Hollis, secretary to the JPC, and Sir Andrew Noble, formerly at the Rome Embassy, for the Foreign Office. Both the COS and the FO were now opposed to the talk taking place at all, but it was pointed out to them that it had already been advertised in *Radio Times*. Its cancellation would inevitably lead to questions in the Commons, accompanied by just the kind of uncomplimentary remarks about Italy which official vetting of the talk had been meant to preclude. It was agreed, therefore, that it should go ahead after being rendered 'reasonably anodyne'. Hollis and the Foreign Office would get the JPC to make it 'more innocuous', Backhouse would persuade Richmond to agree to the changes, and Noble would draft a preamble to disarm foreign criticism. Maconachie himself would deal with proposed amendments to the civilian Carr's questions and comments.[17]

After all this anxious debate, the changes made were very few but they were revealing. Noble's preamble merely had Carr asking for the

Admiral's response to those who might see any discussion of strategy at all as 'war talk', and Richmond pointing out that general principles of strategy could be explained 'without bringing into action the armies, fleets and air forces of the Mediterranean powers'. To prevent them even being brought to mind, however, various geographical references and remarks even suggestive of future conflict were to be dropped. For example, Richmond's reference to Great Britain's capacity to attack an enemy in the Mediterranean, even if the channel between Sicily and North Africa was closed, was changed to 'holding up our end in the Eastern Mediterranean', and Carr's observation that Great Britain should be able to count on the help of France, Egypt and others was changed to 'we ought to be able to count on help, seeing that our relations with the Mediterranean Powers are on a friendly basis'. Richmond's own draft had made no mention of Italy at all; now references to France and Egypt as being Great Britain's allies were dropped as well.[18] Yet only a listener totally ignorant of geography and politics could have had any doubt as to what the two speakers had in mind in either version. To judge from these and other trivial amendments to an impeccably academic treatment by Richmond and Carr, it had been deemed dangerous to allow Italy even the slightest pretext for complaint about a BBC broadcast. The sterility of the Rome conversations might not suggest that the effort had been worth much, but it did signify how much was thought to be at stake by the Foreign Office and the Services alike.

The actual peril posed by Italian and, especially, German propaganda in the Middle East was in the minds of the Chiefs of Staff back in London at the time of the Rome conversations. They met on Friday, 13 January, to discuss a memorandum by the Deputy Chief of the Air Staff on the implications for imperial strategy of the forthcoming conference about Palestine. Their advice to Cabinet was forthright and uncompromising. To the familiar identification of the whole Middle East as crucial to imperial defence and, specifically, to fulfilling the promise to defend Australia and New Zealand by prompt naval aid via the Suez Canal, they added a warning that Egypt and the Arab states must be convinced by the outcome of the conference that maintaining their treaty obligations and ties of friendship to Great Britain was in their interests. The Axis Powers were striving to subvert Great Britain's predominant position in the region and to undermine its reputation in the eyes of the Muslim world. If 'our future policy in relation to Palestine is such that it cannot be accepted by the Arab states as equitable, and is not a clear earnest of intentions to maintain their friendship, these states who are already shaken in their belief in our good intentions will at last become alienated – if not actively hostile.'[19] In other words, the government must use the conference to demonstrate its readiness to sacrifice Zionist aspirations on a scale which would reassure its Arab allies.

While ministers and officials were making their way back from Rome, a shift was taking place in the forecasts offered to the Foreign Office as to Hitler's next move. Between Wednesday, 11 January, and the following Sunday, diplomats tried to find out what had transpired between Hitler and Beck. They failed, and so they could not interpret confidently the one fact which did emerge, namely an arrangement for Ribbentrop to visit Warsaw on 26 January. Initial speculation that Beck had agreed to a German railway across the Corridor and to some deal regarding Danzig quickly faded. It was followed by still more dramatic suggestions that Hitler intended to reward co-operative neighbours in Eastern Europe with a share in the colonial territories he meant to extract from Great Britain, France, Belgium and Holland.[20] Yet grounds for scepticism about Hitler's alleged plans for the Ukraine, to which these rumours were linked, were provided by a despatch from Moscow which reached the Foreign Office on Saturday, 14 January. It was from George Vereker, Chargé d' Affaires at the Embassy while awaiting the arrival of a new Ambassador.

Vereker argued that a move against the Ukraine by Hitler at this point was inherently improbable. It would have to involve either the promotion of a nationalist movement or a war of conquest, or both. Since Soviet political control over the Ukrainian population was total, there could be no reliance on the first course. Conquest would require the co-operation, enforced or otherwise, of either Poland or Roumania, and the former would not relish the implications for its own Ukrainian population or the prospect of yet another frontier with Germany. The Ukraine was economically and strategically vital to the Soviet Union, 'the life-blood of European Russia'. An attack on it would undoubtedly be met by all-out war and, despite the recent purges, the Red Army would be formidable in its defence. Vereker's exposition, free of the customary cautious reservations, implicitly demolished the idea emanating from the Berlin Embassy that the Ukraine was the most likely objective of the brief and limited military operation expected from Germany in the coming weeks.[21]

His argument carried conviction in the Foreign Office. As head of the Northern Department, whose remit included the Soviet Union and Poland, Laurence Collier strongly supported the view that the Ukraine could not be detached without a large-scale invasion and that the Poles would fight rather than allow Germany to mount an invasion from their own neighbouring territory with its five million Ukrainian inhabitants. They might be forced to remain neutral if a German attack was launched through Roumania, or they might join in for the sake of the spoils, but 'the ultimate consequences to Poland are so obvious that it would require the very strongest pressure, coupled with the conviction that they could get no support from France, to make them amenable to any scheme of this sort.' (19 January) From the Central Department, Strang (20 January) and Speaight (17 January) agreed with Vereker's analysis. Sargent thought it a good despatch (21 January) and Cadogan added two considerations which pointed away from the Ukraine: he doubted whether the Poles would be as relieved as they appeared to be by Beck's interview with Hitler if collaboration against the Ukraine had been agreed; and he thought February and March a very odd season for military action to achieve it. (21 January) To Cadogan, the despatch and the comments made on it all seemed to make sense. 'And that might point to the conclusion that Hitler, if he feels he must explode, will explode towards the West first.' (23 January) Vansittart was, of course, glad to agree that 'if there is any inference to be drawn from all this, it is the one drawn by Sir A. Cadogan. Such an amazing amount of facile nonsense has been talked about the Ukrainian project, that it is well to have the almost insuperable difficulties plainly put. There are no ripe plums in the Ukraine.'[22] (25 January)

These minutes were being penned while, and perhaps in part because, an alternative speculation had been gaining ground, namely that the postulated military operation would be directed against Holland or Switzerland or both. On Saturday, 14 January, the same day that Vereker's despatch arrived, a telegram was received from Sir Robert Clive, Ambassador at Brussels, reporting the views of the Chief of the Belgian General Staff. The latter claimed that the German General Staff had been studying recently a plan to seize the Dutch ports and coastline; the plan would not involve violating Belgian neutrality.[23] On that day, too, in Geneva, Harvey introduced to Halifax a Dutch foreign correspondent, based in Berlin, who expected Hitler to occupy Holland in the spring 'in order to hold us up to surrender'.[24] A new memorandum from Goerdeler, dated 15 January, had been dictated to Arthur Young by Reinhold Schairer at the Kenilworth Hotel; Young took it to the Foreign Office. It claimed that rumours about the Ukraine were a smokescreen and that the real plan was for a simultaneous attack on Holland and Switzerland; the object would be to force the Western Powers to meet

German claims in respect of colonies, loans, raw materials and world markets.[25]

Set alongside Vereker's persuasive argument, these reports were taken seriously in the Foreign Office. Strang, Sargent and Vansittart linked them to the expectation that Hitler would raise again the question of colonies in a speech he was to give on 30 January. Sargent suggested that he would pose as the champion of all countries which thought they deserved colonies, including Poland, and that he would demand the redistribution of all colonies, not just the return of Germany's. Roberts contemplated a German threat to lay London in ruins if colonial demands were not met, though he saw Roumania as more likely to be the next target of German aggression; the reported plan against Holland was more likely to be a case of Germany's generals trying to anticipate a variety of possible decisions by Hitler.[26]

Cadogan used the morning of Tuesday, 17 January, to assemble a paper on this and other recent evidence that an attack on the West was to be expected in the near future. He showed his notes to Halifax when the latter got back from the Continent in the afternoon.[27] On the following Monday afternoon, 23 January, the Foreign Policy Committee (FPC) met to discuss memoranda and notes on the matter by Halifax, Vansittart, Cadogan, Strang, Jebb and Kirkpatrick, along with Clive's telegram of the previous evening reporting his discussion over dinner in Brussels with the Belgian Minister of War, the French Ambassador and the French Military Attaché. The assembled ministers and officials faced a difficult task. As Halifax put it, they were all 'moving in a mental atmosphere much like that surrounding a child in which all things were possible and impossible, and where there were no rational guiding rules'. His colleagues probably felt that they had become used to that. They were now expected to devise an appropriate policy for anticipating Hitler's next aggressive act, the nature of which was as yet unknown. That there would be some such action at least seemed a reasonable assumption. Although numerous reports before them from 'secret sources' offered, bewilderingly, support for almost every current speculation as to Hitler's plans, they did share, as Halifax pointed out, one general tendency, namely that 'Hitler is contemplating a *coup* early this year, the danger period beginning towards the end of February.' Memoranda before them by Vansittart and Jebb had summarised these reports, but neither official felt able to claim that anything more specific than that could be firmly deduced.

Only one of these allegations, however, envisaged a situation for which no provisional policy had yet been devised. This was an invasion of Holland alone, so as to pose a direct threat to Great Britain while leaving Belgium and France untouched. The FPC, therefore, focused on how Hitler might be warned against attacking Holland and on what to do – and on what France and Belgium might or might not do – if the warnings were ignored. It was tacitly assumed that a crisis would have to be manufactured by Germany as a pretext for any attack, and everyone was aware of the criticisms made of their predecessors in handling the crisis of July 1914. Vansittart several times stressed the importance of warning Germany ahead of Hitler's speech. Three measures were agreed upon by the Committee. First, Roosevelt was to be informed immediately in the hope that his diplomatic weight would be employed. Secondly, broadcasts to Germany were to be such as to strengthen the imagined forces of moderation in Berlin. Thirdly, if a crisis was engineered, a proposal for arbitration might wrongfoot Hitler in the eyes of the German public. There would be an obvious difficulty, in that case, in finding an acceptable arbiter. Chamberlain thought that American arbitration would be generally unwelcome in Germany, but, ever confident in his own reputation, that Hitler might risk unpopularity if he were to reject British arbitration. Chamberlain was urged by Stanley and MacDonald to use the speech he himself was to give on the following Saturday to warn Hitler. Halifax offered to draft an appropriate passage. Chamberlain was non-committal; he might employ some such expression as long as it could not be construed as involving any new commitment.[28]

Whether there should be a new commitment was a question put to the Chiefs of Staff once the meeting was over. Inskip told them that the answers were required urgently because a public statement might have to be issued in the immediate future if their answers justified it. They were to report, in time for Wednesday morning's Cabinet, on whether Holland was so strategically vital as to require British intervention in the event of German aggression. They were also to decide, before Thursday's meeting of the FPC, what forms any such intervention could take.[29] During the evening a long telegram was drafted at the Foreign Office, detailing the causes for alarm, and it was sent to the Embassy in Washington for Roosevelt's 'personal and secret information', together with a hint that some public announcement by the President before Hitler's speech might help matters.[30]

The main work of producing answers about a threat to Holland fell to the JPC of Captain Danckwerts, Brigadier Kennedy and Group Captain Slessor. Their drafts were adopted, with significant changes, by the COS as their recommendations to the Cabinet and the FPC. Dealing with the first question, the JPC recalled opinions expressed in 1934, 1936 and 1937 as to the vital importance of both Holland and Belgium, the permanent occupation of which by Germany would endanger Great Britain, although not as much as would the defeat of France. It was doubtful whether British air power could prevent the use of Dutch ports by Germany for submarine warfare; this might mean diverting all sea-borne trade away from London. From Holland, Germany's short-range bombers would be able to attack London and other targets, probably with fighter escort, though this advantage was unlikely to be decisive. The German Army would be the better able to attack Belgium and France. Overall, German occupation of Holland would be to Great Britain's strategic disadvantage, not only in Europe but also in Asia if the Dutch East Indies came under German control. Arguably, these were short-term disadvantages and not in themselves sufficiently serious to warrant going to war, especially as British intervention, even if combined with that of France, could not prevent a German conquest of Holland. 'On the other hand, our failure to intervene would have moral and political repercussions which would seriously undermine our position in the eyes of the world and would be likely to deprive us of support in the subsequent struggle between Germany and the British Empire.'

It was this last consideration which persuaded the JPC to opt for intervention, on the long-term view that 'failure to intervene would have such moral and political repercussions on foreign and Dominion opinion that our ultimate security would be undermined to a vital extent.'[31] The implication of this was that war with Germany at some point would become virtually unavoidable once Holland was conquered; the British response must not be such as to undermine the prospects of building an effective coalition against that day.

The Chiefs of Staff hesitated to accept this conclusion. They acknowledged that failure to intervene might – not 'would' – have the effect predicted by the JPC and they accepted that Holland's integrity was so vital a strategical interest to Great Britain as to call for intervention if it was violated, but there had to be some doubt about intervention unless the country's defensive preparations were reasonably complete. Until they were clear as to the answer to the second question, they could not make a definite recommendation.[32] This was a tactful way of telling the Cabinet that if premature war against Germany with inadequate forces led to defeat, there would be little comfort in having impressed potential allies by a spirited response.

When the Cabinet met at 11 a.m. on the following day, Wednesday, 25 January, it discussed, therefore, only the political implications of the rumoured threat to Holland. Even without any COS recommendation, Chamberlain made his own position so plain that only Halifax sought to modify it. Despite the hesitations of the COS, the Prime Minister had already concluded that British intervention would be politically unavoidable if Germany actually attacked Holland. At the same time, he was firmly opposed to issuing promises to Holland or warnings to Germany. The Dutch government had sought no promises from Great Britain, and in certain circumstances, which he did not specify, a precisely defined commitment might prove embarrassing. He made a comparison with undertakings made to France, in terms which would have disturbed that country's leaders, so recently reassured by his public statements. Although France had undertaken to come to Great Britain's assistance in the event of an attack, such an attack could come only from Germany, whereas France might be attacked from more than one quarter. Great Britain's obligation to France was, therefore, potentially more onerous; hence his recent declaration that British obligations towards France passed beyond specific treaty obligations. He would deprecate any attempt to define the position more narrowly, and for much the same reason he thought that, for the moment, it would be undesirable to enter into a precise and definite obligation to intervene if Holland were attacked. He certainly wanted to wait for the answer by the COS to the second question.

The Prime Minister apparently still hoped to avoid involvement in a Franco-Italian war as opposed to a Franco-German war, and was questioning whether British involvement was certain if Germany subjugated Holland by means short of war. It would leave the impression that the British Government had deserted the Dutch if any kind of public commitment had been made to Holland or any kind of warning to Germany. Yet within two months he made just such a commitment and uttered just such a warning in respect of Poland, which, in contrast to Holland, had not been hitherto seen as strategically vital to Great Britain.

In face of clear resistance by the Prime Minister to a specific commitment, his colleagues approached the matter cautiously. Simon, Kingsley Wood and MacDonald concurred. Hore-Belisha acknowledged the difficulties of intervening. There was emphasis on the urgency of general military precautions by Inskip, Hoare, Stanley and Winterton. Halifax alone openly expressed unease. He agreed with Chamberlain that active intervention would have to follow a German attack whatever the reservations of the Service chiefs, but he would have preferred an immediate statement. He hoped one would not be ruled out indefinitely, despite

Dutch resistance to any move which undermined their neutral status.[33] No one appears to have taken seriously a suggestion by the First Lord of the Admiralty that much of the information may have been planted with some ulterior object by the Germans themselves, or to have gone on to speculate which Germans, and with what motives, those might be.[34] Even if they had done, it would have made little difference. Although Chamberlain and his colleagues still hoped, by diplomacy and propaganda, to avert war, they had come to accept, since the latter part of November, that war might be forced upon them at any time in unpredictable circumstances. All discussions of policy took account of that and, in an atmosphere increasingly akin to that of wartime, ministers tried to anticipate all possible contingencies. The rumours were a useful stimulus to this mental preparation. There was, therefore, no paradox in Chamberlain's combining an unequivocal readiness to fight if Holland were actually attacked with reluctance to spoil, by public warnings or guarantees, what prospects for diplomacy remained.

Meanwhile, the COS discussed a draft answer to the second question and asked the JPC to revise its structure and add to the content by 4 p.m., so that a final debate and revision could be undertaken in time for Inskip's deadline.[35] The final version spelled out, in even starker terms than the answer to the first question, the dilemma with which the Cabinet would be faced if Germany did invade Holland in the immediate future. The most that the Dutch could do on their own against a German attack would be to resort to their traditional defence of inundation, which would slightly delay the process of rapid conquest. If France and Belgium remained neutral, there was virtually nothing Great Britain could do to affect the issue. Sending troops and planes would not only be a futile gesture, but it would precipitate a war with Germany in which all available troops and planes would be needed to defend the United Kingdom. If France and Belgium were also prepared to fight for Holland, the position would be little different. Neither proposed to send troops to Holland. The British Field Force could be sent to France as planned, and the availability of Belgian air space would facilitate allied air attacks on Germany, but none of this would save Holland from swift occupation.

Nonetheless, the COS endorsed the JPC's conclusion that the consequences for Great Britain of *not* going to war in these circumstances were likely to be even more dire than would be those of intervention. They even omitted the only hopeful observations made by Danckwerts and his colleagues, namely that the prospect for Germany of war with the British Empire would have a deterrent effect, that British naval power could at least safeguard Dutch territories overseas and their seaborne trade, and that Great Britain's stand might attract allies enough to secure Germany's eventual defeat. They kept to the almost unqualified gloom of the main conclusions. These were that German domination of Holland would facilitate a direct attack on Great Britain; that the destruction of Dutch authority in the East Indies would undermine the British position throughout the Far East; and that a German attack on Holland must, therefore, be regarded as attacking Great Britain's own interests, a military response to which would mean war with Germany, almost inevitably Italy and possibly Japan, with only France as a possible ally at the outset. The final paragraph of their report was central to the debate on the following afternoon in the FPC:

> 22. If we were compelled to enter such a war in the near future we should be confronted with a position more serious than the Empire has ever faced before. The ultimate outcome of the conflict might well depend upon the intervention of other Powers, in particular of the United States of America.
>
> Nevertheless, as we have pointed out in our first Report (paragraph 12), failure to intervene would have such moral and other repercussions as would seriously undermine our position in the eyes of the Dominions and the world in general. We might thus be deprived of support in a subsequent struggle between Germany and the British Empire. In our view it is hardly an exaggeration to say that failure to take up such a challenge would place Germany in a predominant position in Europe and correspondingly lower our prestige throughout the world. Therefore, we have, as we see it, no choice but to regard a German invasion of Holland as a direct challenge to our security.[36]

On the following day, Thursday, 26 January, the FPC met to consider the COS memorandum. Newall, for the COS, observed that he and his colleagues, having advised that aggression against Holland would directly threaten the security of Great Britain, had, nevertheless, 'refrained from giving any precise answer to the question whether we ought to intervene'. He did not repeat the reason given, namely that the country was not yet sufficiently equipped for war. Nor, of course, had the COS been able to suggest any effective form of intervention, apart from declaring war on Germany and eventually restoring Dutch independence if and when the war was won. Instead of answering either question directly, they had implied that the government had a choice of risking, if they did so intervene, early defeat by too many powerful enemies, or, if they did not intervene, of suffering defeat at a later date because they would have alienated all their potential allies.

The FPC preferred the first of these risks. Most of them, including Chamberlain and Halifax, were convinced that the Dutch would resist a German attack, in which case no one present disputed that British intervention must follow. As Halifax put it, 'failure on our part to intervene would undermine our position in the world and would only mean that at some later stage we should have to face the same struggle with fewer friends and in far worse circumstances'. Chamberlain and Simon agreed. MacDonald pointed to the impact on the Dominions of failure to intervene. Australia and New Zealand would be sensitive to any threat to the Dutch East Indies; South Africa would be readier to fight over Holland than over any other issue; even Eire would be disturbed by an attack on a small country. If an invasion of Holland evoked no British response, 'the Dominions would conclude that our sun had set'.

Nor was any dissent recorded when Halifax raised the related question of a possible German attack on Switzerland, provoking French intervention and French expectation of British support. Halifax's view was that existing obligations required such support since the German move could only be in pursuance of aggression against France. Chamberlain agreed that, in the cases of Holland and Switzerland alike, intervention would be a necessary part of countering aggression against Great Britain and France, but he also invoked a more general principle. Great Britain would not be fighting for the security and integrity of Holland or Switzerland, but in defence of the freedom of all neutral countries. No one was recorded as having questioned or commented on this, though its implications were wide-ranging. Switzerland's neutrality was written into the public law of Europe, and the British Government was among those which could be expected to defend it even if their own security was unaffected, but the Low Countries and the Scandinavian states merely laid claim to various forms of neutrality which they hoped would be respected.[37] If Chamberlain really was taking it for granted that Great Britain would fight on behalf of all or any of them, then the first question posed to the COS had been unnecessary.

An urgent note was struck by Chamberlain when the Committee turned to the question of staff conversations. He brushed aside suggestions of delay while attitudes in Brussels and The Hague were being ascertained. The French government should be told immediately of the general policy provisionally adopted by this Committee, ahead of next week's Cabinet meeting. If, in the meantime, the French expressed agreement, Cabinet would then be in a position to authorise staff conversations right away. He agreed with Halifax that the conversations must assume war against both Germany and Italy; the Italians were involved in joint planning with Germany against France and Great Britain, and would probably be surprised to know that there was as yet no parallel planning between Paris and London. He saw no danger of Italy using such conversations as an excuse to pick a quarrel. He shared French anxiety about the Near East, and discussions should certainly include Egypt, Libya and Tunis. Even the Far East should not be ignored, though Japan was unlikely at present to widen its war with China. In reply to a question from Newall, he confirmed that, henceforth, actual plans were to be discussed with the French.

Chamberlain's sense of urgency was, however, confined to allied preparations for war. When Halifax referred again to the draft warning he would soon have ready for Chamberlain to insert in a forthcoming speech, the Prime Minister made it clear there was no immediate hurry. It would not be needed for Saturday's speech; the Commons debate on 3 February, after Hitler's own speech, would be the right time – if any. The distinction between preparations and a warning was understandable. Chamberlain's confidence, displayed in Cabinet on 21 December, that by personal diplomacy in Rome he could engineer crucial changes in the policies of both Italy and Germany had been temporarily undermined. In reporting to Cabinet he had been reduced to inviting admiration for Mussolini's loyalty to Hitler. The very possibility of a German occupation of Holland and the consequently increased vulnerability of his country to air attack had now made expediting defence preparations a matter of the greatest urgency. The very fact that these were to include Staff Conversations with France and Belgium would serve as a warning to Germany, if it became known to them. This is presumably why Chamberlain told the meeting that the predictable leaking of such information from Paris would not necessarily be disadvantageous, and why Halifax, Kingsley Wood and Hore-Belisha agreed with him. An implicit warning of this kind would carry at least as much weight as a public warning, without the risk of a dangerous retort. Halifax, however, continued to favour both.[38]

Alongside these speculations that Hitler might soon make war in Western Europe, there was relatively solid evidence that he was not, at any rate, preparing a military offensive in the East. Beck's meeting with Hitler had been followed by Ribbentrop's visit to Warsaw on 25–26 January, the outcome of which proved equally difficult to ascertain.

Kennard reported the general impression among his fellow diplomats that Hitler's purpose was to bring Poland into the Axis sphere of influence, ensuring its neutrality in coming developments, such as a bid to control the oil of a then isolated Roumania. Consistent with this interpretation was a planned German trade mission to Moscow, which might arrange a supply of war materials uninterrupted by naval blockade, and the notable absence from Hitler's speech on 30 January of his customary diatribe against Soviet Communism.[39]

Chamberlain's speech to the Birmingham Jewellers' Association on Saturday, 28 January, echoed the firm line adopted at the FPC meeting. Although he predictably defended both the Munich settlement and the Rome visit against their critics, and stressed that only if war was avoided could people look forward to 'higher wages, shorter hours, better food and better clothes', he dwelt more on the threat of war and on the need for 'unrelenting vigour' in the task of rearmament. He compared his position with that of the Younger Pitt, whose ambition for financial and other domestic reform was cut short by events abroad 'and, reluctantly, after long resisting his fate, he found himself involved in what was up to then the greatest war in our history'. He hoped that his would be a happier lot, but, with the British position having been repeatedly made clear, 'it is time now that others should make their contribution to a result which would overflow with benefits to all'. He alluded to the provisions of the Anglo-German declaration at Munich as a means to peace and conciliation, 'but until we can agree on a general limitation of arms let us continue to make this country strong'. Then, with the consciousness of strength, 'let us go forward to meet the future with the calm courage which enabled our ancestors to win through their troubles a century and a quarter ago.'[40] It was with this reminder of a successful war in the distant past, not of his own recent diplomacy, that he concluded his speech.

The speech lacked clarity in one respect. Referring to Roosevelt's New Year message, he endorsed the President's view that peace could be endangered only by 'a demand to dominate the world by force', a challenge which 'the democracies must inevitably resist'. Although the phrase, in fact, neatly encapsulated Hitler's dream, Chamberlain's use of it required amplification. The question whether Great Britain should go to war if Holland was attacked had been straightforward in that, whatever the answer, there would be no dubiety as to whether Holland had or had not been attacked. By contrast, it was not obvious how 'a demand to dominate the world by force' could be recognised. The words 'demand', 'dominate', 'world' and 'force' were open to too many interpretations to constitute a clear warning to Hitler. Two days earlier, Chamberlain had strongly agreed with the Chiefs of Staff that Great Britain must inevitably regard an attack on Holland as an occasion for war, but would such an attack amount to 'a demand to dominate the world by force', even if it meant the Dutch East Indies changing hands as well? Yet the Prime Minister was publicly warning Hitler against making a demand apparently devoid of specific meaning, while reluctant to warn against an action which would, in fact, trigger war with Germany.

The FPC's recommendations about Holland and Switzerland supplemented the very brief list of events which the Foreign Office assumed would involve Great Britain in a European war. Its political review, appended to the COS strategic appreciation dated 26 January, had considered that a postulated war in April, involving Great Britain, would most probably result from a direct attack by Germany on France or on Great Britain itself. An Italian attack on France would not necessarily do so unless Germany came to Italy's aid. The third possibility would be war arising from a German attack on a neighbour in East or South-Eastern Europe. This was the least likely to involve Great Britain in war 'for, even if Germany, of the various courses of action open to it in Eastern and South-Eastern Europe, were to attack Poland or the Soviet Union, to which France is bound by treaty engagements, or even Roumania, it is highly improbable that France, without a guarantee of assistance from us, would go to the assistance of the victim of Germany's aggression. As regards Czechoslovakia, although we and France have guaranteed its new frontiers, it is most unlikely in present circumstances that a war will arise in the near future on this issue.' As a German attack on Holland or Switzerland was to be regarded as a means towards attacking Great Britain or France, respectively, the Committee's recommendations did not affect this order of probabilities. The memorandum implied that assistance for France, in the event of German aggression against Poland, Russia or Roumania, was unlikely to be forthcoming.[41]

Planners from the three Services were making similar assumptions at this time. In preparing for an exercise, scheduled for 17 February, testing the recently constructed War Rooms, they constructed a hypothetical narrative in which war began at midnight on 16 February. After putting the most alarming possible interpretation on the current international scene (and correctly adding a deadlocked conference on Palestine to come), they imagined that, in 'this thoroughly poisoned atmosphere', Hitler and, to a lesser extent, Mussolini would 'throw discretion to the winds'. Suspected German preparations for war in the spring would become more open. There would be intense pressure on Holland, Denmark and Roumania, and the democracies would be vilified by propaganda in the Middle East. On 12 February, arrogantly worded demands would be made in London and Paris for an immediate 'discussion' of German and Italian colonial claims. These would be hotly debated by M.P.s and Deputies, but spiritedly rejected by both Powers. Within a few hours, an atmosphere of impending war would spread all over Europe and the Middle East. Troop movements and air activity would point to imminent war, and the British Cabinet would put its plans for home defence into operation, including the evacuation of children from vulnerable areas. Last-minute appeals for peace by Chamberlain and Roosevelt would fall on deaf ears and, at midnight on 16 February, they reported that once more 'the lights are going out all over Europe'.[42]

It was a scenario 'not deliberately related to reality', but there would have been little point in a scenario deliberately divorced from a perceived reality. All of it would have seemed not at all unlikely to insiders in government and the armed forces at the end of January.

6
Continental Commitment

Chamberlain had questioned the widespread assumption that Hitler's speech to the Reichstag on 30 January would resolve these doubts and speculations one way or the other. His guess, if such it was, proved correct. The Fuhrer did boast of his triumphs to date and he did reiterate his arguments for the restitution of Germany's former colonies, but he also stressed that such a problem could not be a cause of war. Nor did Germany have any other demands on Great Britain or France. He acknowledged the help of Mussolini, Chamberlain and Daladier in the matter of the Sudetenland, and hoped that the Czechs would not revert to the policies of Benes. He expressed satisfaction at Germany's relations with Poland and lesser European states, all mentioned by name apart from Albania.[1] His failure to mention the Soviet Union at all on this occasion amounted to a friendly gesture, given his past routine of denunciation. Foreign governments knew better than to take all this at face value, and the mood abroad of unease and uncertainty was not dispelled. His intentions were no clearer than before, but the speech was, at least, not obviously designed to prepare the German people for imminent war.

After the speech, as before, the British Government assumed two possible courses of events during February and March. Either, Germany would start a war, in which case ministers and officials must be clearer than hitherto as to the form their diplomatic and military responses should take; or, peace would be preserved long enough for an indirect attempt to change Hitler's policy by influencing the German people as a whole through propaganda, and the political, military and industrial elites through personal contacts. During February, both tasks were tackled with more urgency.

Success in the latter task would, in Chamberlain's eyes, reopen the path to appeasement. In a Commons debate on 31 January, he even claimed that the policy of appeasement, far from having failed, was 'steadily succeeding'. He did not offer any evidence for this imprudent claim. It was made in the course of defending the Government's rearmament record and of asserting the Empire's inherent strength, which, 'probably, if we were ever engaged in a life and death struggle, would ensure us victory in the end'. (An added reference to friends and allies helped to reassure M.P.s after the honest but unnerving 'probably'.) He did, however, make clear that settling differences around a table depended on a favourable international atmosphere such as did not currently exist, and that concrete evidence of a willingness for arms limitation must precede 'the general appeasement of Europe'. He was careful, too, to claim no more for Hitler's speech than that it did not suggest 'a man preparing to throw Europe into another crisis'.[2]

If Chamberlain's public reference to ultimate appeasement might be seen as no more than a diplomatic acknowledgment of Hitler's speech, he reverted next day, in the privacy of Cabinet, to more immediate concerns and in the tone of his Birmingham address. It became clear that his enigmatic warning against any attempt to dominate the world by force was more than oratory. He used the formula twice in recommending to Cabinet the Foreign Policy Committee's (FPC) conclusion that a German invasion of Holland must involve Great Britain in war. Although the circumstances of German aggression could not be foreseen and might not be such as to require an immediate declaration of war, 'any attempt by Germany to obtain military control of some kind over Holland by threat of force would be such evidence of Germany's intention to dominate Europe by force as to require this country to treat it as a *casus belli*'. Similarly, 'a German attack on Switzerland would be clear evidence of an attempt by Germany to dominate Europe by force, and that from this point of view a German attack on Holland and an attack on Switzerland were in the same category.'[3]

Chamberlain thus clarified his vague public warning by substituting 'Europe' for 'the world' and by giving specific examples as to how an attempt to dominate Europe by force was to be recognised. This represented an extension, too, of the motive for war as defined by Service chiefs and by his colleagues on the FPC, namely that an attack on Holland would threaten Great Britain's security and an attack on Switzerland that of France. Chamberlain's much wider formula was, rather, of a piece with his earlier talk of fighting in defence of neutral states within the European system: a matter of general principle, not merely of immediate national security.

His use of the term *casus belli* caused concern in the Foreign Office, lest it should imply to America and the Dominions an automatic resort to war even if the circumstances offered scope for diplomacy. Cadogan suggested a distinction between an invasion of Holland, which would require a resort to war, and some other German action, which might or might not be interpreted as a disguised attempt at military control over Holland. As long as this was a matter for doubt, it should be treated as 'a menace to the security of this country' rather than a *casus belli*. In response, Chamberlain agreed to substituting the former phrase for *casus belli*. Indeed, he wanted the circumstances in which the British Government would feel its country thus threatened to be described in language as elastic as possible. Hence, his preference for stressing the manifestation of force or the threat of force against Holland as signalling a German attempt to dominate Europe, whether or not 'military control' was involved.[4] In a subsequent meeting of the FPC, he explained his intended procedure if German troops actually crossed the Dutch or the Swiss frontier: 'In such an event, it might be anticipated that we should deliver an ultimatum to the German Government requiring them to withdraw their troops before a certain time, failing which we should declare war upon Germany.'[5] Thus did the January speculations give rise to the formula eventually used when Poland was invaded.

Chamberlain had rejected Halifax's proposal of a public warning to Hitler against attacking Holland. The Foreign Secretary's own advisers were also wary about the issue of any warning as specific as that which had proved counter-productive in May 1938. Ogilvie-Forbes (1 February) feared the consequences of any warning about Holland leaking to the press. Roberts (3 February) was 'fully alive' to the danger of another May 21st. Strang (4 February) agreed that this point was 'in all our minds'. Sargent (6 February) warned that 'any statement about Holland and Belgium will have to be drafted with this consideration in view' and must be based not on rumours of Hitler's intentions but on his assurances that he had no such intentions. Cadogan (6 February) endorsed these views.[6] Ministers and officials alike, however, acknowledged the need at this point for explicit public support of France. On 26 January, Bonnet had told the Chamber of Deputies that, in the case of a war involving their two countries, the forces of Great Britain would be at the disposal of France just as all the forces of France would be at the disposal of Great Britain. This gave rise to a Commons question on 6 February.

To the surprise of Cadogan, who had been uneasy beforehand as to how much support Bonnet might claim, Halifax prepared 'a very strong draft, really promising help in all circumstances. To my greater surprise he later put it across P.M.'[7] Chamberlain confirmed that Bonnet's statement was 'in complete accordance with the views of His Majesty's Government.' He went on to say:

> It is impossible to examine in detail all the hypothetical cases which may arise, but I feel bound to make plain that the solidarity of interest, by which France and this country are united, is such that any threat to the vital interests of France from whatever quarter it came must evoke the immediate co-operation of this country.[8]

Such clear agreement as to a diplomatic and military response to aggression had yet to be matched, on the British side, by clarity as to how an ensuing war should be fought. The original plan of restricting the Army to defend the British Isles, the empire and the Commonwealth, and of attacking the enemy by economic blockade and aerial bombardment had at least the merits of simplicity and coherence. Yet the slow erosion of this resolve to commit no troops at all across the Channel had resulted in a dangerous compromise; the proposed expeditionary force appeared too small and ill-equipped to play its tentatively assigned role of reinforcing both British relations with France and French defences against German attack. When the COS resumed their discussion of Hore-Belisha's compromise proposals on Wednesday, 18 January, the general standpoints of Newall, Backhouse and Gort were reiterated. Newall urged the need for strategic mobility and was reluctant to concede in advance any commitment at all of the Army to the continent; Gort reasserted its inevitability and the indefinite magnitude of a commitment once made; and Backhouse wanted a defensive commitment limited enough to allow of strategic mobility. Bridges tried to persuade them that a decision on equipping the Army did not depend on prior agreement as to its deployment in war. As even Newall accepted the possibility of some assistance to the French on land, the discussion ended in unanimous support for Hore-Belisha's proposals.[9]

The government had no intention of abandoning its assumptions as to how a war against Germany would eventually be won, but one of those assumptions had been that France's defensive strength on land was such as to avert defeat while the superior resources of the two defending empires were being mobilised. This particular assumption had been challenged in reports from the British Military Attaché in Paris of his conversations with the Head of the *Deuxième Bureau* and other leading French soldiers.[10] The COS had been asked, therefore, on 12 January to pronounce on whether, if British help was no more than currently contemplated, France could withstand a German attack; on the effect of a simultaneous attack by Italy; on how long French forces could hold the frontier; and on what difference would be made by the postponement of war for a year or so. The questions were passed to the Joint Planning Committee (JPC), whose draft answers were made available to the COS on 25 January.[11]

Even while stressing that they could not take into account surprise, morale and other incalculable factors, the JPC gave markedly pessimistic answers to all four questions. Their draft was then revised by the COS to sound vague and non-committal. As to the first question, the JPC thought that the French could probably hold the Maginot Line, but that if the Germans turned the northern and weaker sector of the Line by attacking through Holland and Belgium, France would be less likely to withstand a German attack. Here, the COS only changed 'less likely' to 'less able', and they did not amend at all the view that Italian intervention would seriously weaken France's power to resist a German attack. It was the answers to the third and fourth questions which the COS seem to have found disconcertingly specific. They accepted the JPC's view that it would be 'unsafe to assume that she could hold out indefinitely', but dropped the qualifying words that 'it would be surprising if her lines were seriously penetrated in less than six weeks'. They preferred to say that 'we do not feel able to formulate an opinion, which would have any value, as to the period during which the French frontier defences could hold out.' As to the question of how conditions might be expected to change in one or two years' time, the JPC thought that France would probably be much stronger and Great Britain certainly so, and that the latter would be able to give far more assistance to France on land and in the air than at present. They could not be certain whether the two allies would be relatively stronger. They added, however, that 'if the totalitarian states can maintain their present rate of progress, it is doubtful whether the capacity of France, with our assistance, to withstand attack by Germany and Italy will show any marked improvement, either in one or two years' time.' The COS omitted this passage altogether. The relative pessimism of the JPC replies had obvious implications for the very problem on which neither the COS nor the Cabinet were able to agree, namely the extent to which Great Britain should help France on land.[12]

Nor were Cabinet divisions on the issue resolved on 2 February, when Hore-Belisha was able to cite COS support for his proposals. He described them as modest. A formidable combination of the Prime Minister and the Chancellor of the Exchequer disagreed. Chamberlain emphasised that the financial aspect could not be ignored, 'since our financial strength was one of our strongest weapons in any war which was not over in a short time'. The financial position looked to him 'extremely dangerous'. He dismissed the argument that the French might withhold help without a greater British commitment on land; such particularised comparisons should be replaced by a discussion of 'how the combined resources of the two countries could best be utilised', in which the French might come to realise 'not only what a gigantic effort we had made, but also that in the common interest the best course might be that we should not attempt expand our land forces'. The French might even prefer a smaller force than that which Hore-Belisha now proposed, since it could be despatched to France more quickly. Simon detailed the already huge financial burden of defence, and pointed to other costly additions to come, which were also described as urgent and necessary. The country's financial strength might already be slipping away; during the autumn it had been difficult to maintain the level of sterling. Once financial confidence was lost, there would be no way of arresting it. 'We might be faced with a financial crisis as grave as that of 1931 but with the added difficulty that the foreign situation was now far more serious.' Hoare pointed out that one of those costly additions would be in the air defence programme; agreed priorities in defence should not be altered. Kingsley Wood suggested that proposals for the Field Force and Air Defence of Great Britain (ADGB) should examined together. Chamberlain opposed any decision in the absence of the new Minister for the Co-ordination of Defence; Chatfield had yet to examine Hore-Belisha's proposals.

Support for those proposals was also formidable in that it was led by the Foreign Secretary. Halifax went beyond his now familiar argument that France must be assured of substantial help on land, and tried to resolve the Cabinet's difficulty in having been presented with 'two sharply contrasting necessities, each commanding their intellectual allegiance'. An answer to these difficult questions could not be delayed for more than a week or so. He conceded the force of Simon's argument, but he 'was satisfied that the present state of tension could not last indefinitely and must result either in war or in the destruction of the Nazi regime'. In such abnormal and temporary conditions, borrowing for current defence expenditure was justified. Halifax's speculation that the Nazi regime might soon be destroyed as an alternative to war, rather than as a result of war, showed how seriously he was taking the prospects of dissension and revolt within Germany.

Stanley, on whose forthcoming visit to Berlin rested the main hope of improving relations with that regime through commerce, nevertheless supported Halifax, as having expressed what many of the Cabinet were thinking. He contended that Simon's argument about the unaffordability of such a defence programme conflicted with the reality that, in a sense, 'we were already at war and had been for some time'. The current situation could not last much longer, perhaps not for another year; the present year was probably crucial. Like Halifax, he did not elaborate. Elliot was prepared to support the arguments for equipping the Army properly, however the arguments as to its role were resolved. Chamberlain insisted that the additional spending could not be authorised before a decision as to its use. Since there was obviously to be no consensus on this, a decision should be postponed at least until the new ADGB proposals had been presented and until Chatfield, whose support he obviously anticipated, had taken up his duties in the following week. Chatfield could then join Hore-Belisha and Simon in examining the whole problem.[13]

If Chamberlain had appointed Chatfield in hope of his support on this issue, he was to be disappointed. The Prime Minister chaired two meetings of the three ministers involved, along with Morrison, who dealt with defence in the Commons. Chatfield backed Hore-Belisha's proposals, so that Chamberlain, having insisted on the importance of the new minister's opinion, could do no other than recommend them, with some minor changes, to Cabinet on Wednesday 22 February. Simon was 'gravely disturbed', but conceded that the military aspects outweighed those of finance.[14] Why Chatfield had changed his mind is not altogether clear. He told Cabinet that the position had greatly changed during the previous six months, and that the proposals would provide a good basis on which to discuss war plans with the French. His subsequent explanation, in a book published in 1940 and unreliable as to detail, was that he had 'determined to stand by the side of my Service colleagues against the Treasury'.[15] Since it is clear from remarks he made at the end of March that he was opposed to conscription, the Service colleague by whose side he was standing in particular would have been Backhouse. Halifax, too, saw authorisation of these changes as making it easier to resist French pressure for conscription. So a land commitment on the scale of the last war was still not envisaged in the acceptance of Hore-Belisha's proposals, and an assurance was given that the forthcoming bid for additional expenditure on air defence would not be affected.[16] A continental commitment by the Army had become definite for the first time, but it was still intended by the Cabinet to be a very limited one.

Alongside these mental adjustments to the greater probability of a German attack, there remained a hope, varying in strength among ministers, that war might yet be avoided altogether through mutually beneficial economic arrangements. Establishing mechanisms to facilitate trade between the two countries, with their very different economic and financial systems, had been a rare success, born of plain necessity on both sides, in the development of relations with the Nazi regime. The Trade and Payments Agreement of November 1934 had worked well, and a deteriorating balance of payments and rising unemployment had stimulated further British efforts to increase exports to Germany.[17] So far the benefits to Great Britain had been purely economic. It was now hoped that, if accompanied by hints of consequent political discussions, the current and forthcoming trade talks might tempt the Nazi leadership to anticipate negotiated gains on such a scale as to render the risks of general war unnecessary. This optimism survived the dismissal, in January, of Schacht, who had fostered it, and was reinforced on 28 January when representatives of the British and German coal industries finally settled their differences over exports.[18]

Stanley's forthcoming visit to Berlin was intended to extend the prospect of such deals, while the political atmosphere was to be stimulated by visits from the Foreign Office by Ashton-Gwatkin and from the Air Ministry by either Kingsley Wood or Newall. The Berlin Embassy wanted the Air Minister himself to go, but the Foreign Office was uneasy at the prospect of a return visit to London by Göring at this point; they preferred to keep the exchange at a Service level.[19] The focus of all these hopes was, nevertheless, still Göring. Halifax's belief, expressed in Cabinet on 2 February, that they had entered a critical period in which the days of the Nazi regime might be numbered, as long as the British diplomatic cards were skilfully played, surfaced again on this issue. Agreeing with his officials that the Chief of Air Staff (CAS) should go to Berlin, he observed: 'I think that when the invitation is renewed, it would be all to the good if the CAS could find a good reason for fixing his visit but deferring the date till middle or end of March. The more time we can gain the better.'[20]

Of these intended visits only that by Ashton-Gwatkin materialised. He had now the opportunity to prove that his official German contacts were more valuable than his covert links with Goerdeler and his associates had proved to be. In October, Prince Max von Hohenlohe, a familiar intermediary, had encouraged him to have a talk with Göring, who was 'impressed by the difficulties of autarky and feeling his way towards a freer policy'.[21] During November, he had been in touch with the German Embassy about a possible private visit to Berlin to explore the prospects of increased trade; he had expressed the hope of meeting Göring. The response was encouraging, and towards the end of January he was being pressed by Emil Wiehl, roughly his opposite number in the German Foreign Ministry, for a definite date. On 1 February, the Prince rang him to say that 'Göring's people had been enquiring if and when I was coming; he wants authority to telegraph Göring's people tomorrow to say I will be in Berlin 17–28 Feb.'

His colleagues did not show any marked enthusiasm. Kirkpatrick thought that the absence of any concrete offer might merely irritate Goring. Roberts noted that Hitler's speech, boasting of Germany's self-sufficiency, seemed an unfavourable prelude to talks aimed at modifying it, 'but in so far as Göring is leader of moderate wing of Nazi Party, it might be unwise to postpone visit further, especially as Göring is reputed to be less well-disposed these days.' Strang acknowledged that he could not withdraw from the visit, so it was better that he should go. Sargent and Cadogan thought that he should go provided that it was made clear in advance that he would be bringing no proposals with him. Halifax agreed. 'With economics so much in the air', he noted, 'and a prospective visit from Dr. Funk imminent here, I don't suppose it will arouse any adverse comment here'.[22] On 3 February, Ashton-Gwatkin telegraphed his expectation of being in Berlin on the dates mentioned.

Meanwhile, the Foreign Office and the War Office continued to try and divine Hitler's intentions. They were now paying less attention to the continued spate of rumours. 'Our sources of information', observed Cadogan on 2 February, 'have lately become so prolific (and blood-curdling) that I am beginning to regard them all with a degree of suspicion'.[23] On 8 February, Strang learned from Brigadier Beaumont-Nesbitt at the War Office that there was nothing to indicate early military action by Germany in the West, East or South, nor of any plans for aggression against Holland. Colonel Benfield, formerly Military Attaché in Vienna, told Roberts on 13 February that the War Office had gone through all the evidence as to whether German mobilisation could be expected in the near future; he thought that many of the stories had been deliberately planted, especially those about an attack in the West and, more recently, about German troops being issued with tropical helmets for service in Tunis. He was suspicious of some of Mason-MacFarlane's military informants, and the Military Attaché himself now thought that the note of alarm in his reports from Berlin had been overdone.[24]

Nevertheless, even if all the rumours were discounted, there remained much in the observable situation to cause puzzlement and concern. Although there was much uncertainty as to the nature of Hitler's conversation with Beck and of a temporarily aborted German commercial mission to Moscow, these did suggest that Hitler was trying to improve relations with both Poland and the Soviet Union. Dr. Hassan Nashat Pasha, the new Egyptian Ambassador at London and recently Minister at Berlin, told Halifax on 31 January of talk in the German capital that a political deal with Moscow was on the cards. Sargent noted reports that Germany had helpfully betrayed alleged plotters to the Soviet authorities. If Hitler was promoting *détente* in the East, it might be preparatory to aggression in the West. Cadogan wondered if Hitler now saw the Soviet Union as a source of unlimited supplies of raw materials in such a war, and one secure against naval blockade.[25] Even if this was the case, it made Hitler's immediate intentions no more certain. These moves in the East might have no more significance than Hitler's readiness for trade talks in the West. Whatever that might be.

The continuing lull was similarly open to contrasting interpretations. Halifax told Cabinet that 'the relative quietness of the atmosphere was regarded by some people as an ominous symptom.'[26] Cadogan was puzzled by it. 'This is a critical time. There's a curious lull in Germany. Either there's an internal tug-of-war, or they're preparing some awful devilment or – they're feeling devilish uncomfortable.' He thought that Chamberlain's statement on the 6th might have been 'psychologically just very well timed'.[27] Roberts suggested that the firmer British line on colonies and rearmament, British support of France against Italy, recent outspokenness by Roosevelt, and Germany's own economic problems may have combined to show Hitler that he would not be able to do what he liked in 1939. He would postpone matters for a year or so, while maintaining international tension. In Mason-MacFarlane's view, one soon to change, that would suit the German Army.[28] Depending on which set of untestable assumptions was favoured, it was, therefore, as logical to say that the present lull was disquieting as to argue the opposite.

What was certainly disquieting were reminders during February of how inopportune for Great Britain a war just then might be. A COS memorandum on 1 February recalled that in the last war Germany had come near at times to 'obtaining peace on favourable terms' even against an alliance which had at one point included Great Britain, France, Russia, Italy, Japan and America. Now, in the event of a renewed German challenge, any Italian or Japanese involvement would be on Germany's side. In such a world-wide conflict, could Great Britain still adhere to the undertaking, given at the Imperial Conference of 1937, that 'in the event of war with Japan, we should send a Fleet to Eastern waters irrespective of the situation elsewhere'? The memorandum claimed that the importance of so doing was undiminished. The Fleet's presence would deny to Japan the naval control needed to attack India or either of the Dominions, and confine its forces to island raiding. Admittedly, that might give Japan advance bases in North Borneo, New Guinea, the Solomons, New Hebrides and even Fiji, but, given their military commitment in China, possible threats from Russia and America, and the expected arrival of the British Main Fleet, they could scarcely commit very large forces in these operations. Sufficient naval strength would still be available in British home waters to contain the German Fleet, while it would be for the French Navy to limit Italian naval action in the Mediterranean.[29]

With the need reaffirmed, the practicability of meeting it in present circumstances came under scrutiny. The occupation by Japanese forces, on 10 February, of the island of Hainan, scarcely of use to them in trying to break the stalemate in China, could only confirm suspicions of Japan's aggressive intent towards the European and American colonies. Halifax told Dominions' representatives of his suspicion that the move had been co-ordinated with the Axis Powers.[30] It certainly reinforced the case for maritime deterrence. How precise that commitment should be was another matter. On 6 February, Backhouse pointed out to Ismay that, in the event of an attack by Japan when British naval forces were already engaged in a European war, the despatch of a fleet to Singapore might have to be delayed. The commitment to relieve Singapore within 70 days would have to be qualified or revised.[31] Backhouse made his case at a meeting of the COS on Wednesday, 15 February. It was agreed that the JPC should update the 1937 document accordingly. Further discussion of Backhouse's paper was to be postponed until the CID had ruled on revising the period before relief. Ismay expected the change to come as a great shock to the Australian government; it might give rise to 'rather awkward questions'.[32]

Nor was it possible to feel confident that comparable dangers in the Middle East could be avoided. The British Ambassador at Cairo, Sir Miles Lampson, had warned that the hostility of the whole Arab world would result from British failure to halt Jewish immigration into Palestine.[33] The Chiefs of Staff warned that the security of British forces in the Middle East and of their lines of communication depended on the continued readiness of Arab rulers to fulfil their treaty obligations; it was, therefore, essential that the conference on Palestine, which opened on 7 February in London, should be handled by the Colonial Secretary in a manner acceptable to them.[34] Axis propaganda was trying to exploit Arab resentment at the methods employed by British forces to restore order in Palestine. Those forces, moreover, constituted far too large a proportion of the Army, given the likelihood of a major conflict in Europe.

As with the Far East, there was no immediate danger. At the end of the conference's first week, MacDonald reported to Cabinet on his fruitless attempts to find common ground between delegations of Palestinian Arabs and Jews, who refused even to occupy the same room, but he had also noted that the equally intransigent public stance of representatives from the neighbouring Arab states was accompanied by private reassurances of their readiness to co-operate behind the scenes.[35] The Joint Intelligence Committee produced a report on 20 February, arguing that, while Egypt, Iraq and Saudi Arabia might exploit Great Britain's involvement in a European war, they were not expected to side with its enemies.[36] Nevertheless, these latent threats to imperial interests were an added incentive to averting a prolonged war in Europe.

The prospect of so doing seemed to improve during the second half of February, when the mood in Downing Street and in the Foreign Office quite suddenly became more relaxed. In the case of Chamberlain, it was induced by news from Henderson, soon after his return to Berlin on 13 February. He had exchanged diplomatic pleasantries with Ribbentrop on 15 February about peace, assuring the Foreign Minister that the 'noisy outcry of a section of London opinion and Opposition press' did not represent 'the mass of public opinion in England'.[37] In the evening he was due to speak at a dinner given by the *Deutsche-Englische-Gesellschaft*, his themes being the defensive character of British rearmament and the necessity of Anglo-German co-operation. He sent an advance copy of his speech to its President, Duke Leopold of Saxe-Coburg-Gotha. He gathered that the Duke's own address was then revised 'under higher direction', the text being passed to the speaker to read out only at the very end of the dinner. Henderson convinced himself that Hitler had had a hand in drafting it.

Referring to the importance which Hitler, in his speech on 30 January, had attached to co-operation with Great Britain, the Duke hoped that the personal contact between Hitler and Chamberlain at Munich would lead to 'a further clarification of international relations' based on 'reciprocal understanding for the needs and vital rights of the other party'. He saw an instance of this reciprocity in the recent coal agreement, an encouraging prelude to forthcoming talks between German and British industrial leaders in Berlin. Henderson's telegram on 16 February, reporting the speech at length, was seen by Chamberlain, who was much elated by it. On 19 February, having reluctantly the day before yielded to demands for greater expenditure on preparations for continental warfare, he readily endorsed Henderson's interpretation of the Duke's speech as evidence of Hitler's own peaceful intent. 'It seems', he wrote, 'to come closer to that response for which I have been asking than anything I have seen yet. Of course it would have been worth more still if Hitler had made it himself but, if he approved it, it is good and I shall make some sympathetic allusion in the same sense when I speak at Blackburn on Wednesday.'[38]

He then went straight to what seemed to him a logical sequence of events. 'Things look as though Spain might clear up fairly soon. After that the next thing will be to get the bridge between Paris and Rome into working order. After that we might begin to talk about disarmament, preferably beginning with Mussolini, but bringing in the Germans pretty soon. If all went well we should have so improved the atmosphere that we might begin to think of colonial discussions. But people have got so frightened and "het up" about them that we should have to approach the subject with the greatest care.'[39] He showed the letter to Halifax, who promptly warned Henderson against such optimism about Franco-Italian relations and pointedly hoped that 'your German friends can really show more than smooth words as evidence of friendly hearts.'[40]

At Blackburn on 22 February, Chamberlain addressed a seated audience of nearly 5000 people, assembled in three adjoining halls, and the relay system carried his speech to thousands more in neighbouring streets. His main theme was unemployment, still topping two millions, exacerbated by an international situation which damaged trade. This gave him the opportunity for an incidental mention of trade talks with Germany, agreeing with Hitler on the need for co-operation between the British and German peoples, and looking forward to emerging from 'all this fog of armaments and fears of war into a cleaner and saner air, more in accord with the true spirit of Christianity'.[41]

There was irritation in the Foreign Office at Henderson's account of his interview with Göring on 18 February. Instead of simply repudiating Göring's suggestion that, perhaps after the forthcoming election, a successor to Chamberlain might wage preventive war against Germany, he once again attributed such an aim to 'a section of the intelligentsia and of London opinion' and told Göring that the mass of the British people would resist any future Government that was so-minded. He did go on to complain of Germany's own war preparations, 'just as if Munich had never been', but accepted the Field-Marshall's assurance that Germany could ill-afford them and that Hitler had 'vast plans for beautifying Germany and improvement of social conditions just as the British Prime Minister had and his one desire was to prosecute them in peace'. Henderson gained the impression that 'Hitler does not contemplate any adventures at the moment and that all stories and rumours to the contrary are completely without real foundation.' He thought that Hitler 'would now like in his heart to return to the fold of comparative respectability'. This would not preclude his securing soon the reversion to Germany of Memel and a settlement of the Danzig question; 'Czecho-Slovakia may also be squeezed', but 'I doubt whether Herr Hitler wishes to force the pace unless his own hand is forced.'[42]

Scornful dismissal, in the Foreign Office, of Henderson's effusions about a peacefully inclined Hitler did not mean also disputing the Ambassador's assessment of Hitler's immediate objectives as limited and not involving a major war. This they were now only too ready to believe. Hitler might have decided, thought Kirkpatrick, that an immediate crisis did not suit him; he attributed this to British policy. (20 February) Sargent did not believe that Hitler ever had wanted a *European* war. 'What he had until quite recently hoped was that by intensive sabre-rattling he and Mussolini would be able so to intimidate Great Britain and France as to be able to exact yet another success from the Democracies on the lines of the Czechoslovak success last September.' He had postponed for the moment any hope of achieving this 'because the Prime Minister's speech at Birmingham on the subject of our rearmament and his declaration at the beginning of this month regarding Franco-British co-operation in defence of their vital interests and France's moral recovery in the face of Italian demands have combined to make him realise that the policy of intimidation may not work'.[43]

That the Foreign Office became more relaxed at this time owed little, however, to Henderson's reassurances, the language of which induced exasperation. An unexpected item of news passed to Ashton-Gwatkin in the course of his mission to Germany contributed to the change of mood, though the mission itself failed to reinforce his hope that a development of commercial relations would lead to political *détente*. Ashton-Gwatkin arrived in Germany on the evening of Sunday 19 February and left in the evening of the following Sunday. He went and returned via Paris, taking the opportunity to talk with officials in the Finance Ministry and in the Economic Department of the Foreign Ministry. In Berlin, he met several banking and other officials, but his most important, and most discouraging, talks were with Ribbentrop, Funk and Göring.

Both Ribbentrop and Göring, predictably, rejected Ashton-Gwatkin's opening gambit that a settlement of economic issues between their two countries depended on some prior improvement in the political atmosphere through, say, arms reductions. Ribbentrop responded with a lecture, which lasted half an hour but the upshot of which was very simple. Germany was not interested in any negotiations until the Four Year Plan was sufficiently advanced to make it relatively independent. Then there could be a broad settlement of colonial, trade and armaments questions, and of Italy's claims against France. Göring was friendlier, but even more obviously intent on lecturing Ashton-Gwatkin, who had to sit in front of a dais from which Göring addressed him behind a high desk. The Field-Marshal told him that the 'political confidence' he sought would arise from recognising Germany's needs in such matters as the supply of raw materials and the revision or cancellation of debt. Germany's Balkan plans, he stressed, would not involve the exclusion of British trade. He had assured Hitler that 'of course, we can work with England'. Ashton-Gwatkin wondered why he had to assure him.

If some economic settlement had to precede political discussions, the latter were very far off to judge from Ashton-Gwatkin's conversation with the Minister of Economics. Funk suggested that a necessary prelude to Germany's removal of exchange controls, as sought by the British and other governments, would be that an International Banking Consortium should buy up Germany's foreign debt and arrange for conversion into a new loan at much lower interest. Great Britain must persuade the United States to agree to this. Funk admitted that German internal prices would, nevertheless, be kept isolated from the rest of the world for a long time. Ashton-Gwatkin, therefore, saw no reason to believe that the machinery of exchange controls would be dismantled. G.H.S. Pinsent, the Berlin Embassy's Financial Adviser, who read Ashton-Gwatkin's report, agreed that, even if Germany's creditors could be persuaded to accept terms so disadvantageous to them, exchange controls would remain in place. Whatever German business might prefer, the Nazi leadership saw exchange control, import control, and the control of internal investment, distribution of raw materials, prices and wages as essential to the regime's economic independence. He concluded that, while the continuing trade talks might bring some mutual benefit, there was no prospect of general economic co-operation because the two governments had incompatible political aims. The British wanted it with a view to bringing about arms limitation; if Germany's leaders wanted it at all, it would be so as the better to finance their armaments drive.[44]

Ashton-Gwatkin's report of his various conversations was unpromising, but it was, at least, a useful corrective for ministers in receipt of Henderson's reports and of assurances of Nazi benevolence conveyed by such as Lord Brocket, recently returned from a private mission to Germany.[45] The item of news welcomed by the Foreign Office was in respect of Hitler's immediate intentions. At the beginning of his visit, on the morning of Monday, 20 February, Ashton-Gwatkin spoke with Emil Wiehl about the series of discussions between British and German industrialists, which Wiehl thought the most practical course of action at present. Wiehl expected German trade with Great Britain and France to expand as long as peaceful conditions continued. He thought that they would so continue, but he hinted at 'some adjustment that must be expected in a part of Europe where England was not concerned'. That evening, Ribbentrop assured Ashton-Gwatkin that Great Britain, France and Belgium were under no threat from Germany, with whose government they had agreements, such as the Munich Declaration and the Naval Agreement. 'But', he added, 'there were other countries which lie in Germany's sphere of influence.' Ashton-Gwatkin asked him if this sphere was political or economic. Ribbentrop replied that it was perhaps both. 'We do not mix in England's affairs; we expect England not to mix in our own sphere.'

The next day, Ashton-Gwatkin asked von Hohenlohe how he explained 'this recurrent hint of some adjustment in a part of Europe where England had no business to intervene'. The Prince 'was sure (from his recent talk with Hitler) that this referred to Czecho-Slovakia, and to nowhere else – not to Hungary or Roumania. It indicates a further extension of German influence over the Czech state. The Czechs would retain their nationality, passports, &c., but a German Resident in Prague would direct policy.'[46] His conversation with Hitler had taken place at Friedrichsruhe at the time the *Bismarck* was launched. He told Ashton-Gwatkin that 'Hitler intends to deal further with the two "historic lands" so that he can get the whole industry of Central Europe under German control.'[47] Roberts minuted (28 February 1939): 'This paper, and the penultimate paragraph of C2345 bears out the recent suggestions that Germany's next design may now be the complete absorption of Czechoslovakia.'[48]

The 'recent suggestions' were those received by Vansittart from sources in Germany, indicating a punitive expedition to Prague, once Germany had fomented a Slovak revolt to serve as a pretext.[49] The reliability of this forecast might have been questioned in that the aggression to the West, which his sources had been so confidently predicting, had not materialised, but Ashton-Gwatkin's report came close to official confirmation. It was now reasonable to assume that Hitler's next move, whatever form it might take, would be against Czechoslovakia, the direction deemed least likely by Mason-MacFarlane at the beginning of the year.

The relief expressed by officials and ministers at this news was understandably immense. For over two months they had faced the prospect of imminent aggression by Germany, involving the bombing of London and the conquest of Holland, neither of which they could prevent, but either of which would plunge them, still ill-prepared, into a war which was likely to acquire global dimensions and which might end in catastrophic defeat without quite undependable intervention of America and Russia. A degree of callousness about the unfortunate Czechs, who were apparently to suffer a mere 'adjustment', was to be expected. In Roberts's view, it signified that 'Germany does not intend to make serious trouble in the immediate future.'[50] Vansittart suggested that 'a brutal move of this nature is in reality a confession of failure and impotence, for it is based on Hitler's assumption that this further outrage can be perpetrated without fear of dangerous consequences, whereas adventures either East or West would at the present moment be too risky for him.'[51] There was, of course, still the matter of the 'moral guarantee', but the implications of that had so grown in ambiguity over the intervening months that it was no longer taken seriously.

Moreover, if this was to be Hitler's next move, there was general agreement within the Foreign Office as to the reason. A burgeoning scepticism about the spate of rumours, as expressed by Cadogan at the beginning of the month, had been fortified by growing confidence that Chamberlain's recent pronouncements had actually deflected Hitler from whatever major act of aggression he had been planning. There was agreement, too, that the government must continue to show its determination to resist. 'Any slackening of effort on our part', wrote Cadogan, 'or any relaxation of vigilance would be extremely dangerous'.[52] Kirkpatrick feared that Hitler was still unconvinced of Great Britain's readiness to fight, but Sargent thought that assumption had recently been seriously undermined by Chamberlain's speeches and statements, 'and Göring's wild and whirling words are evidence of the effect which the undermining of this comfortable belief is having on Nazi leaders.'[53]

As a result, confirmatory evidence in early March of growing Slovak hostility towards Prague and of Slovak contacts with Berlin was treated in the Foreign Office as reassuring rather than alarming. When Henderson, in a despatch received on 2 March, anticipated 'in the immediate future a period of relative calm', Czechoslovakia's troubles did not feature in his arguments nor in the reaction of Halifax and his officials to them. Henderson suggested that internal difficulties had accounted for the relatively moderate tone of Hitler's speech on 30 January, and that 'economic needs may have for the first time outshadowed political aspirations'. Given the hope that 'the forthcoming discussions with British industry may help to relieve a serious economic situation', he thought that 'it may therefore be felt to be wiser in the interests of Germany not to spoil the atmosphere in advance by any untoward incidents.' The worsening state of Franco-Italian relations also rendered untimely 'a serious venture elsewhere'. Only some new incident involving Rome and Paris or some new affront to the sensitive Fuhrer himself by the foreign press would be likely to upset a forecast of relative calm.[54]

There was a mixed response to this proposition within the Foreign Office. Roberts (6 March) noted that 'recent indications certainly support this prophecy', though he found little to reassure him for the long-term in the speeches of Nazi leaders. Strang acknowledged that there was support for Henderson's view in 'our most recent summary of information from other sources'. (7 March) Cadogan and Halifax were more doubtful. The former hoped Henderson was right, but in the meantime it was necessary to 'steer between complacency and hysteria'. (11 March) Halifax agreed. 'There is nothing solid enough here.' He was more interested in the Ambassador's suggestion about the following week's meeting of industrialists in Berlin, namely that just enough should be conceded 'to encourage Germany to hope for more, provided of her own volition she reduces her present rearmament programme'. Halifax thought that was about right and he would instruct Stanley accordingly.[55] (12 March) Among these shades of opinion, there was nothing to suggest that destabilising events in Czechoslovakia need affect Henderson's forecast. The relevance of any German action in response to these had already been discounted.

Nor did the Cabinet exhibit any concern. When they met on Wednesday, 8 March, Halifax told them that they would see from Ashton-Gwatkin's report that 'no immediate adventures of a large type' by Germany were expected, though that did not rule out 'the possibility of further pressure being brought to bear on Czechoslovakia'. No discussion or enquiry as to the implications of such 'pressure' was recorded.[56] This was understandable. To ministers, as to the Foreign Office, this looked like marking an end to the persistent embarrassment of the guarantee, and there was to be no question of getting embroiled again in the nationalist quarrels of Central Europe just when the threat of war with Germany seemed to have receded. At the same time, this German military action would inevitably rekindle in the Press and Parliament the profound guilt and shame which so many had experienced in the aftermath of the Munich crisis. Realisation of the political dangers of this is the most likely explanation of Chamberlain's otherwise bizarre decision, just at this point, to make public his optimistic forecasts about the general international situation, which he had expressed to Henderson on 19 February and which he had sustained in face of Halifax's reproaches.

A general election had to be held sometime during the next 20 months, and the Conservative Research Department (CRD) had begun preparing a manifesto in January in the expectation of an autumn poll. Despite the government's huge majority, which Labour did not expect to overturn, and although the by-elections since Munich did not suggest any really damaging loss of popularity, there was unease within the Party machine. Chamberlain had been warned by the CRD that the by-election statistics appeared inauspicious on closer inspection. So many of their seats were held with small majorities that 'only small turnover of votes would defeat the Government'. Douglas Hacking, the Party Chairman, wanted to 'hold off an election as long as possible'. Newspaper gloom about the international situation was blamed within the Party for undermining the Government's popularity.[57] These worries about the Government's standing would be intensified unless the imminent uproar about Czechoslovakia was countered in advance, by persuading the public to see such episodes in the context of an overall international situation rich with promise.

Chamberlain had already aired this vision of the future privately at a dinner in the 1936 Club on 7 March. 'Chips' Channon noted that he 'foresees no crisis on the horizon, all seems well; he thinks the Russian danger receding, and the dangers of a German War less every day, as our re-armament expands'.[58] Now, in the evening of Thursday, 9 March, he briefed Lobby correspondents on what came to be called a 'rainbow story'. Accordingly, they reported next day greater optimism in political circles due to the country's growing armed strength and to an improved international outlook. The ending of the Spanish Civil War would facilitate a settlement of Franco-Italian differences; a wider measure of pacification in Europe might then be possible, and if this brought during 1939 some agreement about arms limitation, the more settled atmosphere would favour a revival of international trade. Crucial to this would be the state of Anglo-German relations, far better than would appear from German newspapers. 'It is known', said *The Times*, 'that there are at present other interchanges between Britain and Germany – some of them official or semi-official – which are of a very different nature'.[59]

Chamberlain also persuaded Hoare to foster optimism in the annual address to his Chelsea Constituency Association on the following evening. For the most part, Hoare did this in a quite unexceptionable way which did not mislead, as Chamberlain's briefing certainly did mislead. The Air Minister suggested that defeatist tendencies manifest in public opinion the previous autumn had been replaced by confidence and determination. He pointed to the scale of British, French and American rearmament and asserted their determination to resist any attack. He stressed British readiness for trade talks and hoped Stanley's visit would help towards removing barriers to world trade. It was only in his peroration that he incautiously outdid Chamberlain's euphoria. He asked his audience to imagine a golden age of unprecedented prosperity which could be realised if only Chamberlain and Daladier, with Roosevelt's blessing, combined with Hitler, Mussolini and Stalin to guarantee five years free from the arms race and war scares. He called on the other European leaders to share the determination to work for this which Chamberlain had already shown.[60]

On the day that the 'rainbow story' appeared, news from Czechoslovakia indicated that a showdown between the federal power and Slovak separatists was now imminent. The President dissolved the Slovak government and reconstructed it on lines more acceptable to Prague. Walking with Halifax to the Foreign Office on the morning of Saturday 11 March, Cadogan noted that the Slovak crisis appeared to be settled for the moment; 'for God's sake don't let's do anything about it'.[61] Intelligence sources pointed to imminent violation of the Czech frontier by German troops. Slovak independence was proclaimed on 14 March, and on the same day the Czech President and his Foreign Minister were summoned to Berlin. With German intervention certain, discussion within the Foreign Office on 13 and 14 March concluded that cancelling Stanley's visit to Berlin would be the most obvious way of registering disapproval.[62] At 7.25 a.m. on Wednesday, 15 March, news was received from Newton that German forces had begun the occupation of Bohemia at 6 a.m.[63]

In these circumstances, Opposition questioning about the Czech guarantee had become more embarrassing than usual. On Monday 13 March, Chamberlain had provided the Commons with the latest news from Slovakia, but was not to be drawn on questions about the guarantee. On the following day, Sinclair asked if the government still regarded themselves as 'under a moral obligation in regard to the guarantee'. Chamberlain told him that the position had not undergone any change, but in response to questioning from the Leader of the Opposition, he professed puzzlement as to what Attlee wanted the Government to do. What he carefully called the 'proposed guarantee' was one against unprovoked aggression on Czechoslovakia, and no such aggression had yet taken place. Ellen Wilkinson asked whether it was unprovoked aggression 'if a friendly State sends propagandists into another country in order to provoke secession', and protested strongly when the Speaker ruled the question out of order.[64] Seymour Cocks had given notice of a question about the guarantee, to be asked on 15 March. On 13 March, Roberts had observed that since the last time the usual question had been put, on 21 February, they had received from Berlin an uncompromising refusal to proceed, 'clearly intended to leave Germany's hands free to exploit the present Slovak crisis and to effect changes in the present position of Czecho-Slovakia to her own advantage'. This meant that the British and French promise was 'not only incapable of implementation but becomes a very dangerous commitment'. Roberts suggested a temporising reply to Cocks, as any definite statement 'would either irritate the German Government or demonstrate our own weak position too obviously'.

After consultation with Sargent and Malkin, a reply for Chamberlain to use was drafted, pointing out that the present situation had not been contemplated when Inskip's statement was made. However interpreted, that statement could not have meant that Great Britain would try to frustrate a Slovak bid for independence. If successful, however, that bid would render nugatory any commitment to guarantee Czechoslovakia, as re-defined by the Munich Agreement, since its frontiers would have suffered further radical change. Thus, 'in view of the uncertainty of the present position, I cannot foresee whether it will be possible to reach any international agreement for guaranteeing the State or States which may emerge as a result of the present events.'[65] The answer was not required as the question was not put, but its formulation indicated Foreign Office scepticism at that point about any further attempts to 'guarantee' Central and Eastern European frontiers.

When German forces moved on Prague in the morning of Wednesday, 15 March, the worst of the uncertainties, which had confronted British policy-makers since December, seemed to have been removed. War with Germany had ceased to be an immediate prospect, either because the rumours had been false, as Henderson claimed, or because Hitler had been deterred, as the Foreign Office was inclined to believe. There would now be more time both to pursue the rearmament and planning necessary for any war Hitler might launch in the more distant future, and to conduct diplomacy and propaganda in such ways as might avert war altogether.

7
The Challenge of Annexation

Both the Cabinet and the Foreign Office expected the Slovak revolt and German intervention to bring them, simultaneously, embarrassment by exposing the worthlessness of their 'moral guarantee' and relief by ridding them of it altogether. The Foreign Office's attitude was summed up in an exchange between Sargent and Cadogan on 6 March after the Czechs had sounded them as to the possibility of their acquiring neutral status on the lines of Belgium. Sargent was for leaving their Note unanswered at a time when Germany was not only unwilling to proceed with any guarantee but apparently instigating a Slovak bid for independence. The prospect of escaping, by a multilateral guarantee, from the public commitment announced by Inskip had faded and, 'failing that expedient, it is difficult to see how we are to rid ourselves of this dangerous commitment. All we can do is to assume that in the altered circumstances it is already a dead letter. But we cannot say this in Parliament without reopening the whole question and arousing an unpleasant and unprofitable controversy.' He just hoped nothing would occur to provoke a Czech appeal. Cadogan agreed that one had to be cynical; if Czechoslovakia could not be saved by us last autumn, 'we shall not be able to save her from further consequences'.[1]

When the Cabinet met at 11 a.m. on Wednesday, 15 March, they were able to anticipate the scale of public outrage from the reception which the morning papers had given to Germany's action. Even *The Times*, whose leader only on Monday had praised yet again Chamberlain's diplomacy at Munich and had thought the time now ripe for a broader statement of British peace aims, was shocked into an outright and despairing condemnation of Hitler. His declared aim of uniting the German people without aggressive designs on any other people had been repudiated along with other of his assurances. Both Czech and

Slovak leaders had shown their readiness for peace at almost any price, but the Nazi Reich 'appears to be determined not only to expand to its full stature, but also to extend its domination wherever the weakness of other nations may seem to make extension possible'. The Western democracies could now only look to their own security.

Ministers seemed to have hoped that they could ride out the storm. They did not want to be thrown off the course they had set themselves for the longer term by this fresh example of Nazi aggression, given that it was directed against a government already helplessly a part of Germany's 'sphere'. They knew, however, that a clear denunciation of it must be made that afternoon in the Commons, and that the debate asked for by the Labour leadership would revive damaging controversy about Munich. Discussion at Cabinet reflected this difficulty. Halifax reported the known facts about both the German occupation of Prague and the simultaneous Hungarian takeover of Ruthenia; he agreed with the French government that there was no way of opposing or influencing the course of events. Bonnet and Berenger, President of the Foreign Affairs Commission of the Senate, had suggested to Phipps that 'this renewed rift between the Czechs and the Slovaks showed that we nearly went to war last autumn on behalf of a State which was not "viable".' The ostensible compliance of the Czech leaders was noted but not scrutinised. Simon even suggested that, of the two invaders, only Hungary had been guilty of unprovoked aggression. Discussion concentrated on how now to dispose of the 'moral guarantee', on whether the German action was a new departure for Hitler, and on how disapproval of it should be marked.

Halifax proposed to explain away the 'moral' guarantee by portraying it as a temporary device to steady the position while a wider guarantee was being negotiated; there had never been any intention of implementing it unilaterally in the meantime, and those negotiations had never come to anything. Chamberlain preferred a simpler form of repudiation. The disruption of Czechoslovakia might have been engineered by Germany, but German intervention had been under the guise of an agreement with the Czech ministers, so the guarantee was not involved. In his view, 'the fundamental fact was that the State whose frontiers we had undertaken to guarantee against unprovoked aggression had completely broken up.' That fact alone justified an early announcement that 'our guarantee had come to an end'. It was undesirable to supplement it with Halifax's arguments. Simon agreed that the government no longer had any legal or moral obligation under the guarantee.

Opinions differed, too, as to the significance of what Hitler had done. Hore-Belisha and Halifax stressed that it was Hitler's first move to dominate a non-German people. The War Minister forecast a *Drang nach Osten*; he urged a close relationship with Turkey and Roumania, and possibly Hungary, in response. Halifax pointed to the importance of broadcast warnings to the German people about the dangerous path along which Hitler was now leading them. Naked force had now been given preference over the methods of consultation and discussion agreed at Munich. Chamberlain saw no need to interpret events so dramatically. He thought that the move resulted simply from Hitler's disappointment at not having been able to stage a military triumph in the autumn. 'He had for some time past been working for a military demonstration.' The Prime Minister thought, therefore, that 'the military occupation was symbolic, more than perhaps appeared on the surface.'

There was agreement that British disapproval had somehow to be demonstrated and that Stanley and Hudson should, therefore, for the time being drop Berlin from the list of capitals they were about to visit for trade talks. Halifax did not want to withdraw Henderson from Berlin, given the difficulty of then finding any reason for his return, but he favoured the lesser course of recalling him to report. Otherwise, public opinion in America and South-Eastern Europe would assume 'we were inert'. Most of his colleagues, however, thought that even this action would be premature. It should be kept in reserve, while it was seen how the situation developed. Such extreme caution seemed to be the prevalent mood. The wisdom even of dwelling on the fact of military occupation was questioned on the ground that the Czech government had apparently invited it.[2]

This relative insouciance showed that, with the exceptions of Halifax and Hore-Belisha, ministers chose not to regard Hitler's action as being in breach of the Anglo-German Declaration, which he and Chamberlain had signed at Munich. Czechoslovakia was seen as having disintegrated through internal nationalist strife; Hitler had seized the opportunity to exploit the situation by extracting forcibly from the Prague government the sort of concessions advertised in advance to Ashton-Gwatkin. His action was admitted to be reprehensible, but it did not necessarily mean he had abandoned his commitment to Chamberlain. Separate Czech and Slovak states had emerged, but most ministers seemed to be assuming that they would retain just enough of a shell of independence to warrant a claim that the European States System, on whose formal integrity the British Government set such store, had been modified but not critically impaired. Initially, there was some outside support for this expectation. The *Glasgow Herald*'s leader on 15 March pointed to 'the Nazi thesis that people of non-German race must not be allowed to sully the racial purity of the Teutonic Reich'. The logic of this would be to leave the Czechs nominally independent; Nazification would then be imposed upon them by the ruling German minority. This would minimise international difficulties. 'No doubt the Western Powers will accept any arrangement which preserves some fiction of Czech independence.' *The Scotsman* likewise thought that for 'international reasons' Hitler might prefer 'to establish a puppet Government and include the Czecho-Slovakian areas in a German customs union'.

Most publicly expressed opinion was, however, overwhelmingly dismissive of such expectations, and the Cabinet consensus quickly became untenable. Even Henderson had assumed, at 12.35 p.m. on Wednesday, that something more than the postponement of Stanley's visit might be required; it would depend on 'the status to be accorded to Bohemia and Moravia and on future developments'.[3] From the Foreign Office's News Department, Peake communicated to Sargent the warnings of American correspondents as to the damage to Anglo-American relations from 'any appearance of complacency either by the British Government or the British press in the face of what Herr Hitler has done'. He pointed out that Benes was now in the United States amidst a large and well-organised Czech colony and that he could be sure of a sympathetic hearing from the American public. It was important to voice official British displeasure at Hitler's action. Sargent advised that once 'our own minds are a little clearer', a comprehensive review of the situation should be communicated to Roosevelt; the trouble was, as Cadogan pointed out, that 'at the moment, it would be difficult to formulate anything'. Halifax was consulting with Chamberlain about the latter's speech at Birmingham on 17 March, and the Foreign Secretary himself would be speaking on the 20th. 'We may have a clearer line by then.'[4]

It was learned from Phipps on 15 and 16 March that Bonnet expected Roumania to be Hitler's next victim; his view was shared by the French General Staff.[5] The Roumanian Minister at London, Viorel Tilea, told Sargent on the afternoon of 16 March that Roumanian sources expected Hungary to come under German control in the next few months; Roumania would then be dismembered, like Czechoslovakia, prior to becoming a German protectorate.[6] The French press was practically unanimous in concluding that Germany had 'torn the Munich Agreements to shreds, and destroyed the hopes of appeasement'.[7] Commenting, Speaight suggested that Hitler's readiness to allow

Hungary to annex Ruthenia was a sign that Hungary's own independent existence would soon be ended.[8]

The debate in the Commons on the afternoon of 15 March went badly for the Government. The Prime Minister's opening statement was ill-judged in tone and substance. He began by summarising events since 10 March, when the Czech President had dismissed Tiso and some other Slovak ministers. His summary was based mostly on the German communiqués, as he pretended that he had to rely mainly on press statements. He then repeated the case he had made in Cabinet as to why the moral guarantee had ceased to be applicable, and he detailed the changed position with regard to British financial aid. He defended the Munich Agreement against its critics. He taxed the credulity of his listeners in refusing to believe that 'anything of the kind which has now taken place was contemplated by any of the signatories to the Munich Agreement at the time of its signature.' He complained of Germany's failure to notify the other signatories of the despatch of her troops 'beyond the frontier there laid down'. He noted the claim of official Czech acquiescence in what had occurred, but could not regard 'the manner and the method by which these changes have been brought about as in accord with the spirit of the Munich Agreement'.

This downplaying of what he and his colleagues knew perfectly well to have been an act of planned aggression was followed by an attempt to minimise its longer-term significance. He accepted that this new development of a military occupation by Germany 'of territory inhabited by people with whom they have no racial connection' was bound to disturb the international situation and administer a shock to confidence, just when, he claimed, confidence was beginning to revive. He bitterly regretted what had occurred, but 'do not let us on that account be deflected from our course.' Occasional checks and disappointments would not deflect the government from continuing to foster the universal desire for a return to peace and good will or from seeking 'to substitute the method of discussion for the method of force in the settlement of differences'. Thus did he make clear that appeasement remained the government's policy, even though the word was not mentioned.[9]

The debate that followed was predictably acrimonious. The feature likeliest to irritate the government was that none of the ten Conservative backbenchers who made speeches fully supported the continuity of policy pledged by the Prime Minister. Seven of them – Anthony Eden, Viscount Wolmer, Richard Law, Annesley Somerville, Commander Bower, Godfrey Nicholson and Duncan Sandys – forecast worse crises in the immediate future and called for national unity, implicitly or explicitly involving all-party government. They were apparently undeterred by the insistence of successive Opposition speakers that this could only be under a different Prime Minister. Somerville, Nicholson and Sandys did accept that Chamberlain had been right in September, but all seven insisted that a new policy of active resistance, in association with other Powers, was now needed.[10] The three who wanted appeasement to continue – Somerset De Chair, Patrick Donner and Commander Sir Archibald Southby – were so minded because it would allow the Government then to turn its back on continental quarrels altogether and concentrate on the defence of British maritime and imperial interests.[11]

Opposition speeches denounced Government policy in familiar terms, called for Chamberlain's resignation, and advocated some form of grand alliance to contain Nazi Germany. The challenge which caused Simon the greatest difficulty in his much-interrupted reply for the government was that by Hugh Dalton. Dalton picked up a motoring metaphor used by Halifax in a recent speech, in which he had warned Hitler that he was approaching a 'major road ahead'. What 'major road' had Halifax meant? Hungary? Roumania? Poland? Denmark? Holland? Simon tried to ignore the question. He concentrated on undermining the call by Eden and Dalton for a conference of threatened countries, at which a line would be set, any violation of which would meet united resistance. He argued that British governments had been traditionally opposed to commitments obliging them automatically to go to war when a foreign government interpreted circumstances as warranting it. Very effectively, he quoted remarks to that effect, made by Eden himself when a minister. The effect was spoiled by Dalton's persistent enquiry about Halifax's remark, which seemed to advocate just such an indefinite commitment. Simon refused to list the possible countries, and suggested that the Foreign Secretary had been referring to Italy's quarrel with France. He then quickly brought his speech to a close, reiterating that events had not discredited Chamberlain's policy and that the Government was resolved to continue with it.[12]

If a week is a long time in politics, the three weeks which had elapsed since Halifax's remark had been more than enough to blur the memories of Dalton and Simon alike as to its context and meaning. On the afternoon of Thursday, 23 February, the Lords had debated Anglo-French relations. The Labour peer, Addison, had asked Halifax about the statement Chamberlain had made to the Commons on 6 February, committing Great Britain to go to the aid of France against attack from whatever quarter. Addison wanted an assurance that this did not mean the abandonment of attempts to remove international grievances by conference diplomacy. Russia especially should be involved in this. He was critical of France's earlier attempts to use the League to form 'a sort of iron ring round Germany, and to fence in many of the unjust provisions of the Treaty of Versailles'. After Crewe had disputed this view of French diplomacy, Halifax reiterated in forthright terms British determination to back France and condemned attempts to play down Chamberlain's assurance. It would be 'a profound error to suppose that any mental reservation of any kind accompanied the Prime Minister's words. That declaration was indeed quite clear and unmistakable. If I may translate it into terms of a homely parable, it was in the nature of one of those signs which we now see in many places on our highway system, carrying the device "Halt: Major road ahead." That was its purpose.'[13] So the only country 'ahead' was France. Dalton's question was thus pointless, yet Simon's recollection was too hazy to dismiss it.

On Thursday morning the press referred to the 'annexation' of Bohemia and Moravia, undermining any case the government might wish to make that some semblance of Czech autonomy had been preserved. The Cabinet's predominantly sanguine reading of events was finally shattered between 5 and 6 p.m. that day. Two messages were received from Henderson, making clear that Bohemia and Moravia had indeed been annexed to the German Reich. A decree just issued did not even offer a verbal disguise to which optimistic politicians or diplomats might cling. Henderson was aghast. His recent forecast of relative calm had been dramatically discredited. His notorious readiness to give Hitler the benefit of any possible doubt was cast aside, as there was now no possible doubt. 'The utter cynicism and immorality of the whole performance defies description', he declared. There had been some moral justification for Hitler's previous acquisitions. 'The annexation of Bohemia and Moravia is on a completely different plane and cannot be justified on any grounds which weakened opposition to incorporation of Austria and Sudetenland. It is entirely contrary to right of self-determination and utterly immoral. It constitutes a wrong which will soon call for redress and though it may have afforded Herr Hitler and Herr von Ribbentrop a facile triumph it would be sad not to believe that in the end it will prove a costly error.' He pointed to the violation of the agreements which Hitler had made at Munich. 'His Majesty's Government will doubtless consider what attitude to adopt towards a Government which has shown itself incapable of observing an agreement not six months old and which is apparently set on domination of the whole of the Danube basin.'[14]

In Chamberlain's eyes, too, this formal confirmation of a violent change to the European States System was manifestly of concern to Great Britain, as to all other members of the System, and thus a matter on which the statement of 30 September bound Germany to consult with Great Britain. He had taken the commitment very seriously. Although he had been obliged to take even more seriously the subsequent rumours of imminent German aggression, when these died down he had reverted to his normal optimism during the first two weeks of March. He had not been disturbed in this by the well-signalled German moves, as Göring and Ribbentrop had been at pains to stress to Ashton-Gwatkin that action against the Czechs would not be such as to concern the British Government. Now that he was forced to realise that Hitler did not regard the overthrow of a neighbouring government and the annexation of its territory as a question to 'concern our two countries', Chamberlain's mood swung as dramatically as had that of the Ambassador. He was suddenly shocked and angry.

Evidence of this is to be found in a 'secret and personal' letter which he wrote on the following afternoon, Friday 17 March to his Cabinet colleague, Runciman, who was abroad on a sea voyage to restore his health.

> My dear Walter,
>
> The events of the past week – a surprise as usual – have changed the whole situation. They show I am afraid that settlement is impossible with the present regime in Germany, since they cannot be relied upon to carry out any assurances they give.
>
> In these circumstances there seems to be little left of the differences between Anthony and myself and I think he would like to come back to the Government. So long as his return would be regarded as a change of policy when policy had not been changed I could not consider it. But now that Hitler has made the policy impossible – for the present at any rate, – I am bound to open my mind again.
>
> I have come to no final decision yet and am just off to Birmingham to make a fateful speech but I may want to act quickly next week and you very generously left me a free hand when you saw me before beginning your voyage. Accordingly I wired you today
>
>> 'Circumstances which you will understand may compel immediate acceptance publication your offer of February last. Writing Sydney today. N.C.'
>
> and this will I hope reach you in good time to prepare for any announcement next week.[15]

Chamberlain's readiness even to consider a course so distasteful to him as inviting Eden back into the Cabinet was a measure of the shock he had received. So was the speech to which he had referred in the letter and which he delivered in the evening to the annual meeting of the Birmingham Unionist Association. He had consulted more widely than usual as to its content, and had been sensitive to the views of Halifax and the Foreign Office. For example, on receiving an urgent phone message from the Foreign Office, shortly before delivering his speech, that the King of Roumania had asked for public affirmation of British and French interest in South-Eastern Europe, he took care to insert an appropriate remark.[16]

In the speech, he came close to apologising for the impression of unfeeling detachment conveyed in his remarks to the Commons on Wednesday; he said he would use the present occasion to show how mistaken that impression had been. He made no apology for his role in the Munich settlement, which he defended at length along with his general policy of appeasement; his only doubt was as to the appositeness of the word itself. Hitler's actions over the past few days had shattered the hopes embodied in that settlement. Even if there were any disorders of the kind so absurdly claimed to threaten Germany, they had been fomented from without. He had unilaterally destroyed the settlement by armed force and without even consulting other signatories to the Agreement. The annexation of Bohemia and Moravia had been accompanied by the appearance of the Gestapo and the usual wholesale arrests.

> Every man and woman in this country who remembers the fate of the Jews and the political prisoners in Austria must be filled to-day with distress and foreboding. Who can fail to feel his heart go out in sympathy to the proud and brave people who have so suddenly been subjected to this invasion, whose liberties have been curtailed, whose national independence has gone? What has become of this declaration of "No further territorial ambition"? What has become of the assurance "We don't want Czechs in the Reich"? What regard has been paid here to that principle of self-determination on which Herr Hitler argued so vehemently with me at Berchtesgaden when he was asking for the severance of Sudetenland from Czechoslovakia and its inclusion in the German Reich?'

Previous violations by Hitler of the international order might have been thought justified, in their outcome if not their method, but his present actions were in complete disregard of Germany's own proclaimed principles. They gave rise to three questions:

(1) Is this the end of an old adventure, or is it the beginning of a new?
(2) Is this the last attack upon a small state, or is it to be followed by others?
(3) Is this, in fact, a step in the direction of an attempt to dominate the world by force?

These questions became the most quoted section of his address. Their very enunciation in a speech broadcast internationally gave the impression that Chamberlain inclined to the second alternative in each case, indicating a return to his mood of late January and early February, when he had told another audience in Birmingham that evidence of such an attempt would constitute a *casus belli* for Great Britain. The impression was reinforced when he went on to announce that every aspect of national life must be reviewed from the point of view of national safety. The Government would consult with the Commonwealth, France and all other nations who valued freedom even above peace.[17]

Yet on both occasions Chamberlain seems to have been puzzled about Hitler's intentions; the questions he was now posing appear to have been quite genuine. He continued to find it incredible that Hitler would deliberately expose Germany to the hazards of a general European war, but, embarrassingly soon after sharing his roseate prophecies with the nation, he had been forced to realise once again how unsafe it would be to make that assumption in devising policies. Profoundly shocked by the annexation, which he regarded as a betrayal of him by Hitler, he promptly reverted to the policy of warning and deterrence which he had acknowledged to be the only appropriate course in early February and which he had prematurely acclaimed a success. He did not make clear, however, whether this meant abandoning altogether the policy of appeasement, or whether he believed that he could this time devise new forms of deterrence so effective that Hitler would have no alternative but to accept a revision of Versailles by peaceful methods alone.

During the hours on Friday when Chamberlain was preparing and delivering his speech, the shock of recent events was also being registered at the Foreign Office by the untypically maladroit way in which Halifax, Cadogan and Sargent responded to a report of German pressure on Roumania. At his meeting with Sargent on the afternoon of 16 March, Tilea had pointed out that Roumania's recent arms contracts with the Czech government were now likely to be aborted, and he broached the question of a loan to buy alternative supplies from British, Belgian and American firms. Although Sargent was non-committal, the request had a good chance of being met. Of the thirty-six countries seeking arms from Great Britain, Roumania was currently ranked eighth in order of priority by the COS (after Egypt, Iraq, Belgium, Portugal, Turkey, Greece and the Netherlands),[18] and Cadogan did not anticipate problems with the necessary legislation in present circumstances. Nor would there have been any problem with instructions received later that day by Tilea and his counterpart in Paris to urge greater assertiveness in South-Eastern Europe by the two Western Powers. Both were already considering what form this might take, and King Carol's aim in this was simply to preserve a diplomatic balance in the region once the current negotiations for an economic agreement with Germany had been completed. Before he could carry out these instructions, however, Tilea was told by telephone, at 6 a.m. on Friday, 17 March, details of demands made by Germany. The caller, from Paris, was an employee of a Roumanian industrialist, Nicolae Malaxa. It was Tilea's premature use of this report which led to premature action by the Foreign Office.

The report was related to the prolonged negotiations with Germany. The policy of King Carol and his Foreign Minister, Grigore Gafencu, was to secure from Germany a guarantee of Roumania's territorial integrity, long at risk from Hungarian, Bulgarian and Soviet claims, in exchange for the economic concessions sought by the German government. At the same time, they did not intend to rely for their continued independence on German restraint, and encouraged also the assertion of British and French influence in Roumania and the rest of the region. Despite this policy of equilibrium, their readiness to deal with Germany met with some opposition. Malaxa was among the opponents. So was the Minister-President, Armand Calinescu, who had recommended Tilea for the London post. Tilea himself feared German designs on Transylvania, where he had been born.[19] Seeing the report as a means of reinforcing the case he had to make to the British Government, Tilea asked his influential fellow-Roumanian, Marthe Bibescu, to spread the report through her network of political contacts, thus giving an impression of independent testimony. Her message reached Halifax's Private Secretary, Oliver Harvey, shortly before Tilea arrived at the Foreign Office. Before the end of the day, Tilea had also spoken with Jebb, Cadogan and Vansittart, with the American, Russian and Turkish Ambasadors, and with the Greek Minister. His Military Attache had been in touch with Hore-Belisha.[20] Tilea told Halifax that 'during the last few days the Roumanian Government had received a request from the German

Government to grant them a monopoly of Roumanian exports, and to adopt certain measures of restriction of Roumanian industrial production in German interests. If these conditions were accepted, Germany would guarantee the Roumanian frontiers.' This had seemed to the Roumanian government 'something very much like an ultimatum'. In the evening, he had told Cadogan that his government had rejected the proposals and that further proposals, of which he had no details, had then been presented.[21]

An obvious reflection would have been that an ultimatum could not, by definition, be followed by further proposals, and that 'something very much like an ultimatum' might have been normal Nazi heavy-handedness in negotiations with a lesser Power. An obvious course of action would have been to instruct Sir Reginald Hoare by telegram to check the report. Instead, Halifax, Cadogan and Sargent agreed that instructions to act on the report should be sent that evening to British diplomats in Moscow, Warsaw, Ankara, Athens and Belgrade.[22] The telegrams were routinely repeated to Hoare for his information, but he himself was sent a despatch, which merely summarised Tilea's interview with Halifax and did not enquire as to its accuracy and implications.[23] Possibly, the three men had been so taken aback by the annexation of Bohemia and Moravia that it seemed safer to assume Tilea's claim to be an understatement, rather than an exaggeration in pursuit of diplomatic support. Moreover, Lloyd, usually well-informed on Roumanian affairs, assured Halifax on 20 March that the story was essentially true, despite official Roumanian denials.[24]

In Moscow, Sir William Seeds was instructed to ask the Soviet government whether they would, 'if requested by Roumanian Government, actively help the latter to resist German aggression'. He was to explain that Tilea had enquired as to Great Britain's position in the event of such aggression following upon the apparent ultimatum, and that an essential element in the British response 'would be the knowledge of what would be the attitude of other Governments'.[25] The other telegrams implied that the British Government could more easily define its position 'if Poland and Roumania agreed to make treaty provision between them clearly applicable as against German aggression and if Balkan Entente proclaimed their joint determination to guarantee each other's frontiers'.[26]

The same urgency to act was apparent next morning. At 11.15 a.m. on Saturday, 18 March, Chatfield, Wilson, Bridges and Sargent met the Chiefs of Staff and members of the Joint Planning Committee (JPC). Wilson and Sargent told them of the reported ultimatum, and Sargent read out the telegrams sent by the Foreign Office the previous evening. Chatfield set out four questions to which answers by the COS were required in time for a Cabinet meeting at 5 p.m. It was arranged that the COS would meet to decide on their answers at 3 p.m., by which time the Joint Planners were to have ready for them an *aide-mémoire* for their discussion. The JPC, meeting at 12.30 p.m., had good cause for resentment at the brief time thus allotted to them, and they expressed it in a heavily underlined passage, pointing out that 'the conclusions reached could not and did not receive the full consideration which it is desirable that matters of such importance should receive.' Nevertheless, from their debate, the Secretary, Lt. Col. Hollis, was able to produce in time clear and somewhat discouraging answers to the questions which Chatfield had posed.

The first question seemed more a matter for the Foreign Office, as it concerned the advice to be given to Roumania if its government asked how it should deal with an economic ultimatum and, in particular, whether it was in British interests that Roumania should reject it. Slessor and his colleagues, however, had no doubt that its strategic implications were far-reaching. Economic control of Roumania would allow Germany to dominate South-Eastern Europe, including Greece, and to gain an outlet to the Mediterranean. Germany would approach self-sufficiency; and would no longer have to fear a war on two fronts or the economic pressure, which would be Great Britain's principal weapon against her. By contrast, the British would be left without friends in the region. Even Turkey and Greece would realise that they had nothing to hope for from Great Britain and would become subservient to Germany. Hence, on a long view, the government should advise Roumania to reject such an ultimatum, which would bring her wholly under German domination and would threaten British vital interests.

The second question assumed such an answer to the first, and asked whether Great Britain could do anything to protect Roumania from the consequences of rejection; if nothing, which countries were best placed to do so? The JPC answered that Great Britain could give no direct assistance to Roumania by land, sea or air; only Russia, Poland or Yugoslavia could do that. If, however, 'we took the lead in organising combined resistance to German aggression against Roumania – and nobody else will if we do not – the threat of an unlimited war may act as a deterrent.'

The third question assumed the failure of diplomacy to avert a German invasion. In that case, ought Great Britain to go to war, and with which allies as a pre-requisite? To the JPC, the necessity of war in such circumstances derived from their answer to the first question. As broadly based a coalition as possible should be organised, though at present only France's alliance could be assumed. The keys to the military situation would be Poland and Russia, with Turkey and Yugoslavia next in importance as facilitating pressure on Italy and Bulgaria. Given her long frontier with Bulgaria, there was a case for keeping Greece neutral unless Turkey regarded her participation as essential. Detaching Italy from the Axis, avoiding Arab hostility, and securing Japanese quiescence by an American fleet in the Pacific would all be of great importance in such a war.

Chatfield's final question arose from the five telegrams which the JPC had heard Sargent read out that morning. If those five countries were ready for joint action to prevent Germany from dominating Roumania, what should be Great Britain's military contribution? Unsurprisingly, the Joint Planners could think of no direct action at all. Naval action would be the same as in any war against Germany; despatching the Field Force to France might be a less urgent matter if Germany was occupied in the Balkans; action in the air would be in response to that by Germany, with the proviso that British attacks must not involve heavy civilian casualties.[27]

At 3 p.m. the JPC discussed their *aide-mémoire* with the Chiefs of Staff. They were then joined by Chatfield, Morrison, Hore-Belisha, Kingsley Wood and Stanhope, to whom Newall summarised the agreed answers to Chatfield's questions. Roumanian acceptance of such an ultimatum would mean German immunity from the effects of economic warfare, but, if the government advised its rejection, Great Britain must be prepared to fight and, possibly, to fight alone. Going to war alone, or with France as the only major ally, would not prevent German expansion to the Mediterranean and the elimination of Turkey and Greece as potential allies. Germany would have to be defeated in the West, and the outcome of a conflict there would be problematical. The aim must be to engage Germany on two fronts by the involvement of Russia and Poland. Such an alliance just now, accompanied by an ultimatum, might deter Germany from seizing Roumania. It would be up to Russia and America to keep Japan neutral. No further military advice could be offered until the attitudes of Russia and Poland were known.

Newall did, however, go on to make clear to the ministers how important it would be to involve both Russia and Poland, if there was to be war. If both those Powers intended to remain neutral in the event of German aggression against Roumania, and if Great Britain's only allies were to be France, Greece and Turkey, the COS 'have no hesitation in saying that they could not recommend the Government to challenge

Germany to the extent of risking war'. If Poland joined Great Britain in the war, but Russia remained neutral, the answer would be much the same. 'We should expect the Poles to fight stoutly, but surrounded as they are on three sides by Germany, they would be confined to the defensive and with their inferior communications it is improbable that they would contain any considerable portion of the German Army or Air Force.' If Russia joined us in the war, while Poland remained neutral, 'the position would alter in our favour' in that its fleet could interfere with Germany's supplies of iron ore from Sweden and her forces in the Far East might delay or even deter Japanese expeditions against Singapore or Australia and New Zealand. 'But even so the prospects are not such that, from the purely military aspect, we would feel justified in recommending the Government to challenge Germany over the Roumanian question.' Finally, he reiterated an earlier warning by the COS that war against Japan, Germany and Italy simultaneously would be 'a commitment which neither the present nor the projected strengthening of our defence forces is designed to meet, even if we were in alliance with France and Russia, and which would, therefore, place a dangerous strain on the resources of the Empire.'[28]

The sense of urgency had subsided somewhat by the time the Cabinet met at 5 p.m. because of a total repudiation of Tilea's story by his own government. At 12.30 p.m. Sir Reginald Hoare had briefly advised cancellation of the telegrams and he provided a full explanation at 3.40. The Roumanian Foreign Minister had assured him that there was not a word of truth in the story and that the economic negotiations were proceeding normally; if anything, 'the tone of the German negotiations was more conciliatory since the Czech *coup* than before.' He was bewildered by Tilea's misrepresentation; he assumed it to result from excess of zeal. He did add cautiously that there was no threat to Roumania's political or economic independence '*for the moment*'. So far, there had been no attempt to bring politics into the discussions.[29] This news that Germany was *not* threatening Roumania eclipsed authentic evidence from Riga at 1.45 p.m. of Germany's intention shortly to occupy Memel. Presumably because it had so long been a development taken for granted, this was not discussed by the Cabinet and, therefore, its possible value as an indicator of Hitler's current priorities was not examined.[30]

Halifax suggested to his Cabinet colleagues that, although Tilea's report had proved to be unfounded, it might be as well to consider what should be done if that kind of situation actually did arise. He took the view that 'if Germany committed an act of naked aggression on

Roumania, it would be very difficult for this country not to take all the action in her power to rally resistance against that aggression and to take part in that resistance herself.' Chatfield, who had met the defence ministers at 4 p.m. 'for a few minutes' to discuss the recommendations of the COS, briefly summarised these but did not comment on them. Subsequently, Stanhope and Hore-Belisha stressed the importance which the COS had placed on securing the military alliance of *both* Russia and Poland. The First Lord took up their point that Hitler would be averse to simultaneous battlefronts in the East, against Russia and Poland, and in the West, against Great Britain and France. Ensuring such a prospect would greatly reduce the likelihood of Hitler going to war, and make his defeat much more likely if he did so. Hore-Belisha urged a new policy of open alliances with such countries as Poland and Russia.

The Prime Minister repeated the points he had made at Birmingham as to the impossibility of continuing 'to negotiate on the old basis with the Nazi regime'; he added, mysteriously, that this 'did not mean that negotiations with the German people were impossible'. Another step by Germany 'in the direction of dominating Europe' would mean that Hitler had accepted his challenge. 'Roumania was, therefore, more than a question whether Germany would thereby improve her strategic position; it raised the whole question whether Germany intended to obtain domination over the whole of South-Eastern Europe.' He agreed with Halifax that 'if Germany was to proceed with this course after warning had been given, we had no alternative but to take up the challenge.' Chamberlain was less clear, when pressed, about how this challenge was to be taken up. He was not asking his colleagues to decide there and then to declare war if Germany invaded Roumania; nor did he want a decision as to 'the moment at which we should make our stand'; nor did he intend that Great Britain alone should resist German aggression. The next move, rather, was to 'ascertain what friends we had who would join with us in resisting aggression'. This caution was welcome to Maugham, Kingsley Wood and Zetland, all of whom preferred to postpone a challenge involving war until British preparations for one were more advanced. The Air Minister suggested that another six or nine months were needed.

Halifax disagreed. After his 'reflections through the night' about the Godesberg meeting, he had envisaged the destruction of Nazism as the ultimate end, which he wished to see accomplished. He now invited his colleagues to consider, as he had done on 25 September 1938, the possibility that, if Hitler was driven to war, the result might be to help bring down the Nazi regime.[31] Allies were certainly desirable in resisting

German aggression; Germany's attitude was either bluff, 'in which case it would be stopped by a public declaration on our part; or it was not bluff, in which case it was necessary that we should all unite to meet it, and the sooner we united the better. Otherwise we might see one country after another absorbed by Germany.' At the same time, even without an alliance embracing France, Poland, Turkey and the USSR, and 'even if the reports of feelings in Germany and Italy were discounted, a war which did not have immediate and conclusive success might have important internal reactions in Germany. It might be that such a reaction would only follow under the pressure of Germany getting rashly engaged in war.'

No one else seemed tempted by this singular idea that the opening of hostilities might bring internal upheaval of the kind which, in recent wars, had been associated only with disastrous defeat. Nor did anyone venture to contest it. Similarly, no one probed Chamberlain's puzzling assumption that 'Poland was very likely the key to the situation'. His suggestion was that the attitude of other countries 'would obviously be affected' if Poland agreed with his view that 'the time had now come for those who were threatened by German aggression (whether immediately or ultimately) to get together.' Yet it was far from obvious what the effects would be. It would still be as difficult as ever to predict Soviet reaction. It was not at all obvious that Poland and the Balkan states would show a capacity for effective co-operation, nor that Hitler would be unduly disturbed if they did. The only obvious way in which Poland might seem to Chamberlain to be the key to the situation would be if Hitler, once deterred from seeking 'world domination', were to welcome a negotiated deal about Danzig and the Corridor. This might have been in the Prime Minister's mind as an eventual outcome, but his immediate concern was undoubtedly deterrence and he seems to have been confident that it could be effected by this kind of 'barrier', centred on Poland.

The upshot was agreement on Chamberlain's proposal for an immediate approach to all the countries mentioned at the meeting, so that 'we could make a strong pronouncement of our determination to resist further German aggression with the knowledge that we should be supported in that action.'[32]

Replies to Halifax's premature telegrams began to arrive in the early evening, so that his overnight instructions to suspend action were already too late. By Sunday evening, all the governments contacted had given their replies. Each of Roumania's partners in the Balkan Entente reaffirmed their obligations, but none of these applied to an attack on Roumania by Germany alone; internal consultations were promised, which, it was stressed, would be facilitated by prior knowledge of Great Britain's own intentions.[33] Beck did not believe the report, but would consult with his colleagues and with the Roumanian government if it proved to be accurate.[34] From Moscow alone came a constructive response, and it was embarrassingly specific. Litvinov was sceptical about a change in British policy, wondered why he had received no direct approach from Bucharest, and told Seeds that 'no good purpose would be served by various Governments enquiring of each other in turn what action others would take before making up their own minds.' He proposed a meeting at Bucharest of British, Soviet, French, Polish and Roumanian delegates to discuss 'possibilities of common action'.[35]

On the following day, Sunday 19 March, Chamberlain, Halifax, Simon and Stanley met at 11.30 a.m. and again at 4.30 p.m. At the morning session, attended also by Cadogan, they considered what form the planned pronouncement was to take. Chamberlain suggested that the signatories should merely agree to consult together in the event of a threat to the independence of any state in South-Eastern Europe, thus avoiding the difficulty of an advance commitment to military action. This public warning would be followed by private consultation as to what each country could do. Initially, Russia, France, Poland and, perhaps, Turkey would be invited to sign; the smaller countries later, as consulting them would involve considerable delay. The Prime Minister made a distinction, not altogether clear and unlikely to impress those involved, between a violation of frontiers, on the one hand, and, on the other, an attack on the integrity and independence of a state. The declaration would not apply to the former. His example was that of Danzig. He appeared to mean that British involvement would depend on whether Poland, in whose integrity and independence Great Britain was interested, risked both by deciding to fight on the issue of Danzig. The British aim was to prevent German domination in East and South-Eastern Europe. It was not surprising, given their continued readiness for peaceful treaty revision, that discussion led the ministers to substitute the word 'security' for that of 'integrity'. The term 'South-Eastern Europe' was first broadened to 'Eastern and South-Eastern Europe' so as to include Poland and Lithuania, and then dropped altogether in view of the existing concern for Holland and Switzerland as well. Although the Foreign Office had routinely warned that Hitler should not be allowed by British actions to exploit the German fear of 'encirclement', Cadogan thought this joint declaration a good idea. The proposed signatories were certainly all around Germany, but it was presumably now thought to be more in Great Britain's interest to exploit that fear.

The harmony of the meeting was broken when Chamberlain, pursuing a favourite obsession, proposed to ask Mussolini if he could take any action should Germany seek world domination. Halifax countered by a suggestion that Mussolini should, instead, be warned that the French would respond to provocative claims by him in like spirit and that Great Britain would be bound to support France. Chamberlain retorted that to do so might expose him to a rebuff, as Mussolini might think it as interference in his business, a curious concern in that even an implied threat to France was unquestionably Great Britain's business. No decision was taken, but Chamberlain agreed to show a draft of his letter to Halifax.[36]

At the afternoon session, relations with Russia and America were discussed. Chamberlain wondered if Roosevelt might be willing to send the American fleet to Honolulu if Great Britain got involved in war with Japan as well. Halifax and Stanhope would discuss the terms of a telegram instructing Lindsay to make the necessary soundings. Halifax had seen Maisky earlier in the afternoon, and had expressed his doubts as to whether a conference at present would serve. The reasons by which he tried to avoid giving offence were scarcely convincing, namely that no minister could be spared and that a conference might be dangerously unsuccessful. He did allow Maisky to report that it would not be ruled out altogether. Further verbal changes were made to the draft, and texts of the proposed telegrams were to be put before Cabinet on the following morning.[37]

When the Cabinet met at 10.30 a.m. on Monday, 20 March, these ideas were developed. Ministers were able to concentrate on how to word the telegrams, as the new policy itself encountered no dissent. Its exposition by Chamberlain and Halifax did throw some further light on the thinking behind it as well as leaving some aspects obscure. Halifax, for example, explained that rapid action was needed, but that 'if we attempted too much we might end by achieving no positive results for a long time.' If 'too much' meant prolonged negotiation of military alliances with France, Russia and Poland, this would have been true, but ostentatious diplomatic activity signalling to Germany that these five Powers were moving towards such pacts could have been set in motion immediately by, for example, Litvinov's proposed conference. It would have been far more likely to have the 'immense political significance' and 'steadying effect', which Halifax sought, than from a vague public declaration that the four governments would 'consult together in the event of any action being taken which appears to constitute a threat' to the security or independence of European states.

Chamberlain anticipated any criticism that the declaration did not define such a threat or explain how it was to be countered. He argued that although it 'did not involve us in any actual new commitment, public opinion would certainly attach significance to such a declaration signed by the four Powers, and they would assume that if we consulted together some action would follow'. His concern for British public opinion was understandable, but the more important question was surely whether Hitler would make that assumption. On this he did not speculate, though it was clear from what he said in the privacy of the Cabinet that Hitler was to have every reason for doing so. Whichever neighbours were involved, if Germany 'showed signs that she intended to proceed with her march for world domination, we must take steps to stop her by attacking her on two fronts'. The four Powers should, therefore, decide 'what military action they could take in order that such a war could be conducted to the best advantage.' Clearly, the declaration was to mean much more than it said. It was not clear how Hitler was supposed to deduce this and be deterred.

The implications for the armed forces were of concern to Chatfield, to whom it sounded like guaranteeing 'the independence of practically every State in Europe'. He preferred a looser commitment 'to stop any action which constituted a threat to the general security of Europe'. Chamberlain conceded that it might be so interpreted, but it was eventually agreed, as a basis for consultation, that 'European peace and security may be affected by any action which constituted a threat to the political independence of any European State.' Chamberlain resisted a call for 'may' to be replaced by 'must' so as to exclude trivial complaints, and he went on to qualify the commitment still further in response to Halifax's interpretation of what was being declared. The Foreign Secretary saw it as a resolve that 'if Germany showed that she intended to attempt to dominate Europe by action designed to coerce a particular European State, we, in concert with other Powers, would have to take steps to stop her.' Chamberlain promptly stressed that the declaration would not mean 'a guarantee of the existing frontiers or of the indefinite maintenance of the *status quo*'. Someone raised the obvious question: 'Would German aggression against Danzig and Memel come within the scope of the formula?' The only test suggested was 'whether the action proposed was such as to constitute a threat to the security and independence of Poland'. Who was to determine that was left open, but Chamberlain showed the direction of his thinking by the significance he attached to the word 'interest' in any formula. 'Germany had on several occasions taken the line that what happened in Central and Eastern

Europe was of no interest to us and it was important to make it clear that this was not the case.' His hope seemingly persisted that, once deterred, Hitler would resign himself to negotiating any further revision of Versailles.

Chamberlain and Halifax repeated in Cabinet the substance of their exchanges about a letter to Mussolini. Their colleagues took cover and left them to settle the terms of a letter 'on the lines indicated', tactfully ignoring the absence of agreement between the two as to what those lines should be.[38] In the event, Chamberlain rejected Cadogan's advice to warn Mussolini against making 'demands with menaces' to France. 'I am rather afraid', wrote Cadogan, 'his inference from this letter will be that we and the French have lost our nerve and that he *can* bounce us'. The furthest Chamberlain would go, when Halifax discussed amendments with him at 3.45 that afternoon, was to incorporate 'the earnest hope' that the Duce 'may feel it possible, in any way that may be open to you, so to act in these anxious days as to allay present tension and partially restore the confidence that has been shattered'. Nor did the Prime Minister alleviate Cadogan's fear that the letter would convey to Mussolini the impression that Chamberlain was seeking another Munich. He did drop the phrase 'turn to you again', of which Cadogan had particularly complained, but only amended it to 'feel impelled to address you again'.[39]

Helped by mental adjustments already made in response to the rumours of January, ministers had responded quickly to the actualities and new rumours of March; they had at least sketched the outlines of a general strategy in response. It was only ten days since Chamberlain's 'rainbow story' had appeared, expressing in exaggerated form the growing confidence felt in Whitehall. On 15 March, Hitler's forces had occupied Prague, and the annexation of Bohemia and Moravia had been announced on the following day. On 20 March, the Cabinet had agreed on diplomatic moves to promote a coalition with those Powers deemed essential by Service advisers to the containment or defeat of Germany. Just as, during the last fortnight of January, the occasions for war had been re-defined in response to rumours, now, in only five days, a mixture of hard fact and speculation had persuaded ministers at least to consider an immediate challenge to Nazi Germany, if necessary to the point of war.

8
The Quest for Coalition

A diplomatic containment of Germany would make most sense within a general strategy to counter the nascent alliance of Germany, Italy and Japan. Violent attacks on the international system by these Powers had been uncoordinated, and moves towards a formal alliance, with commitments more specific than the vague pledges of the Anti-Comintern Pact of 1936–7, had so far failed, but neither had America, Great Britain, France and Russia yet tried to form the only counter-coalition likely to deter or defeat them. In their internal discussions, British ministers, for example, had merely expressed a hope that Russian and American power in East Asia and the Pacific would be sufficient to contain Japan if British and French forces had to be concentrated in Europe. Negotiating commitments to possible war was, of course, always difficult, the more so when preparations for war were far from complete. Some of the difficulties quickly surfaced in the wake of the new British initiative.

In a series of meetings on Tuesday, 21 March, ministers and officials tackled the implications for defence and diplomacy of their new policy. It was thought that 'rebuffs' such as Chamberlain's speech might provoke Hitler to initiate immediate hostilities. At 10 a.m. Chatfield chaired a meeting of the CID, at which Sir Horace Wilson portrayed Hitler as in 'a towering rage' and capable of a 'mad dog' act. The critical period would be the next few days; the danger was a 'bolt from the blue', yet 'if we took any major step to accelerate our readiness for war, this would be certain to be interpreted as an earnest of our intention to encircle Germany.' The Prime Minister was reported to be uneasy about the length of time needed to deploy the defences against air attack, and, with a French presidential visit due to begin that day, to be in favour of immediate rehearsals for the protection of London. The COS had been asked what covert precautions against air attack might be taken straightaway without exciting undue publicity.

A provisional answer from the JPC was not reassuring. Half measures would be more dangerous than no measures at all, since they would be scarcely less difficult to conceal and might precipitate the very event to be averted. If there was a risk of secrecy being lost, it would be better 'to get full value by taking off the mask at the outset and instituting full war preparations on a national scale'. Discussion of this at the meeting led to the view that nothing much could be done without declaring a state of emergency, even though the effect on Hitler of such a decision might be the same as if full mobilisation had been ordered. Concern was also expressed at the possible reaction in provincial towns if such measures were confined to the defence of London.[1] At 12 noon, Chatfield, Morrison and the Service ministers discussed these findings with the Prime Minister. Chatfield explained that, for complete readiness against an attack in the next few days, all five anti-aircraft divisions of the Territorial Army (TA) would have to be called up; this would require a state of emergency to be declared, as employers might not release enough men for a voluntary exercise. A state of emergency was, nevertheless, adjudged premature and the immediate deployment of regular AA units alone, in the guise of a practice, was agreed.[2]

During the afternoon, the Deputy Chiefs of Staff worked out the implications of this. Regular AA units would, by Wednesday evening, have deployed 76 guns and 48 searchlights to cover the eastern half of London from Chelsea to the London Docks. Long-range RDF stations on the east coast would be manned continuously and there would be arrangements with the SIS to monitor all German wireless activity. The whole of the RAF's Regular Fighter Force would be ready to take to the air, and the operations rooms could work at short notice.[3] Chatfield got these arrangements approved by the CID at 5.15 p.m.[4]

While the implications of a hypothetical air raid were under discussion, real difficulties in the way of the government's diplomatic initiative were being experienced. The first objection had been offered before the proposed declaration was sent off to the various capitals. After Monday morning's Cabinet meeting, Halifax, due to speak in the Lords that afternoon about the annexation of Bohemia and Moravia, instructed Cadogan to get a draft declaration into shape for Chamberlain's approval. At 5.45 p.m. the French Ambassador called on Cadogan, who read it out to him:

> We the undersigned hereby declare that inasmuch as the security and political independence of European States are matters of common

> interest and concern, we have pledged ourselves immediately to consult together in the event of any action being taken which appears to constitute a threat to the security or independence of any one of them.

Corbin surprised Cadogan by his horrified reaction. It would confirm the impression that the Powers 'were not disposed to take any action and would only talk when a threat arose'. It would have an especially bad effect on Beck, who was coming to London to try and get 'some kind of guarantee from us, in default of which he would return to Poland and reinsure with Germany'. The danger was that Beck 'might interpret this declaration as indicating that he would not be able to get any actual guarantee'. It would be better to publish nothing at all than this. Consultation should take place right away, not when the danger arose.

Cadogan was impressed by Corbin's criticism and held up despatch of the telegram. At 7.15 he consulted Chamberlain, Halifax and Wilson, and the text was revised to widen the scope for intervention and to stress that consultation would be a prelude to action:

> '... inasmuch as peace and security in Europe are matters of common interest and concern, and since European peace and security may be affected by any action which constitutes a threat to the political independence of any European State, our respective Governments hereby undertake immediately to consult together as to what steps should be taken to offer joint resistance to any such action.'

Telegrams proposing this form of joint declaration were sent at 11.5 p.m. to the Ambassadors at Paris, Moscow and Warsaw.[5] On the following morning, Tuesday, 21 March, the Polish Ambassador went to see Halifax, hoping for British diplomatic aid to prevent a clash between Roumania and Hungary. Halifax replied sympathetically, but he had already heard from Kennard of Beck's evasiveness as to Poland's attitude if Germany were to attack Roumania. He took the opportunity to ask Raczynski, who made the usual reply that Poland's obligation to help Roumania applied only to an attack by Russia, but he added that Poland most probably would have to 'come in'. When Halifax told him about the proposed declaration, the Ambassador pointedly referred to Poland's 'difficult position between her two powerful neighbours' and to the past attitudes of Great Britain and France. On the second point, Halifax assured him that if, in the course of negotiations over Danzig or Memel, Germany threatened the independence of Poland or Lithuania, the British 'would have to treat it as a question which was of the gravest concern to themselves'.[6]

During the afternoon, Halifax learned that Roumania and Turkey were also looking to him for a more clear-cut commitment to action. Hoare reported the Roumanian fear that a pact of mutual assistance would merely provoke Hitler; they wanted Great Britain and France to declare openly that they would allow no further frontier changes and that they would go to war in support of any state defending its independence. The Turkish Ambassador was indifferent to what Russia or Poland might decide about the declaration; Turkey would undertake new obligations only if assured of Great Britain's own commitment and of its active alliance with Turkey.[7] Nor had the amended declaration impressed the French. At 5 p.m., Bonnet, who had accompanied the President to London, went with his private secretary Bressy to meet Halifax and Strang at the Foreign Office. Their exchange of views lasted an hour and three-quarters; it was marked by disagreement as to what could and should be done.

Bonnet did not share Halifax's confidence that the declaration drafted by the British would lead to the states of the Balkan Entente joining with Great Britain, France, Poland and Russia to deter or defeat German aggression. French military advice since Munich had been that the country's security required Poland, Roumania and Yugoslavia to constitute a second front against Germany, and that they would have to be supplied with the necessary armaments by Russia.[8] The French government sympathised with the Polish refusal to allow Russian troops on their soil, but Bonnet pointed out to Halifax the present reluctance of either Poland or Roumania to collaborate with Russia even about the supply of arms, and the military consequences, especially for France, if war occurred in the absence of such collaboration. Without Russia as their arsenal, these states would be ineffective allies, while, lacking a common frontier with Germany, Russia could not operate directly against it. If Halifax's declaration provoked rather than deterred Hitler, France would be left to deal with a German attack virtually alone, given that 'British help on land would at first be very small.' Hence he urged on Halifax the need for their two governments to bring the strongest pressure to bear on Beck, who must be convinced of the imminent threat to Roumania and of Poland's need for Russian arms.

Halifax agreed perfunctorily, but he argued that the real question was whether Great Britain and France, with or without allies in Eastern Europe, could 'so damage Germany that they could achieve their purpose of checking her'. He suggested to Bonnet, as he had done to his

Cabinet colleagues, that there was 'some evidence to show that, if Herr Hitler brought the German people into a major war, this might well be followed by internal consequences in Germany disastrous to the Nazi regime. The same might be true of Italy.' In any case, 'even if no assurance of Poland's collaboration could be obtained in advance – and this would, of course, affect Russia's capacity to help – it would still be very difficult for France and Great Britain to take no action if there was a further act of aggression by Germany.' It was decided to resume discussion on the following day when Chamberlain and others could contribute.[9]

Overnight telegrams from Kennard, who had earlier on 21 March reported a German ultimatum to Lithuania for the immediate cession of Memel,[10] explained Polish disquiet at being asked to sign the declaration. Beck and his colleagues would find it embarrassing to refuse, but dangerous to accept in view of their vulnerability to German retaliation. Their frontier with Germany was long and practically undefended, while Hitler could make trouble for them over the status of Danzig and the Corridor, as well as among Poland's German and Ukrainian minorities. They had to ask themselves 'whether there is any actual threat to their independence which would justify them in provoking German displeasure' and 'whether other signatories are prepared and in a position to see them through not only eventual war but also period of uneasy peace which might follow such a declaration'. Kennard thought that some safeguard would be welcomed, but 'officials as recently as last night were expressing reluctance to trust in collective guarantees except in case of immediate danger and even then only in military commitments.' They seemed to prefer strengthening present agreements with France, Roumania and even Russia 'rather than provoke Germany by signing and *publishing* a new one aimed at her'.[11]

In the evening of 21 March, Beck dined with Kennard and Hudson, the latter in Warsaw on his trade mission. Conveying his first reaction to the British proposal, Beck echoed the apprehension expressed by his colleagues. Poland had tried to keep a balance between Germany and Russia, but to join Russia in signing such a declaration 'would definitely place Poland in the Soviet camp and the reaction in Germany, especially given the Führer's mentality, would undoubtedly be serious'. Beck's forthcoming visit to London had already caused annoyance in Berlin. Nevertheless, he might be able to associate Poland with a declaration if the Russians were not involved.[12]

Aware of Polish resentment at having been excluded from the negotiations culminating in the Munich Agreement, the British had this time distinguished between Poland and the smaller states of Eastern Europe. Halifax, in his conversation with Raczynski that morning, had been careful to explain that members of the Balkan Entente had not been invited to sign the declaration because it was deemed essential 'to obtain, first of all, the co-operation of the Great Powers chiefly concerned. If that co-operation could be secured quickly, this would provide a rallying point for the smaller Powers.' Whether Poland was a Great Power, in the acknowledged sense, was a crucial question in these circumstances. Although, after Russia and Germany, by far the largest of the Central and Eastern European states in terms of population and territory, it was by no means obvious that she had the military and industrial strength for success in single combat against either neighbouring Great Power. Kennard's reports confirmed this. Beck had long hoped to compensate for this basic inferiority by trying to align Poland with Hungary, Yugoslavia and Italy. He had failed. For him, the question now was whether this proposal from London would be a viable alternative or simply a new danger.

When the Cabinet met at 10 a.m. on Wednesday, 22 March, Halifax's report showed that the British proposal had fallen flat. Only the French government seemed ready to sign, apparently out of politeness to an ally rather than with any enthusiasm or conviction. Halifax was now inclined to be less dismissive of Litvinov's proposal for a conference. Discussion moved to the prospect of war. Chamberlain and Chatfield reported on the emergency measures taken to protect London against sudden air attack, and on the accompanying problem of readily available manpower. This re-opened the question of conscription, with Hore-Belisha favouring the Swiss model. Chamberlain, however, noted that in the afternoon there was to be a meeting of the TUC, the Parliamentary Labour Party and the National Council of Labour; there was now some prospect of these bodies openly supporting the Government's foreign policy, 'subject only to the reservation that they would not support conscription'. Chatfield made a singular observation. He said that 'he did not think that the Defence Ministers or the Chiefs of Staff had ever considered what advantages would be derived from conscription. The general feeling that conscription would add greatly to our military strength needed, of course, a great many qualifications.' Chamberlain welcomed the idea of an enquiry into the matter. It appeared that, even with a general European war in the offing, French pressure for conscription had been without effect on most ministers. Great Britain's contribution to such a war was still likely to be confined to professional and volunteer forces.

This may have been a case of Chatfield's continued preference for a war requiring no more than defence against air attack and help for the French in holding the Western front, while Germany was strangled by blockade. That the question of conscription was not seen as urgent by the rest of the Cabinet may have been due more to confidence among ministers that deterrence was going to work. Even Halifax, who had appeared readier for war than most, did not expect a resort to it on this particular occasion. He made this clear when dealing with the problem of 61 German officials who ran Nazi organisations in London. Halifax wanted some of them deported, and one of his arguments was that 'this was a good time to take this step, since our relations with Germany could hardly be worse than they are at present. It would be a pity to postpone action to a later date when our relations might be improving.' Thus, although confident that war would quickly bring down the Nazi regime, he seemed not to expect the present crisis to end in war as long as the Western Powers demonstrated their determination to contain any further German aggression.[13]

At 12.15 p.m., however, the Foreign Office was warned by Ogilvie-Forbes against assuming that Germany would be deterred. The reported intention to set up 'a democratic front against Germany' had been greeted by the old cry of 'encirclement', which was 'making a deep impression on all Germans regardless of class or political opinion'. Publication of the proposed declaration would reinforce this, and Ogilvie-Forbes was also apprehensive of its effect on an 'excited and elated' Hitler.[14] When Halifax met the Dominion High Commissioners that afternoon, he found a similar concern that a policy of 'encirclement' might provoke war. For South Africa, Ter Water argued that, instead, Mussolini should be persuaded to approach Hitler in search of a diplomatic solution. Halifax told him that such a move would merely convince Hitler that 'our proposed declaration was only words', reinforcing von Ribbentrop's constant claim that 'the British Empire would never fight whatever the provocation.' Both Hitler and Mussolini would certainly follow a policy of aggression if convinced that they could get away with it. Ter Water retorted that this 'meant getting to the point of war before suggesting to the dictators that there might be a way out'.

Halifax acknowledged the danger, but 'if it came to war we should be resisting, not an attack on Roumania, but aggression *as* aggression, and such an attack would mean absolutely that Germany was aiming at world domination. In spite of the fact that our rearmament was incomplete – and we were bound to be more conscious of our own weaknesses than of the weaknesses of others – he felt that it would be better to run the risk of war now, if this was the alternative, than to have to go to war in six months' time with Germany in possession of Roumania, with public opinion in this country in a state of despondency, and with public opinion in the United States, in reaction to what would certainly be considered the supine attitude of the democracies, determined not to let herself be embroiled in any European quarrel.'[15]

At 5 p.m. a further Anglo-French conversation took place, this time in Chamberlain's room at the Commons. As well as the Prime Minister himself, Cadogan, Phipps and Corbin were additional contributors to the second meeting. It was on a day when Lithuanian troops were evacuating Memel, when the Lithuanian Foreign Minister was in Berlin signing away his country's right to the territory, and when Halifax had been able to offer Bronius Balutis, the Minister at London, no more than his deep sympathy in 'a situation in which no legal rights were respected'.[16] Its significance was so obvious that they wasted no time discussing this latest and long-expected annexation. Bonnet confirmed his government's readiness to sign the declaration, but, in view of Poland's attitude, the British ministers now accepted the need to consider an alternative course. The French plan was the obvious alternative, especially as only the timing and the occasion in Tilea's story had been thought by French leaders to be misleading. There was also an obvious difficulty. Roumania, Poland, Yugoslavia and Turkey could muster between them numerically impressive forces, but lacked the arms with which to equip them. France's capacity to export arms was limited, as was that of Great Britain. Yet Roumania and Poland refused to be associated with Russia, the only Great Power positioned to supply arms to them promptly in the event of German aggression.

This was not the only flaw in the plan, as the present crisis had revealed. Litvinov's conference proposal showed that Russia could not be confined to the supporting role assumed for it. Roumanian leaders saw a pact of mutual assistance as likely to provoke a German attack, and simply wanted a declaration by the Western Powers that they would fight in defence of any state whose integrity or independence was threatened. Nor did Beck show any interest in the active role assigned to Poland in respect of Roumania. Daladier was not, however, discouraged by all this, as the British knew from Phipps's account of a conversation with him on the afternoon of 18 March. Earlier that day he had made clear to Beck that the latter's request for help in the event of a German move against Danzig would depend on whether Poland had concluded a defensive alliance with Roumania. Hence Bonnet's insistence, during Tuesday's conversation in London, on the maximum pressure being exerted on Beck to do this. Daladier had also told Phipps that their two governments should do all they could to encourage Poland and the countries of the Balkan Entente to guarantee each other's frontiers, and to assure them of French and British support.[17] At Wednesday's conversation, the British accepted this as a basis for joint action.

A sequence of moves suggested by Halifax was then endorsed. This amounted to ascertaining, first, that Roumania would resist German aggression, and then convincing the Polish government that, if they went to Roumania's aid, both France and Great Britain would go to war in support of them both. As Cadogan put it, 'we and French should offer to guarantee a Polish–Roumanian mutual Guarantee Pact.' Thus had the guarantee, so recently discredited as a diplomatic device, taken exactly a week to be brought back into play. Once agreement on these lines had been reached with Roumania and Poland, it was to be suggested to these governments that 'they should not raise any objection to our doing our best, both in their interest and in our own, to secure Soviet participation.' What form the involvement of any of these Powers was to take was left vague. Bonnet hoped to persuade the Russians simply to supply the Poles and the Roumanians with the means to fight, while Chamberlain assumed that British and French assistance would take the form of 'pressure' on Germany's western front.[18] The reason for the vagueness lay in the assumption that Germany was bound to be deterred by such a wide-ranging alliance, and war thus averted.

It was, perhaps, this assumption which made use of the word 'guarantee' seem acceptable again and so soon, even to the British ministers, tired of Opposition taunts. The Czech guarantee had never taken its intended form owing to the attitudes of Germany and Italy, while the 'moral guarantee' unilaterally offered by Great Britain in October had lacked credibility from the start, becoming both a source of embarrassment and a target for derision long before the Ides of March. The guarantees proposed by France on 22 March could be seen as of a different order, if they were meant to be the prelude to a formidable military alignment, which would include the three Great Powers which had opposed German expansion in 1914. Its realisation would, of course, depend on Poland, Roumania and Russia agreeing to co-operate with one another in the roles planned for them. Yet it was through their reluctance to co-operate at all that even a much less demanding declaration proposed by the British Government was now on the verge of being discarded. The French did realise the difficulty, not only with the governments of Eastern Europe, but, to judge from a conversation Bonnet had with Halifax after lunch on the following day, with Great Britain's own role in the absence of military conscription.[19]

Nevertheless, during the next two days the Foreign Office received from Rome, Warsaw, Moscow and Berlin reports which seemed to reinforce the arguments for this policy. Both the British and the French governments received reassuring hints about Italy, such as Dingli's message to Ball that Mussolini was very anxious to avoid war.[20] Kennard had sent an assessment by his Military Attache, Lt. Col. E.R. Sword, of the military dimension to Poland's current diplomacy, and parts of it were highly reassuring. Sword suggested that Poland's reluctance to fight in support of Roumania could be overcome if its leaders were 'absolutely convinced that her entry into the war would immediately invoke the previously guaranteed military aid of France and Great Britain and at least the benevolent neutrality of the U.S.S.R.' Sword believed also that Poland would accept war material from Russia. He thought it possible that a guarantee against aggression, backed by France, Great Britain and Russia, might 'enable the wiser elements in the Reich to restrain Herr Hitler'. Even if the British commitment fell short of definite military support, anything which increased Poland's strength and solidarity might make Germany pause, and 'thus gain time for the completion of our armament programme, and assist in the maintenance of our prestige'.[21]

This part of Sword's appreciation ensured its welcome in the Foreign Office. As Strang noted, it 'provides arguments in support of the policy which we are about to broach (with the French) to the Polish and Roumanian Governments.'[22] Similarly, warnings from Sir William Seeds that Russia would keep out of any war between Germany and the Western Powers unless directly threatened itself did not disconcert the Foreign Office, as it was accompanied by his prediction that any Russian assistance to East European countries attacked by Germany would take only the form of 'war material, provisions and technical help'.[23] This would conform precisely to the role envisaged for Russia in the Franco-British plan. Furthermore, a terse analysis in some two hundred and fifty words by Mason-MacFarlane, telegraphed from Berlin on the evening of Saturday 25 March, advised the government, on military grounds, to do just what it was planning to do. His argument reinforced the Foreign Office's view that Hitler must know that he would be fighting on two fronts if he precipitated a war. Chamberlain and Halifax could the more confidently counter doubts expressed among their Cabinet colleagues in the meetings to come.

The Military Attaché put forward a complicated variant of an obvious enough proposition, namely that Hitler, like Bismarck and Schlieffen before him, would seek to avoid having to fight in the East and the West simultaneously. He believed, moreover, that Germany would be in danger of defeat only if forced into this position and effectively blockaded at the same time. As things stood, therefore, Germany was in a dangerous situation. War just now with the two Western Powers would involve it also in immediate war in the East, as she would need to seize and hold those of its resources essential to its war effort and to surviving an allied blockade. Yet the German Army, he believed, would take two or three years to acquire the capacity so to fight on both fronts simultaneously. In the immediate future, however, there was a danger that these eastern neighbours of Germany would succumb to its threats and concede economic agreements, which made their conquest unnecessary. It was, therefore, essential to convince their governments now that 'we will permit no further German aggression in the form either of military action or of economic agreements secured by threats.' Otherwise, they 'will almost inevitably slide into Germany's camp'. If they did, and provided Russia remained on the defensive, Germany could withstand a blockade, at least in the short term. Meanwhile, Hitler could concentrate his forces in the West against France and Britain.[24]

Mason-MacFarlane's claim was arguably at odds with another part of Sword's assessment, namely that of Poland's extreme vulnerability to German attack. Although Poland might be able to deploy 54 divisions and 500 first-line aircraft, she lacked the resources to maintain them in a prolonged conflict. She was exposed to simultaneous invasion on three fronts by German forces: along the open western plains, from East Prussia and, since Germany's recent treaty with Slovakia, from the Carpathians. Both its outlet to the sea and the industrial area of Silesia were within easy grasp, and Warsaw was only 150km. from the frontier of East Prussia. German bombers could destroy any Polish city. Nor would alliance with France and Great Britain be of much help. France could keep part of Germany's forces in the West, but the only direct role of the two Powers would be in the supply of war material, a difficult task given German control of the Baltic. Sword clearly did not think it would take much for Germany to defeat Poland. Halifax preferred Mason-MacFarlane's assessment.

On Saturday, 25 March, Halifax met with Vansittart, Cadogan, Sargent, Malkin and Strang to discuss the policy agreed in general terms with the French. He argued that Russia must not appear to be in the forefront in view of Poland's attitude and because 'we should not make it too difficult for Italy to betray her Ally.' This was not to underestimate Russia's importance in the scheme, as 'both for internal reasons and because of her ultimate military value, if only as our arsenal, we must keep her with us'.[25] The results of their discussion were embodied in a draft memorandum by Strang. This was revised by Cadogan on Sunday. In the evening he and Halifax went to Downing Street to discuss with Chamberlain and Butler the 'approach to Polish and Roumanian Governments – involving our guarantee'. The Prime Minister 'approved in principle'.[26]

During the afternoon of Monday, 27 March, instructions to Kennard and Hoare were drafted in the Foreign Office. A meeting of the Foreign Policy Committee (FPC) was summoned for 5 p.m. to discuss the proposed policy and to examine the drafts before their despatch that evening. Chamberlain told the Committee that an emergency Cabinet meeting for this purpose might have caused undue publicity, an odd reason given the aim of making Hitler realise how seriously the British Government were taking the situation. Possibly he wanted a rehearsal of the arguments about sidelining Russia before the full Cabinet met. If so, he got his wish. Of the seven Cabinet colleagues present, three – Hoare, Chatfield and Stanley – were eloquent in their criticism and were too important for it to be brushed aside.

Having explained the Polish attitude and Beck's counter-proposal, the Prime Minister claimed that a front against German aggression simply could not be formed if Russia was openly associated with it. He listed the countries which were expressly antagonistic as Poland, Roumania, Finland, Yugoslavia, Italy, Spain, Portugal and certain South American Republics, and warned, in addition, that Russian involvement would make it more difficult to influence and maintain good relations with Italy and Japan. All he could find to set against this was left-wing suspicion and distrust in Great Britain and France at Russia's exclusion. It was a list of varying relevance, and his colleagues would have been unsurprised to hear that Mussolini, Franco and Salazar were hostile to Russia. Chamberlain proceeded to show how deterrence could be made to succeed without Russia, using the arguments timeously provided by Mason-MacFarlane. The immediate German threat was to Roumania and its resources; Poland might be ready to go to Roumania's aid if Great Britain and France proclaimed their support for both states; faced by the prospect of a war on two fronts, Hitler would have to abandon his planned aggression. If deterrence did fail, against Chamberlain's obvious expectations, Russia might agree secretly to come to their aid as well, perhaps through some adaptation of the Franco-Soviet Pact.

Chamberlain hoped that Poland would also agree, as part of the deal, to enter a war in which Germany attacked Great Britain and France, but even without a reciprocal arrangement 'we should be prepared to give her the unilateral assurance as regards the Eastern Front seeing that our object was to check and defeat Germany's attempt at world domination.' He did not, however, see any need to seek Polish aid for Yugoslavia, as Italian interest in that region made a German attack unlikely. Neither did Halifax expect Polish help in that quarter, but his reasoning was different. He cited Yugoslav suspicions that Hitler and Mussolini were planning their country's partition; since Poland was unlikely to get involved, help for Yugoslavia would have to be a direct concern of Great Britain and France.

Hoare, who had had first-hand experience of Russia during the last war, was unconvinced by Chamberlain's case for excluding it and thought it would be widely seen as 'a considerable defeat for our policy'. There should be at least an arrangement for parallel action by Russia. In rejecting this and some later arguments, Halifax may have been ill at ease as his customary lucidity is not evident in the minutes. His reply to Hoare seemed to boil down to three assertions. First, Poland was more important than Russia as being able to give 'the greater value'. By this he presumably meant that Poland, unlike Russia, could engage Germany directly and so create the essential second front. Secondly, it was imperative not to offend Beck at present, and Beck would be offended by a parallel arrangement or by modification of the Franco-Soviet Pact, either of which would have to be disclosed to him. He did not explain why Beck, as Foreign Minister of a vulnerable country in need of support, must not be offended; possibly it was for the same reason, in that an irate Beck might make some territorial deal with Hitler, ruling out a second front of any significance as well as depriving Roumania of direct help against Germany. Thirdly, Russia would admittedly make mischief, but this would not matter as long as British Labour leaders could be convinced that its exclusion was not the Government's fault.

Of the ministers present, only two – Chatfield and Morrison – had attended the meeting on 18 March at which the Chiefs of Staff had warned against war with Germany unless an alliance with *both* Russia and Poland could be formed. Chatfield now developed this argument in the light of developments since then. If there was to be a war, maximum support must be secured on the eastern front and he acknowledged that Poland would probably provide the most useful military assistance there. Russian involvement, however, 'would act as a greater deterrent' to Hitler's embarking on war at all, an important argument given that this was the British aim. He went on to challenge the assumption behind the policy proposed, namely that Roumania was to be Hitler's next victim. A commercial treaty was a strange preliminary to war; a more likely explanation was that Germany wanted it so as to secure Roumania's oil and other resources prior to an attack elsewhere. In any case, Roumania would be an unsatisfactory ally for the Western Powers, as she was dependent now on Germany for the military equipment formerly supplied by Czechoslovakia. 'He wondered whether from a military point of view Roumania was worth the candle.' She would count for something militarily, but the question was 'whether we could do anything effective on the West which would stop Poland and Roumania from being overrun and absorbed by Germany'. Would such a campaign draw off enough German forces to enable France to attack and breach the Siegfried Line? As far as he knew, this question had not been examined.

The Prime Minister and the Foreign Secretary were oddly fatalistic in their responses. They dwelt upon the consequences of inaction rather than upon whether the particular action proposed would be effective. Chamberlain argued that if it was decided to do nothing, Germany would try to make Roumania work the commercial treaty in Germany's interests. Their success in this would mean that Roumania had been forced to sacrifice its independence without invasion or the use of any military force. He cited this as an example of Hitler's new technique. He did not go on to consider whether such exploitation of its inherent strength by a Great Power in its commercial relations with a lesser Power – hardly unprecedented in international politics – would warrant a general European war. Inskip did. He found the words 'may undermine these countries' independence' vague and indefinite, and suggested that they were 'inconsistent with what we had already publicly stated in regard to Germany's right to reasonable expansion', a reference to Halifax's policy of conceding German economic predominance in the region, provided British trade was not totally excluded.

Halifax, however, now found German economic expansion sinister, but, having reflected on Chatfield's anxieties, he agreed that there was probably no way in which French and British forces could prevent Poland and Roumania from being overrun. 'We were faced with the dilemma of doing nothing or entering into a devastating war.' Doing nothing would ensure a great accession to Germany's strength and a corresponding loss of sympathy and support for the Western Powers in America, the Balkans and other parts of the world. 'In those circumstances, if we had to choose between two great evils, he favoured our going to war.' Chatfield conceded, perhaps too readily, that these were the choices. 'In a sentence we were in a weak military position to meet a political situation which we could not avoid.' He might have followed up this pithy summation by commenting on Halifax's curious preference for war from a weak military position to a search for other ways in which the unavoidable political situation might be temporarily met. Why did both Chamberlain and Halifax assume that the only alternative to war was 'nothing'? Graduated forms of pressure and persuasion would have been the diplomatic norm at such a time, when rearmament was far from complete and when Staff Conversations had only just begun with Great Britain's one certain ally.

During the previous September, an inner cabinet of four ministers had formulated policy as the crisis developed. Of these, Hoare was ill at ease with what Chamberlain and Halifax had devised, and Simon now made his reservations plain in the two questions he posed. First, he asked whether there was reason to believe that French and British assurances to Poland and Roumania would influence German policy. Chamberlain did not answer the question. He referred instead to advice that the action proposed would greatly strengthen the morale of other states and tend to bring them on to our side. Simon then asked what was meant by the undertaking in the draft telegrams that Great Britain and France would be prepared 'to support' Poland and Roumania. The Prime Minister's answer, which might have surprised the governments in Warsaw and Bucharest, was that 'by manning the Maginot Line we should be holding up large German forces which otherwise would be available for overrunning Poland and Roumania.'

Halifax suggested that any support from the Western Powers would give Beck at least some ground for hope; without it, 'Poland's position was hopeless'. Earlier in the discussion, he had been asked by Chatfield whether the Foreign Office had received any appreciation of Poland's strength on land and in the air. Halifax said that he knew of 'nothing very recent' and Cadogan did not correct him. (Sword's appreciation had reached the Foreign Office on the previous Friday; the first minute on it, by Speaight, was penned on the day of the FPC; Cadogan and Halifax did not read it until 30 March). Now it occurred to Halifax to ask whether the Staff Conversations had yet dealt with the problem of Poland's military position. Chatfield told him that he had discouraged the COS from doing more than estimating the number of troops France and Poland could mobilise; he was awaiting the political decisions which would define the military problem. Possibly this was the wrong way round.

Morrison re-introduced the question of Russia's exclusion. Halifax had observed that until it became possible to make a statement to Parliament, various elements there would have to taken into the government's confidence 'to obviate inconvenient and embarrassing questions'. Morrison questioned whether such secrecy could be preserved on any arrangements relating to Russia, and, recalling the latter's preference for a large conference, he expected it to 'react actively' on learning of its exclusion from the pact. Halifax thought she might 'just sulk', and Chamberlain suggested a gentleman's agreement of a verbal character. Stanley disagreed, and expected its exclusion to have serious consequences. He urged some new form of declaration in which Russia could join. At present, their propaganda was accusing the Western Powers of pushing Germany into conflict with Russia. There should be a separate agreement by which Great Britain and Russia would come to one another's aid if attacked in Europe. Hoare then resumed his own challenge about the neglect of Russia. He referred to Chatfield's point that Russia 'constituted the greatest deterrent in the East against German aggression. All experience showed that Russia was undefeatable and he was apprehensive of the possible consequences that might result if at this juncture the enmity of Soviet Russia towards this country was increased.'

After further, unrecorded, discussion, the adverb 'generally' qualified the FPC's approval of the policy proposed by Chamberlain and Halifax. Simon was to join Halifax in settling the final form of the draft telegrams in the light of the Committee's discussion and suggestions.[27] The telegrams were sent off to Kennard and Hoare at 11.30 p.m.[28] Copies would be available to the rest of the Cabinet when it met on Wednesday morning. One paragraph of the message was re-worded to stress Russia's proposed role, in response to Hoare's criticism, and it was clear that the approach to Poland and Roumania would have to be followed by a much more serious attempt to involve Russia than Chamberlain thought necessary.

On the following afternoon, Tuesday, 28 March, at 2.30, the JPC met to discuss the military implications of an Anglo-French guarantee to Poland and Roumania. They were to assume that Russia would be friendly, neutral and ready to supply arms to its neighbours. They were also to examine the effect of any Italian intervention. Discouragingly, Danckwerts, Kennedy and Slessor professed themselves unable to assess the deterrent effect of the guarantee in which the political leaders had such confidence. They were, however, concerned lest it encourage an intransigeant attitude in Warsaw and Bucharest and 'thereby tend to precipitate a European war before our forces are in any way fully prepared for it, and such a war might well be started by aggression against Danzig alone'. They were also concerned at the omission of Turkey from their terms of reference, given its great importance in any war involving Germany and Italy. Having previously[29] discussed the implications of a war with Germany in which Powers to the East were neutral, they had now to examine the likely differences if Germany was engaged on both fronts. Naval and air warfare would be little affected by the involvement of Poland and Roumania. The main differences would be on land.

Germany's defences in the West were strong enough to resist an allied offensive, and Great Britain and France could give these allies no direct support by land, sea or air to resist German invasion. Nor could they supply them with armaments, for which they would have to rely on Russia. German forces could be expected to occupy Roumania quickly and to defeat Poland within a matter of months, though they would then have a long frontier with Russia to defend and would thus have fewer divisions for an offensive in the West. If, instead, they concentrated first against the Western Powers, they would still not be strong enough to break the Maginot Line, but they would probably overrun Holland and perhaps part of Belgium, with the serious consequences for Great Britain examined in earlier papers. Even if Italy did not immediately enter the war, its hostility would have to be assumed, adding to allied military worries and reducing any deterrent effect on Germany of the guarantees.[30]

Chatfield had said it was essential that he should be able to outline the views of the Chiefs of Staff at Wednesday's Cabinet meeting, so the COS met straightaway to discuss and revise this JPC report. Newall, Cunningham and Adam also disliked the proposed guarantees and expressed their misgivings more forcibly. They warned that if an appeal for help by any one government had to be answered automatically by all the others, 'we will have surrendered the issues of peace and war with Germany to the action of Governments over whom we have no control, and at a time when our defence programme is far from complete.' They assumed, or pretended to assume, that safeguards against this would be written into any agreement. At the same time, they were more sanguine about the likely course and outcome of a war in which Germany was engaged on two fronts, as long as its initial offensive was to the East. While Poland's defeat could only be a matter of time, the difficult nature of the country would reduce the chances of an early decision. Although the Western Powers could expect no rapid or spectacular success against the Siegfried Line, given 'the internal situation in Germany, the dispersion of her effort and the strain of her rearmament programme, we should be able to reduce the period of Germany's resistance and we could regard the ultimate issue with confidence'. If, however, Germany attacked in the West, they agreed with the JPC on the fate of the Low Countries with all its consequences, but they hoped that a Polish offensive would relieve the pressure on the Western Powers. As it was the COS assessment which Chatfield would report to his Cabinet colleagues, there was some encouragement here for taking the risk of immediate war implicit in the policy proposed by Chamberlain and Halifax.[31]

That war was being risked with the aim of deterring Hitler from its immediate use was clear from the proceedings of Cabinet the day after. When it met at 11 a.m. on Wednesday, 29 March, Halifax explained to Ministers the difficulties which had been experienced in trying to implement the decisions made at their last meeting, and he turned their attention to an alternative means of countering German aggression. On the assumption that Germany was as yet unable to conduct a war on two fronts simultaneously, the Western Powers should ally with Poland and Roumania as the most likely objects of German aggression in the immediate future. Copies of the telegrams already sent to Warsaw, Bucharest and Paris were distributed. Halifax explained that it might be necessary to exchange, at very short notice, mutual undertakings of the same kind with Turkey and Greece, should there be war in the Mediterranean.

Once again, the question of Russia came to the fore, and Halifax told how he had redrafted a paragraph in the telegrams so as to accommodate Hoare's concern. Chamberlain believed that he had brought home to the Labour leadership the importance of Polish involvement, the price of which had to be Russia's exclusion. He realised that others in the Opposition would be more difficult to convince. So, indeed, were Hoare and Elliot. Hoare reiterated the need for the French to exploit their alliance with Russia and was puzzled at their failure to do so. Elliot took up the suggestion which Stanley had made in the FPC meeting of a separate British agreement with Russia, by which either would come to the aid of the other if attacked in Europe. Since Germany could attack Russia only through Poland or Roumania, this need not mean any new British commitment. If Roumania lost its independence and became a base for a German attack on the Ukraine, 'this country would not be able to stand aside.' Halifax was not encouraging. He expressed readiness to try and keep in with Russia, but not if it meant the loss of Poland's co-operation.

The success with which a sense of urgency had been communicated to Ministers was indicated by De La Warr's enquiry as to whether the position could be held while awaiting Beck's arrival at the weekend. Halifax assured him that the extent of British concern was already so clear to Berlin that 'Germany would think twice before she involved herself in a major war.' The Poles were already engaged in talks at Berlin, and Danzig was apparently not the only subject under discussion. This and the fact that Beck's travelling arrangements were unaltered 'did not point to any sudden disturbance', impossible though it was to predict the future. The sense of the meeting was, nevertheless, of eventual war and of the need for much more time to prepare for it, rather than of hope that it could be averted altogether. For example, an urgent War Office proposal to mount guns near Port Said and Suez, to protect the Canal and the passage through it of vital oil supplies, aroused no dissent, despite realisation that it would probably violate the 1851 Convention and certainly annoy Mussolini. Even the Prime Minister, normally anxious to avoid offence in that quarter, suggested no more than attempting to camouflage the guns.

Halifax reminded his colleagues of the need to gain time for further rearmament and 'for Germany's difficulties to develop', which suggested that he was now less confident that war just at that point would provoke internal revolt. In their speeches, he told them, they should not use language 'which suggested that we were anxious to attack Germany, since this might encourage Germany to make an immediate attack on us'. Chamberlain added that personal attacks on either dictator should be avoided. Although it was not on the agenda, the Prime Minister had decided to bring up the question of conscription, long on the back-burner but now requiring urgent consideration. He had been under pressure from his backbenchers to boost recruitment to the TA, and from Halifax to provide some dramatic evidence that aggression would be resisted. He had met Hore-Belisha the previous afternoon and had asked him if there was some alternative to conscription, one which the TUC might accept. The War Minister suggested doubling the TA, though he warned that he had not worked out the implications, nor had he consulted the generals. There would certainly be difficulties over equipment, accommodation and instruction. Chamberlain, however, accepted the idea.[32] He now told his colleagues that his pledge not to introduce conscription in time of peace was inapplicable to present circumstances, 'since though we were not at war, it was scarcely peace either.' He did not, however, wish to imperil the helpful attitude of the Labour Party and the TUC towards emergency working practices in the armaments industry. Greenwood had seemed to favour Hore-Belisha's proposal. Simon, whose consent to the additional expenditure had been obtained in advance, called it 'a severe, but unprovocative, warning to Germany of our fixed determination to resist aggression'. The rest of the Cabinet agreed.[33]

At lunchtime on Wednesday, 29 March, therefore, the Franco-British plan of guaranteeing a Polish–Roumanian mutual guarantee pact and of arranging Russian arms supplies to both countries was still in place, though how it was to be implemented was altogether unclear. Poland, regarded as the key to the plan, appeared quite unwilling to play the roles assigned to it of guaranteeing Roumania and of co-operating with Russia. Bonnet and his colleagues, distant in their relations with Beck for obscure reasons,[34] made it clear that it was now up to the British Government to put the strongest possible pressure on him during his visit to London.

9
The Guaranteeing of Poland

At ten to six in the evening of Wednesday, 29 March 1939, the Foreign Office received French agreement to the proposed course of action, and at 9 o'clock Kennard and Hoare were told to act on the instructions they had already been given. At half-past nine, as an afterthought, it gave Kennard the option of communicating with, say, the Polish President in view of 'reasons which we have for lack of confidence in M. Beck'.[1] During that evening, however, a modification to British policy was being decided upon, which was to have unintended consequences for the overall plan.

The immediate occasion for this was a journalist's story of German preparations to attack Poland immediately or in the very near future. Rumours had abounded since 15 March as to Hitler's next move. Now that Memel had been seized, the most likely objective seemed to be Danzig, whether by negotiation or by force or by a mixture of the two. Diplomats and foreign correspondents in Berlin strove to identify what was authentic among the numerous and conflicting stories in circulation there. One of the correspondents was Ian Colvin of the *News Chronicle*, commended to the Foreign Office by its chairman, Sir Walter Layton, and by Lord Lloyd, whose private 'intelligence agency' he also served. Back in January, 'a reliable source' had told Colvin that a victualling contractor to the German Army had been given an order for the same quantity of rations as he had provided in September 1938. They were to be made ready by 28 March for delivery to forward dumps in an area of Pomerania pointing towards Bromberg, which was a railway junction in the Polish Corridor. On 23 March, Colvin asked Lloyd to arrange for him to meet British ministers.[2] When German newspapers on 27 March reported harassment of the German minority in Bromberg, he was reminded of comparable reports from the Sudetenland prior to the crisis of September 1938. Colvin consulted Mason-MacFarlane and passed on the story he had heard in January. The Military Attaché agreed that it might foreshadow a rapid move to cut the Polish Corridor. He advised Colvin to go immediately to London with his news, as written reports seemed to have no effect – odd advice, given that he himself was about to follow his telegraphed assessment of Germany's current military limitations with lengthy written advice to the Foreign Office to force a war on Germany straightaway. Possibly he thought that Colvin's story, delivered personally at the Foreign Office beforehand, would add strength to his own recommendation.

Colvin flew to London on Tuesday, 28 March. At the Foreign Office's News Department, he contacted Leeper, who arranged for him to meet Halifax and Cadogan on the following afternoon. By then, he had already spoken with Churchill and Simon. At the Foreign Office he put forward a number of reasons for believing that an attack on Poland was imminent and that a conspiracy to overthrow Hitler, aborted last September, would be carried through if, this time, conflict with the Western Powers was certain. Colvin was surprised that this 'appeared to be a completely new aspect of the German problem to Lord Halifax'. As it was no such thing, of course, Colvin had misinterpreted the Foreign Secretary's manifest interest in this part of his exposition. Halifax's reaction was understandable. He had been trying, without much success, to convince both his Cabinet colleagues and the French that the mere onset of war with the West would provoke widespread opposition to Hitler among the German people. Earlier in the year, Goerdeler had given the impression that action by high-ranking military malcontents would be dependent on various prior guarantees by Great Britain and France. According to Colvin, however, the certainty of war would now have the same effect on the generals as Halifax expected it to have on the population at large, and with more immediate consequences.

Certainly it was this aspect alone which his Private Secretary noted in explaining the great impression made on Halifax by what Colvin had to relate. 'He [Colvin] said he was convinced Hitler would attack Poland very shortly unless it was made quite certain that we would then attack him. There would then be a good chance that German generals would stop him or revolt. Generals had been prepared to revolt in September if we had stood up to Hitler.' By contrast, Cadogan was inclined to be sceptical about it all. 'I am getting used to these stories', he noted. Halifax, however, promptly arranged for Colvin to see the Prime Minister. At about 6 p.m. he was taken by Halifax, Cadogan, Leeper and Dunglass (Chamberlain's Parliamentary Private Secretary) to the Prime Minister's room in the House of Commons. A seventh person present was assumed by Colvin to be Admiral Sinclair, the head of SIS. After the meeting broke up, Halifax stayed behind and persuaded Chamberlain that, as long as there was Polish and French assent, there should be an immediate guarantee of Poland alone, without awaiting the outcome of diplomatic moves already taken. He returned to the Foreign Office with the news and, after dinner, he, Cadogan, Butler and Harvey worked until 1 a.m. on a draft declaration, to be discussed at Cabinet in the morning, and on draft telegrams for despatch to Paris and Warsaw.[3]

As with Tilea's report of a German ultimatum, Halifax had proved eager to act immediately without seeking confirmation. Yet Colvin's story amounted to very little and merely added to a store of conflicting information, mostly much more recent than the rations story, itself already known to the Foreign Office.[4] Four hours after the meeting at Downing Street, he set down, in a letter for Halifax, the substance of what he had said there. First, there was talk in Berlin that Ribbentrop had been so successful in pressing for plans to attack Poland to be brought forward that 'we may expect an attack on the Polish Republic in twelve hours, three days, a week or a fortnight.' This would give the democracies no time to summon up their courage to resist. As yet, there had been 'no final order either for marching against Poland or for mobilising', but the Army was trained to mobilise swiftly and secretly. Secondly, he cited speeches Hitler was said to have made to various groups of Army officers to the effect that 1939 would be a decisive year, that he would pre-empt the attack which he expected Great Britain to launch in 1940, and that this time the generals must obey him and not cavil as they had done in the previous autumn. Thirdly, there was what Colvin referred to obliquely as 'the subject which interests you most as far as my influence can produce anything of use to the British Empire'. This appeared to refer to the levels of disillusionment, dissidence and conspiracy within Germany since the November pogrom, as at the meeting Halifax specifically asked Colvin to repeat to Chamberlain what he had said about those in Germany who did not believe in Hitler. It was this which appears to have convinced Halifax that immediate advantage could and should be taken of the Polish rumour.[5]

All this was reminiscent of the rumours and gossip from Berlin which had baffled and alarmed ministers at the turn of the year, but this time they referred only to one country as the object of German aggression, and they could be tested routinely against both daily intelligence reports from the War Office and telegraphed Embassy reports. Neither provided evidence that a *coup de main* was imminent nor urged the need for immediate deterrence. There had been hints of both in a consular report on 2 March pointing to a demonstration or an attack on Poland during March; in a claim by a German journalist, passed to the Foreign Office by the American Ambassador in Warsaw, picturing Ribbentrop as having urged such a course on Hitler; and in an SIS report that the German Army had to be in a position to attack Poland by 28 March.[6] On the other hand, a new series of daily War Office reports on German military activity had been available since 21 March, and the latest had dealt with the twenty-four hours ending at 12 noon on 29 March. None of the reports so far had found evidence of troop movements likely to alarm Poland. Memel had been occupied only by troops immediately to hand in East Prussia, and officers there were now being allowed leave again. Tension between Hungary and Roumania had eased and their forces were being pulled back from threatening positions.[7]

Nor were there any threats to report on the diplomatic front. On the morning of 28 March, Kennard had asked Arciszewski if there had been any new moves in relation to Danzig. He was told that within the past fortnight the Polish government had invited discussions about modifying the Statute, but had received no reply as yet. The Vice-Minister for Foreign Affairs expected a demand for annexation, but 'for the moment there is no indication of a threatening attitude on the part of Germany.' Nor did the Poles know of 'troop movements or other measures in Germany indicating possibility of a coup.'[8] That same morning, the Foreign Office learned that, according to Poland's Ambassador in Paris, Jules Lukasiewicz, Germany wanted a settlement about Danzig by Easter, which would be in the second week of April, but that there had been no ultimatum.[9]

The difficulty for British ministers and officials was that this relaxed attitude in Warsaw might signify an impending agreement between Germany and Poland, which would have implications for their policy as disturbing as the imminent attack forecast by Colvin. A bilateral deal changing the terms of the Versailles Treaty would not only frustrate yet again Chamberlain's attempt to restore orderliness and legality to international politics, but deprive the Western Powers of the particular Eastern ally Chamberlain deemed essential to contain German aggression. Poland had been notably reluctant to promise the help to Roumania which the Franco-British plan required; if an arrangement with Germany over Danzig and the Corridor could be negotiated without unacceptably greater insecurity, Polish leaders would lose all incentive to make the commitment. Any prospect of preventing Germany's control of Roumanian oil supplies would then vanish. Not that there had been much hope. When Sargent read a full account, pieced together by

Newton, of Hacha's ordeal in Berlin prior to the march on Prague, he observed: 'I have little doubt that when the same threat is addressed to Bucharest the result will be the same.'[10]

Within the Foreign Office there was uneasy expectation of a deal. Speaight saw the Polish government as ready and even anxious for a compromise; although they would resist a German coup, there was no evidence that Germany was planning one. Makins agreed that Beck seemed 'ready to go a very long way to meet German demands'; he added that, while a deal over Danzig would 'suit us well enough' as it was 'by no means a good *casus belli*', the Germans might moderate their demands in return for a guarantee of Polish neutrality. That would be 'the sort of bargain which might appeal to Beck and the situation will need most careful watching'.[11] Kirkpatrick, trying to assess the evidence about Hitler's current attitude towards Poland, was inclined to think that he was still keeping his options open. While some 'secret sources' did point to plans for an imminent attack, there were also reports that, on the one hand, Hitler would threaten to seize Cracow and other areas if Poland strayed from neutrality or, alternatively, that Hitler had need of Beck for the time being and wanted to avoid conflict with Poland. Kirkpatrick took it for granted that Hitler intended eventually to 'eliminate or neutralise' both Poland and Roumania, though which was to be the first victim remained uncertain. The current press attacks on Poland did not necessarily signal a decision had been made. Sargent suggested that their aim might be to influence negotiations over Danzig or to warn Beck of the risks of making commitments during his visit to London. Cadogan thought Hitler might be trying to divert attention from his main aim of controlling Roumania.[12]

Kennard's conversation with Arciszewski on 29 March left the matter unclear, when his account of it reached the Foreign Office the following day. German proposals as to the future status of Danzig, a motor road across the Corridor, and Poland's adherence to the Anti-Comintern Pact were said by the Vice-Minister for Foreign Affairs to have been discussed over the past fortnight. Kennard's guess was that the demands had been made about a week ago and explained the calling up of Polish reservists. There had as yet been no reply. He observed that it had been very difficult to get straightforward answers from the Foreign Ministry, but he attributed this evasion to fear of the effects of such publicity on the German government and on Polish public opinion. He stressed that 'at the present moment there is no sign of menacing attitude by Germany.'[13] Speaight, however, thought Arciszewski 'scarcely less slippery than Beck', who was 'evidently still on his fence'.[14] Thus, independently of Colvin's story, there was a certain logic in offering Poland alone some immediate offer of military support, given that a deal between Poland and Germany would make impossible the particular form of containment which the British and the French wished to promote.

This sudden decision by Halifax and Chamberlain on the evening of Wednesday, 29 March, to guarantee Poland alone, without even waiting for Beck's arrival on the following Monday, in no way disturbed their advisers in the Foreign Office, where the prevailing mood had been confident and assertive. On 18 March, Sir Reginald Hoare had suggested a dramatic response to any signs that Bucharest was to suffer the fate of Prague. Unmistakable language and lightning speed would be essential. Great Britain, France, Italy and Russia should send their military attachés to the area of trouble within 12 hours, while Hitler had still time to retreat. He urged that, since attempts to deal with Hitler according to civilised conventions had failed, they should be abandoned. See what would happen if an invitation for Göring to visit London was suddenly called off on grounds of the Prime Minister's illness; then, an hour later, announce that the Prime Minister was on board the flagship of the combined Atlantic and Mediterranean fleets in the Heligoland Bight. Sargent (26 March) agreed strongly with Hoare's idea of seizing the initiative in anticipation, and thought his proposed method of doing so was well worth considering. Cadogan (27 March) likewise approved the plan of organising the intrusion of various military attaches, though he would not include Russia in the scheme.[15] Neither expressed an opinion on Hoare's more radical plan. Strang, Roberts and Kirkpatrick all agreed that Germany was in no position at present to fight a general war.

None of them went so far as to endorse Mason-MacFarlane's even more radical recommendation that Great Britain should at once seize the opportunity to launch a pre-emptive war against Germany. Cadogan called it a 'rather hysterical outpouring', in part 'pure gibberish',[16] but they all believed that a policy of deterrence through a threat of war now had a good chance of succeeding. Roberts noted that Mason-MacFarlane's view of Germany's current military limitations was shared by many of his counterparts in Berlin's embassies. Even if Ogilvie-Forbes was right to warn against inferring from this that the political prospects were favourable, it did show that 'we are in a stronger position than we were last September to resist pressure and perhaps even to call a bluff.'[17] Kirkpatrick, drawing on his experience at the Berlin Embassy between 1933 and 1938, agreed with the Military Attaché's assessment that Germany was still vulnerable to a war on two fronts. He thought that it was a view shared by the German leadership; otherwise 'they would not be so palpably nervous of a general war.'

He summed up the case for confrontation when providing notes, on 30 March, for a conversation Halifax was to have with the Turkish Ambassador. Conceding that Hitler was incalculable and 'in a dangerous mood of exaltation', he wrote that, nevertheless, 'we are somewhat fortified by the knowledge that neither Germany nor Italy are in a position to wage a general war for any length of time.' He listed the 'chinks in the German armour' as 'the reluctance of the people to embark on war, a certain weariness produced by shortage of food and intensive preparation for war, lack of raw materials, insufficiency of officers, shortage of equipment, and the necessity for a brief pause to achieve the reorganisation of the newly acquired territory.' Hitler himself had admitted the seriousness of the economic situation and in his most recent speech had declared that Germany must export or die. Yet, Kirkpatrick pointed out, German exports were rapidly declining and that largely as a result of German behaviour. From the point of view of the Western Powers, therefore, the situation was by no means hopeless. Roumania's independence had not yet been destroyed, and the other threatened countries of Europe 'must not fall into the error of thinking that Germany is omnipotent'.[18] It was, nevertheless, realised within the Foreign Office that Germany's very unreadiness to fight a war on two fronts might mean that Hitler, if challenged in the way now proposed, might take immediate action to ensure that he did not have to do so. Sargent pointed out to Cadogan that the effect of the proposed warning might be 'our having to face a German air attack at short notice'. Cadogan saw to it that this reminder was passed on to Halifax on Thursday evening and to Chatfield the following day.[19]

It remained to be seen whether the rest of the Cabinet would think the risks worth while when they met at 11 a.m. on Thursday, 30 March. A policy agreed in advance by both the Prime Minister and the Foreign Secretary would hardly be rejected out of hand, but Halifax recognised that the grounds for action as well as the means and the timing would be open to challenge. In proposing 'a clear declaration of our intention to support Poland if Poland was attacked by Germany', he gave his reasons for thinking such an attack might be imminent, but he admitted that they were based on 'necessarily uncertain evidence'. His hope was that such a declaration would not only make Hitler suspend any plan, but that his having to back down or deny intent might discredit him in the eyes of the German Army, as well as making the German people as a whole realise that he had been risking war on two fronts.

He conceded some obvious objections in advance of their being made. It would give Beck what Halifax assumed he wanted without any reciprocal undertaking having been obtained. It might damage the prospects of current negotiations between Germany and Poland. It could be seen as provocative, recalling the premature warning of 21 May 1938. Roumania would resent its omission, and the negotiations with Poland and Roumania, authorised by Cabinet only the day before, would be at risk. So might the prospects of a settlement between France and Italy, about which Daladier had been speaking. To this impressive list of objections, presumably put to him by Chamberlain the previous evening since Halifax himself had not been influenced by them, he added the reflection that it was a 'rather heroic action to take on the meagre information available to us'. He claimed, however, that the information was from those sources about which there had been undue scepticism in the autumn of 1938.

The Foreign Secretary stressed that he was not asking that immediate action should be taken. He had prepared a draft statement for the Cabinet's consideration, and agreement on its terms would have to be reached with Opposition leaders and with the French government. Dominion leaders would be informed. So would the Polish government, though he did not consider that issuing the statement would necessarily require their consent. It could be published at a moment's notice should the British and French governments think the situation warranted it. In the meantime, while more information was being sought as to the exact position, he asked Cabinet 'whether they were prepared to authorise the Prime Minister and himself to issue a statement on the lines proposed, if circumstances should arise which should render this necessary'. An odd outcome of the meeting was that Halifax's draft statement met with considerable criticism, yet he eventually obtained more than he had initially sought.

The ensuing criticism was understandable, given that the vagueness of the information from which the request arose became even more obvious in his response to questioning. He 'believed' that Hitler had plans for 'a number of adventures, including an attack on Poland', and that the 'real question was which adventure Germany proposed to undertake and at what date.' He claimed that his proposal did not represent 'any material departure' from the policy approved the previous day, namely that of resisting German 'attempts at domination'. If Poland was the next object of German aggression 'we must face the situation at once', and the best means of stopping aggression was 'almost certainly to make clear that we should resist it by force'. Yet the logical response to the situation Halifax had described would be a general warning of British readiness to fight aggression rather than a specific warning in relation to Poland. After all, Roumania had seemed to be at more immediate risk than Poland before Colvin told his latest story, and Colvin's stories were thought by Roberts to be 'sometimes highly coloured and imaginative'.[20]

Moreover, Halifax had not explained what he meant by German aggression against Poland. Simon asked the obvious question. Did Halifax distinguish between a seizure of Danzig and an attack on Poland? In his reply the Foreign Secretary appeared ready to leave it to the Poles to tell the British Government whether such a distinction should be made. He said that he could imagine no better test 'than the decision by Poland whether to regard such an attack as a threat to her independence which she must resist by force'. Maugham responded sharply to the implication that Poland should decide whether Great Britain went to war or not. He would not regard an attack on Danzig as a threat to Poland's independence, and all the signs were that a coup against Danzig, similar to that against Memel, was what was in the offing. Poland should not be encouraged by Great Britain to go to war over Danzig, yet any public statement from London, such as Halifax had in mind, was likely to be so construed.

Chamberlain, who aimed at no more than forcing Hitler to negotiate about matters like Danzig, made obvious his sympathy with these concerns. He pointed to risks and uncertainties even greater than those which Halifax had acknowledged. It was true that the proposal did no more than anticipate action which the Cabinet had already conditionally agreed to take, and that all Halifax now sought was consent to a statement drafted in case of need. Yet all his colleagues should consider the matter carefully 'before they took any irrevocable step'; what was involved here was 'the actual crossing of the stream'. They must consider whether it met the difficulties to which Simon and Maugham had referred. It was important to ensure that publishing such a statement 'would not bring us up against a tremendous decision on some point which did not affect the independence of Poland'. Yet, without it, Hitler might bring off a coup against Poland during the next week which would add its resources as well as Czechoslovakia's to those of Germany. He also expressed his unease as to the secrecy surrounding negotiations between Berlin and Warsaw. 'One possible, but very distasteful, explanation of this was that Polish negotiators were, in fact, giving way to

Germany.' Kingsley Wood enquired if Polish agreement to the issue of this statement was necessary. Halifax replied evasively. He would not issue the statement if the Polish government wished otherwise, unless there was reason to believe their advice in the matter to be 'suspect'. Nor would he undertake to wait for Beck's arrival before issuing it.

While this discussion was going on, the Chiefs of Staff were simultaneously debating what their own advice to this Cabinet meeting should be, an inconvenient arrangement indicative of the prevailing sense of urgency. In Cabinet, Chatfield felt able to anticipate that advice to the extent of saying that, although Poland was likely to be overrun within two or three months, Germany would suffer heavy casualties and have then to maintain a substantial occupation force. If the Western Powers had to go to war with Germany, a Polish alliance was desirable. He pointed, however, to two problems which had still to be addressed: first, whether it would be possible to break through the Siegfried Line while Germany was fighting Poland; secondly, the possibility that Germany might instead decide to stay on the defensive in the East and concentrate first against the Western Powers. No one appears to have responded to these challenging questions. Nor, apparently, was concern expressed as to the prospect of Germany concentrating its forces in the West after those two or three months when Poland had been conquered. Chatfield expected that the need to defend a new frontier with Russia would obviate this. He did not speculate about the consequences if German generals were as dismissive of Soviet offensive capacity as their British counterparts, or if, as the COS did speculate, Hitler and Stalin came to terms.

Zetland questioned the expediency of threatening war on behalf of Poland before the Poles had asked for such support. Agreeing that a draft statement should be ready in case of need, he opposed the suggestion that the Foreign Secretary and the Prime Minister should be authorised in advance to issue it if they saw fit. Cabinet would have to consider the matter in light of all the circumstances before they agreed to its being issued. Inskip agreed that it was inconceivable that Great Britain would ignore a threat to Poland's independence, but he questioned whether the Polish government would want this sort of statement issued in advance of any direct German threat. Wood went further; he argued that its issue might actually provoke an attack which would otherwise not have taken place. Simon also stressed the need to know more about Poland's own policy; how would Poland respond to a threat, only too easy to imagine, that Warsaw would be bombed into ruins within a few days? Only Elliot expressed full support, going even further with his wish that the statement should be issued straightaway to make sure of Poland's resistance. Chatfield offered qualified support. He reverted to a distinction he had made in an earlier discussion between military and political considerations, and suggested that here they pointed in different directions. It had already been agreed that a German conquest of Roumania would constitute a military threat to the Western Powers. 'It might be questioned whether, if Germany over-ran Poland, that would to the same extent constitute a military threat to us, since Germany would then be faced with Russia on her borders.' But 'if Poland were attacked, it was politically impossible for us to stand aside.'

At this point, Halifax circulated drafts of the statement and of the telegrams he wanted to send to Paris, Warsaw and Bucharest. Both aroused strong criticism, notably from Chamberlain and from Simon, who wanted further enquiries to be added to the telegrams. It did not matter that this would mean delay, because Halifax had asked only for approval should urgent action turn out to be necessary. The Prime Minister proposed asking the Polish government whether they had reason to expect a sudden German coup and whether they thought the statement under discussion would be likely to avert it. Simon suggested that Phipps should find out whether the French government intended to honour their treaty obligation to support the Poles in resisting German aggression; if so, they should be assured of British help. This implied that the initiative lay with Paris rather than London, a view already offered by Morrison, who had pointed out that, if Hitler could be deterred by the prospect of a war on two fronts, no further action was needed. If France honoured its obligations 'Germany would *ipso facto* be engaged in war on two fronts.'

The draft statement opened with the assurance that neither the British Government nor those governments they had consulted were pursuing policies 'directed against any legitimate aims or interests of the German Government', but were 'concerned solely with the prevention of further attempts by that Government to destroy by force or threat of force the independence of other states'.

> Apart from other evidence at their disposal that is disquieting, His Majesty's Government have not failed to observe that the German Government have, during the last few days, begun to employ the same methods of violent press attack on Poland that were used to prepare for the forcible absorption of Czechoslovakia.
>
> This is inevitably causing anxiety, and inasmuch as some further time may be occupied in the consultations now proceeding, His

> Majesty's Government think it desirable forthwith to make plain what is their position pending the conclusion of these consultations. His Majesty's Government earnestly hope that their anxieties may be without foundation, and, as they have repeatedly stated, it is no part of their policy to interfere with the adjustment through free negotiation between the parties concerned of any differences that may from time to time arise between them.
>
> At the same time, in the pursuance of the policy to which their present consultations are directed, I wish to say on behalf of His Majesty's Government in the United Kingdom that in the event of resort by the German Government to any action which the Polish Government feels obliged to regard as a threat to their independence and accordingly to resist, His Majesty's Government will at once lend the Polish Government all support in their power.

Discussion of this draft statement showed general unease at its threatening tone, and it was rejected as 'likely to be provocative to the German Government'. There also occurred a significant disagreement between Chamberlain and Halifax. Halifax was ready for war in the event of action by Germany 'which the Polish Government regarded as a threat to their independence'. Chamberlain preferred to make the test 'a threat to their independence which the Polish Government were prepared to resist.' As an example, he said that if the Poles 'regarded the Danzig issue as constituting a threat to their independence and were prepared to resist by force, then we should have to come to their help'. This different wording implied that if the Poles were not prepared to fight even if they did see their independence as being threatened, the British should not go to their aid. This was, indeed, a logical requirement of the policy of deterrence by which Germany was to be threatened with war on two fronts. Halifax complained, however, that Beck 'was most anxious to avoid war with Germany if he could possibly do so'. To judge from this, and from his having encouraged Kennard to bypass Beck in communicating with the Polish government, he wanted any British initiative to be such as would ensure that Poland *did* fight in the event of a perceived threat to its independence.

The Prime Minister's rejoinder was to sympathise with Beck's preference and to suggest that it should be encouraged; the statement 'should end up on a somewhat less defiant note, and should indicate the desirability of settling differences not by threats of force but by discussion'. He went on to suggest that 'we might indicate our readiness to take part in such a discussion, if called upon to do so. Such action would be more in accord with our general policy.' Halifax, possibly taken aback by this sudden reversion to the language of appeasement, said that he was 'a little averse from indicating our willingness to enter into discussions between Germany and Poland'. Chamberlain accepted that a warning of some sort was needed to avert German aggression, and that the warning must be public in deference to the strength of opinion at home, but the exchange illustrated the differences underlying the previous night's agreement to guarantee Poland. Chamberlain wished to use the threat of war to force Hitler to negotiate, appeasement by persuasion having failed. Halifax wished to 'make it plain to important people in Government circles in Germany that Hitler was embarking on action which was likely to lead to war on two fronts'. He expected the threat of war to destabilise the Nazi regime, hopefully removing Hitler from power altogether in the process.

It was the Admiral who supplied the politicians with an apparent compromise. Zetland had once more argued that the statement, even with suggested revisions, could not be issued unless the Polish government wanted it. Chatfield challenged this assumption. The problem with delaying the issue of a statement until the situation became clearer, he argued, was that its issue might then be too late to serve any purpose. He suggested, instead, the issue of a more general statement at an earlier date, thus giving a more timely warning. There ensued a discussion of this, the course of which was not detailed in the minutes, and it is not at all clear why there was eventual agreement with what Chatfield had proposed. What was abandoned had itself seemed a compromise, by which the warning Halifax wanted was endorsed, but he could issue it only if the more cautious Chamberlain agreed. There had then been calls by some colleagues for still further restraint on precipitate action. Instead, it was now decided that, as long as the statement was made less 'provocative', it should be issued almost immediately, even though there had been no confirmation of the threat. Ministers seemed quite confident that they could assess what would or would not 'provoke' Hitler. Its issue was to appear casual and incidental. Rather than resort to diplomatic channels, a parliamentary question was arranged for the following day, which would be answered by the Prime Minister. Chamberlain offered an alternative draft as his answer; after discussion of this, the final warning words of Halifax's discarded draft were added to it. It was agreed to omit any claim that Poland's independence was a vital British interest, apparently because American public opinion might be shocked at such blatant self-seeking! In the meantime, Halifax would contact Warsaw and Paris. Chamberlain had already consulted Opposition leaders, who agreed in general with the government's line of action.

By then, it was five to one, and at that point a brief, informal report from the Chiefs of Staff was passed in to Chatfield, who immediately read it out to his colleagues. A map had been attached, showing the disposition of German forces facing Poland that day. There were four or five divisions on either side of the Corridor, but this was 'practically normal'. More significant was a concentration of forces opposite Silesia, but the Deputy-Director of Military Intelligence interpreted this as 'forming an effective threat in any negotiations with Poland', and not as an intention to invade. It was thought that the present dispositions were designed 'to cover a *coup d'etat* against Danzig only'. There was no hard evidence of a more extensive advance, but they had probably calculated that rumours of such would mean that the relatively minor move would be greeted with relief. It was not believed that Poland would fight if presented by the fact of an unannounced German occupation of Danzig; they would fight if humiliated by having to respond to an ultimatum about Danzig, or if the Corridor was attacked. The COS, therefore, advised that any announcement should make clear that intervention would take place only if there were 'a definite act of aggression against Polish territory' and if the Poles resisted it and appealed for help to both Great Britain and France. The Polish government should at the same time undertake to help if the Western Powers were attacked, thereby ensuring war on two fronts. They also stressed the importance of somehow ensuring that 'Roumania's resources are denied to Germany in the event of war.' They did not venture to suggest how that condition might be met.[21]

The COS, therefore, offered no support at all for the urgency which the Cabinet had assumed was needed, but ministers, having discussed Halifax's proposal for two hours and having with difficulty reached a compromise involving early publication, seemed in no mood to re-start the debate. Besides, they agreed with the actual recommendations of the COS, and they were probably hungry. Chatfield and Hoare did stress the importance of ensuring that the Polish government should consult London before doing anything, which might precipitate hostilities. The Dominions Secretary mentioned a distinction drawn by MacKenzie King between 'consultation', in which his consent was being sought, and 'information', which merely gave him an opportunity to object. Inskip asked which would apply in the case of the telegrams he would now have to send. The Prime Minister was clear that they should be for information, and that there was no need as yet to send the terms of the draft statement. It was left to the Foreign Policy Committee (FPC) to decide that afternoon on the wording of the question and answer by which the Commons was to learn the next day what the Cabinet had decided to do.[22]

When, therefore, the Commons met on Thursday afternoon at 2.45, Chamberlain dealt briefly and non-committally with anxious questions on defence and diplomacy.[23] At 3.45 those members of the Cabinet who constituted the FPC, together with Sir Horace Wilson, met in the Prime Minister's room at the House of Commons for a short meeting. Halifax read out to them the telegrams, drafted after the morning's Cabinet and about to be sent to Paris and Warsaw. The French government were told that, in anticipation of a question in Parliament, Chamberlain wished for their consent to a timely joint warning 'in terms as little provocative as possible concerning any aggression against Poland'.[24] A briefer telegram to Kennard conveyed the gist of the proposed answer for confirmation that it accorded with the Polish government's wishes.[25] The drafts of the pre-arranged Question and Answer were distributed and approved with minor amendments.

> Q. To ask the Prime Minister whether the attention of HMG has been drawn to rumours current as to the imminence of an attack on Poland, and whether he will inform the House as to the view of HMG regarding these rumours and what action HMG would propose to take if these rumours prove to be well founded?
> A. A number of these rumours have reached HMG who must not, however, be taken as accepting them as true.

As regards the last part of the question it will remove any possibility of misunderstanding to point out, as has repeatedly been made plain on behalf of HMG, that it is no part of their policy to seek to interfere with the adjustment, by way of free negotiation between the parties concerned, of any differences that may arise between them. They consider that this is the natural and proper course where differences exist. In their opinion there should be no question incapable of solution by peaceful means and they can see no justification for the substitution of force or threats of force for the method of negotiation.

In the present case I trust (and believe) that the rumours referred to are unfounded, but I feel bound to add on behalf of HMG that, pending the conclusion of the consultations now proceeding with other governments, in the event of any action which clearly threatened Polish independence, and which the Polish government accordingly felt bound to resist with their national forces, HMG would at once lend the

Polish government all support in their power and they have given the Polish government an assurance to this effect.

I may add that the French government have authorised me to make it plain that they stand in the same position in this matter as do HMG.

Halifax explained that, unless there were objections from Paris or Warsaw, the announcement would go ahead 'even if in the interval we had failed to get confirmation of the rumours of an imminent German attack on Poland'. Wilson told the Committee that Mason-MacFarlane had found nothing to report; nor had War Office enquiries that day so far found evidence of significant troop movements. Chamberlain accepted that this 'did not support the theory that Germany was contemplating an imminent military *coup de main*'. Whether to afford Germany the courtesy of advance notice was left open, but it was agreed that the Prime Minister should explain the policy to Mussolini by a further personal letter.[26] Members of the Committee were asked to keep themselves available that evening in case replies from Paris or Warsaw required urgent consideration; otherwise, they were to reassemble at 9.45 the following morning. The telegrams to Paris and Warsaw had been despatched at 3.50 and 4.20 p.m., respectively.[27] It was this activity which presumably led the Foreign Office to cancel a visit by the Russian Ambassador, arranged for 4 p.m.

The question of Russia's role could, however, no longer be avoided. Maisky had not seen Halifax since 19 March and he made clear his frustration when he met Dalton and Greenwood at 6 p.m. The Labour Party Executive met at 9 p.m. and agreed to press for some mention of Russia in the forthcoming statement. Greenwood, Alexander and Dalton went on to Downing Street to see the Prime Minister, stressing not only the hostility he would encounter in the Commons and elsewhere if Russia did not feature in his statement, but the sheer importance of Russian power in a future confrontation with Germany. Chamberlain spoke vaguely of consultation, but stressed the distrust of Russia among many governments. He accepted Dalton's suggestion that the statement due to be made at 11 a.m. should be postponed, though he remained unimpressed by their reason for delay, namely that the conversation which Halifax was to have with Maisky that morning might be taken into account.[28]

At 9.45 on the morning of Friday, 31 March, the FPC reassembled. The Prime Minister reported on his meeting with Labour leaders, who had then disclosed to the Press what he had told them about the latest developments. He gave this as a reason why the planned morning announcement in the Commons had lost its urgency, not the time thereby made available to learn Maisky's views. Indeed, he made it clear that, for Poland's sake, he still opposed any mention at all of Russia, and Halifax strongly supported him in this. There was, however, now time for the full Cabinet to meet again at noon to discuss the final form of the declaration. He would announce the change when responding to the Private Notice question about the European situation, which had been arranged for 11 a.m.

The Prime Minister conceded that the latest information did not point to any immediate *coup de main* by Germany, so that it was as well to omit any reference to rumours, confining the question to 'the European situation'. The obvious objection to this was voiced: if the rumours were of no account, why was a unilateral declaration in support of Poland needed? If it was needed, why make it unconditional, publicly abandoning a valuable bargaining counter in advance of imminent negotiations with Beck himself? Another danger, already much aired, was that the announcement might give rise to the sort of embarrassment experienced on 21 May 1938. It was important to omit prophecies or hopes liable to be falsified by events. It was eventually agreed that the Private Notice Question at 11 a.m. would simply ask the Prime Minister to comment on the European situation, and that this would be promised shortly before the House rose that afternoon. Various changes were agreed to the wording of the statement, and it was in this form that Chamberlain delivered it. To a Supplementary Question on the rumours, the Prime Minister would reply that he was aware of them, but that they were not confirmed 'by any official information in our possession, and the Government must not be taken as accepting them as true'.

On Thursday evening, Kennard, in reporting Beck's immediate agreement to what was proposed, had made clear his own unease. He had pointed out that feeling was such in Poland at present that 'some impulsive action' could not be ruled out if, for example, the Senate in Danzig proclaimed the territory's return to Germany. Polish troops might then be sent in. He suggested that British and French assurances should refer only to 'unprovoked' action by Germany. He added that both Beck and the German Ambassador had confirmed to him that no ultimatum had been delivered and that there was nothing to indicate 'more menacing action in the immediate future'.[29] The FPC rejected his suggestion, presumably for the reason Halifax gave Kennard in his reply, namely that the insidious German technique of aggression might drive the Poles into an act of self-defence which would look like provocation.[30] Instead, it was agreed to warn the Polish government that the forthcoming statement assumed not only on Poland's readiness to resist aggression, but also that 'she would not indulge in provocative behaviour or stupid obstinacy either generally or in particular as regards Danzig.'[31]

At noon, the Cabinet met in the Prime Minister's room at the House of Commons. Chamberlain referred obliquely to the differences of opinion voiced at their previous meeting as a reason for further discussion before a final decision was made. He spoke of his meeting with the Labour leaders. He summarised the proceedings of the FPC and circulated the re-drafted statement. He pointed out that the second paragraph was no longer specifically concerned with relations between Germany and Poland, and that the obligation in the third paragraph to come to Poland's aid 'left us some freedom of manoeuvre' because it 'would, of course, be for us to determine what action threatened Polish independence'. A mere frontier incident would not constitute such a threat.

Discussion concentrated on the question of Russia's role, about which there had been such persistent disagreement within the Cabinet and which Chamberlain knew would be raised after his statement to the Commons. He looked to Halifax for advice, pointing out to him that he would be expected to say whether Russia had offered to participate and whether it had been asked to do so. The Labour Party believed the Government 'were prejudiced against Russia and were neglecting a possible source of help'. His answers to supplementary questions would depend on the results of Halifax's promised interview with Maisky. The Foreign Secretary, however, responded casually and quite unhelpfully. He said that Maisky had been unavailable for discussion that morning, but that he hoped to see him before 3 p.m.; he anticipated that the Ambassador 'would express himself at the interview as perfectly satisfied and would say that the Russians were willing to help if they were allowed to do so'. Possibly this was jocular rather than fatuous, as was his suggestion that, since the Polish government might rather not hear that Maisky 'had expressed complete satisfaction', it would be safer to say that 'the position had been fully explained to the Russian Government, and that there was no misunderstanding between the two Governments.' Hoare, though a strong advocate of Russian involvement, thought that public opinion would understand that priority had to be given to making sure of Poland. He referred to a very moderate article that day in the Manchester Guardian.[32] Hore-Belisha enhanced the sense of urgency by reporting that the latest indications were that 'Germany intended either to occupy Danzig on the 1st of April or to intimidate Poland, at a time when that country appeared to be drawing closer to the Western Powers.' The Cabinet left Chamberlain and

Halifax to consult on how supplementaries might be answered once Halifax had seen Maisky.[33]

When the meeting broke up at a quarter to one, Halifax returned to the Foreign Office, where Maisky awaited him. He read out the forthcoming statement to the Ambassador, who suggested that the phrase 'lend the Polish Government all support in their power' might be 'minimised' by those who sought to question 'the genuine character of British intentions'. Halifax seemed puzzled and was dismissive of this, but Maisky might have been recalling Sir Thomas Inskip's undertaking on 3 October that the British Government would take 'all steps in their power' in the event of aggression against Czechoslovakia. That there was this unfortunate echo had apparently occurred to no one in the process of drafting the present statement. Halifax then asked if the Prime Minister could announce that the Russian government approved. Maisky said that, having been given no time to consult his government, he could not consent to that. Halifax had the impression that the Ambassador did not 'feel any great difficulty' about a vaguer reference to such a move being in line with Russia's declared principles of foreign policy.[34]

At 2.52, Chamberlain rose to make his promised statement to the Commons. He began by reaffirming that the Government had 'no official confirmation of the rumours of any projected attack on Poland and they must not, therefore, be taken as accepting them as true.' He then restated their general policy as one of appeasement, though he did not use the word. 'They have constantly advocated the adjustment, by way of free negotiation between the parties concerned, of any differences that may arise between them. They consider that this is the natural and proper course where differences exist. In their opinion there should be no question incapable of solution by peaceful means, and they would see no justification for the substitution of force or threats of force for the method of negotiation.' Tacitly acknowledging that this general policy was now no more than a pious aspiration, he turned to the special policy called forth by current circumstances.

> As the House is aware, certain consultations are proceeding with other Governments. In order to make perfectly clear the position of His Majesty's Government in the meantime before those consultations are concluded, I now have to inform the House that during that period, in the event of any action which clearly threatened Polish independence, and which the Polish Government accordingly considered it vital to resist with their national forces, His Majesty's

> Government would feel themselves obliged at once to lend the Polish Government all support in their power. They have given the Polish Government an assurance to this effect.
> I may add that the French Government have authorised me to make it plain that they stand in the same position in this matter as do His Majesty's Government.

The Prime Minister was less troubled by the questions about Russia than had been anticipated, perhaps because he did not attempt equivocation; he misled instead by his apparent candour. Greenwood anticipated war as a logical consequence of 'as momentous a statement as has been made in this House for a quarter of a century' unless other Powers, especially Russia, were promptly recruited to the task of deterrence. He wanted an immediate conference of like-minded Powers as the next step. Chamberlain sounded reassuring. His statement had covered only an interim period, during which consultation with Russia and other Powers would proceed. The Foreign Secretary had just been in very full discussions with the Russian Ambassador, whose government, Chamberlain felt sure, fully understood and appreciated 'the principles upon which we are acting'. Further measures would be discussed with the Polish Foreign Minister in the next week so as to 'accumulate the maximum amount of co-operation in any efforts that may be made to put an end to aggression, if aggression were intended, and to substitute for it the more reasonable and orderly method of discussion'. Greenwood was not altogether happy with this formulation. He asked directly whether the Prime Minister 'would welcome that maximum co-operation from all Powers, including the U.S.S.R.?' Chamberlain assured him that 'we should welcome the maximum amount of co-operation.' He did not specify the U.S.S.R., but when asked by John Morgan for an assurance there were 'no ideological impediments between us and the U.S.S.R.', he claimed to have 'no hesitation' in giving it. He insisted, too, that the government had 'no theoretical views about a conference', and would use it or whatever other means seemed most effective. The only really discordant notes, struck by Willie Gallacher and F.J. Bellenger, concerned Chamberlain's fitness to lead the nation at such a time. The general mood among MPs was one of satisfaction that such a clear-cut undertaking had at last been made.[35]

Were they right to be impressed? Neville Chamberlain's statement was provisional and did not, in itself, constitute a 'guarantee' of Poland. Moreover, confining the commitment to 'independence' drew press attention on the following day to the absence of the word 'integrity'.

The leader in *The Times* aroused suspicion by stressing this limitation. A.L. Kennedy, the deputy-editor, privately claimed to have written it precisely on the lines of his conversation with Cadogan the day before the Prime Minister's announcement. Halifax told the editor, Geoffrey Dawson, that Chamberlain's reaction to reading the leader was 'that's just what I meant'. Halifax himself thought it was 'just about right'. Moreover, Cadogan told Kennedy that the Foreign Office had persuaded ministers to drop the word 'integrity'.[36] A bilateral deal, involving veiled threats and territorial concessions, was not thought improbable. In practice, the wording did not much matter. Given the climate of opinion within the Commons and in the press, the government would now have no room for manoeuvre in the event of an actual attack on Poland. They would be obliged, as Chamberlain had said to the FPC on 8 February in anticipation of a similar crisis, to 'deliver an ultimatum to the German government requiring them to withdraw their troops before a certain time, failing which we should declare war upon Germany'. The Prime Minister's statement of 31 March aroused such clear and precise expectations that it was *politically* an inescapable commitment to fight.

10
Diplomacy by Drama

On 3 October 1938, Sir Thomas Inskip had announced in the Commons that, although an international guarantee of Czechoslovakia was still to be negotiated, the British Government 'would certainly feel bound to take all steps in their power' to preserve that country's integrity against 'an act of unprovoked aggression'. Within six months, Czechoslovakia had suffered invasion and partition by neighbouring states. On 31 March 1939, Neville Chamberlain announced in the Commons that if, during the present diplomatic consultations, Poland's armed forces had to resist an action threatening her independence, the British Government 'would feel themselves obliged at once to lend the Polish Government all support in their power'. Within six months, Poland had suffered invasion and partition by neighbouring states. Why had the men involved in the making of British policy come to believe that this second 'guarantee' would be a more effective deterrent than the first?

Psychology has often proved to be an untrustworthy aid to historical explanation, but George Kelly's theory of personal constructs[1] may be an exception in the case of diplomatic history, where what is to be explained are changes in the construing of events by a small number of specific individuals. Policy-makers in any one capital try to construe the intentions of their counterparts in other capitals, and, if those intentions are thought to constitute an immediate or potential threat to the country they represent, they will try to change the thinking which has given rise to those hostile intentions, or at least to make their execution seem too dangerous. At the same time, they will try to promote co-operative thinking by other governments, similarly threatened, in the work of deterrence. In the case of governments bent on intimidation or conquest, their policy-makers will try to facilitate this by undermining thoughts of successful resistance and by seeking allies among governments whose members likewise construe international politics in aggressive and predatory terms. Relatively few individuals are normally involved in such policy-making, even in a democracy, and their task of divining the real intentions of other governments is inevitably difficult and prone to catastrophic error. This process constitutes diplomatic history, a branch of international history. Kelly's theory as to how individuals construe themselves and the behaviour of others, and as to how they may come to construe matters differently, has, therefore, been kept in mind in attempting to explain the behaviour of British ministers and officials engaged in policy-making and diplomacy during these six months.[2]

Neither in September 1938 nor in March 1939 did the British Government choose the simplest and most obvious course in seeking to deter Hitler from further acts of aggression. Co-ordinated action by the conscript armies of France and Russia was, 20 years after the Great War, still the most obvious way by which Germany's conscript Army might be contained in the event of a new war. The obvious British role would still be to reinforce the Western Front by its own yet to be conscripted Army and, through naval blockade, to reduce Germany's capacity to fight a long war. The effect of vastly greater use of air power by all participants was still a matter for both uneasy and hopeful speculation. The obvious British diplomatic role in trying to avert war was, therefore, to help convince Hitler that a combination of these three Powers would be formed in defined circumstances. The events of 1914–18 had shown that even this combination would leave the outcome of war uncertain, but at least Hitler would have to share in the uncertainty. After the annexation of Austria, the most obvious move by Great Britain would have been public or private assurances of support for France and Russia, if their existing commitments with respect to Central and Eastern Europe brought them into conflict with Germany. Instead, in September 1938 and in March 1939, the British Cabinet took the lead at a time when circumstances required from them a supporting role, though one crucial to the success of the two principals.

From mid-November 1938, none of the Cabinet ministers and none of those who advised them challenged the assumption that the Nazi regime constituted a threat, whether direct or indirect, to the vital interests of Great Britain. Their construing of the situation varied only as to what could and should be done to meet the threat. Only the Cabinet could decide, and within the Cabinet anything agreed upon by the Prime Minister and the Foreign Secretary in the field of foreign affairs was unlikely to meet with serious opposition. As, however, there was often disagreement between Chamberlain and Halifax, ministers with relevant expertise or political weight could contribute to its resolution. Cabinet ministers might also allow themselves to be influenced by experts, especially those within the Foreign Office, British embassies, the Service ministries, the Treasury, and the Dominions and Colonial Offices. How each emerging situation abroad was construed might, therefore, vary considerably among the few dozen individuals likely to be involved. In addition, ministers obviously kept an eye on opinions expressed within Parliament, among influential journalists and by prominent persons in their constituencies.

In retrospect, it is apparent that, after Munich, Chamberlain repeatedly misinterpreted Hitler's intentions and Halifax consistently exaggerated his vulnerability to internal opposition, so it is unsurprising that neither succeeded in devising a policy to deter him from further aggression. Chamberlain's goal throughout the year after Munich continued to be one of appeasement, that is general acceptance by European governments that territorial changes should be brought about only by peaceful negotiation and not by war or threats of war. What changed after Munich was, firstly, his assumption that the special relationship he thought he had established there with Hitler would be the means to that achievement and, secondly, his interpretation of Hitler's future goals. He had taken it for granted that Hitler sought to extend Germany's frontiers to include German communities in neighbouring states, and that the problem, therefore, was how to anticipate further aggression in pursuit of this through peaceful revision of the Treaty of Versailles. He was quickly disillusioned. Hitler's hostile public pronouncements immediately after Munich began the process, which was accelerated by his own revulsion at *Kristallnacht* and by reports that Hitler was planning attacks against Great Britain. His alternative hope that Mussolini would persuade Hitler to embrace appeasement faded, if only temporarily, after the Rome visit.

Instead, he had no alternative but to take seriously what were, in fact, false reports of Hitler's intention to launch war against the Western Powers in the *immediate* future, beginning with an air offensive against London or with a land war against either Holland or Switzerland. He did not abandon his goal of appeasement, but he accepted that persuasion had failed as the means. Some form of diplomatic intimidation had to be applied; if that failed and Hitler persisted in a policy of aggression, he realised that Great Britain and France would have to go to war. In particular, Chamberlain had yielded to French demands, strongly backed by the Foreign Secretary, in making his announcement on 6 February of military support for France against German or Italian aggression. By the end of February and in early March, he had convinced himself that deterrence in this form had already succeeded and that Hitler was signalling his readiness for negotiation. The annexation of Bohemia and Moravia shattered this assumption and he promptly reverted to deterrence, this time through co-ordinated action in Western and Eastern Europe, while persisting in the hope that Germany and Poland would then be content with a peaceful revision of frontiers under his auspices. He found Poland and Roumania initially uncooperative, especially in respect of any Russian involvement in the process of deterrence. Nevertheless, he accepted a French plan for a Franco-British guarantee of a pact between Poland and Roumania, despite their reluctance to be so linked or to be armed by a supposedly willing Russia. False rumours of an imminent attack on Poland then persuaded him to try the more immediate and direct deterrence of threatened war.

Halifax's ideas as to what should be done about Hitler and his regime oscillated between September and March. In September, his support for Chamberlain's policy was interrupted by his famous overnight conversion after Godesberg, and he told the Cabinet that his goal was now the overthrow of the Nazi regime. After Munich, he reverted to a policy of appeasement and was ready to concede Germany's predominant influence over most of the states of eastern and south-eastern Europe, looking only for access to British commerce. By the middle of November, the events of *Kristallnacht*, coupled with intelligence reports of Hitler's aggressive intent towards Great Britain, had convinced him once more that a defensive system against Nazi Germany had urgently to be built, centred on a Franco-British alliance. In contrast to Chamberlain, he believed that this meant backing France openly against Italy as well as Germany, and that it required the commitment of substantial British forces across the Channel in the event of war. At the same time, he was sufficiently encouraged by signs of dissidence and economic difficulties within Germany to believe that the mere onset of war would bring about such popular discontent that Army opponents of the regime would engineer its collapse. He, like Chamberlain, had high hopes that a radio propaganda campaign would contribute decisively to that discontent. He failed to convince the Prime Minister that Germany should be warned publicly against attacking Holland; he succeeded in March where Poland was concerned. That Hitler would meet resistance at home remained his belief up to the eve of war. On 30 August, he told Inskip of news from Dusseldorf that 'the crowd is pulling down Nazi posters', and, at lunch on the following day with Cadogan, Wallace, Colville and Wedderburn, he told them that he had had his 'first view of a beaten fox'.[3] His mood in May 1940 may have reflected the scale of his miscalculation.

Between October and March, there were few serious disputes in Cabinet about foreign policy. Of the seven ministers who had strongly backed Halifax at the post-Godesberg Cabinet, only four remained, namely, Stanley, Hore-Belisha, De La Warr and Elliot. Duff Cooper had resigned, Winterton had been demoted, and Hailsham removed on health grounds. Chamberlain had replaced them with the less troublesome Stanhope, Morrison and Runciman. In practice, there was general acceptance of the need to assume impending war, while trying to avert it. The most important dispute concerned the commitment of troops across the Channel. Once this was settled in February, the only crucial controversies were over the terms of the guarantees and over relations with Russia. Ministers concentrated on preparing their departments for war should deterrence fail.

During the second half of March, ministers sensed that publicly expressed opinion so matched a general mood within the nation that 'taking a stand' against Hitler would have been unavoidable even if they had been otherwise minded. As Norton Medlicott put it, writing in the early months of the war, Nazi foreign policy had eventually produced in the British people 'one of its characteristic moods of implacable exasperation'.[4] For example, Sargent urged Raczynski to get a prompt reply from Warsaw about the proferred guarantee, as the Prime Minister was increasingly under attack for a too hesitant response to German aggression.[5] Public opinion did not, of course, impose on the government the particular 'stand' of 'guarantees', which, unless Hitler was thereby deterred, there would be no way of honouring save by a general European war of uncertain outcome. The ultimate rescue of Poles, Roumanians, Jews and others would then come, if at all, only after they had experienced the horrors known by the guarantors to ensue from a Nazi conquest they would be unable to prevent. As the COS had warned, victory in that general war would leave Russia in a position to determine the region's fate instead.

In these circumstances, deals with a neighbouring Great Power had some attraction for the lesser states situated between Germany and Russia. Hungarian and Roumanian leaders saw Hitler as the lesser evil and negotiated terms, which seemed to them satisfactory enough while peace prevailed.[6] Polish leaders, too, saw the advantage of a deal, but not on the terms Germany sought. The vulnerability and military weakness of all these states were obvious flaws in the policy of trying to deter Hitler by threatening a two-front war without Russia being involved. The assumptions were that the conquest of Poland and Roumania would take a few months to accomplish, that this would somewhat weaken the German Army, and that a large part of it would then be tied down in guarding the new common frontier with Russia. All this was expected to reduce Hitler's capacity to strike at the Western Powers by land.

If so, it would be just as well. Service advice, offered to the Strategical Appreciation Sub-Committee on 13 March, had been that 1939 was 'our bad year' and 'in the future we should be in a better position.'[7] Treasury advice was even more discouraging. Under-Secretary Sir Alan Barlow challenged the assumption that 'our financial strength was such that we could support a long war.' 'The position had radically changed for the worse compared with 1914' and to think otherwise would be 'burying our heads in the sand'.[8] The Chiefs of Staff had warned on 20 March that, while Great Britain and France had much latent strength, in 1939 'our state of readiness for war will not compare, as a whole, with that of the nations we have assumed as hostile'.[9] The Joint Planning Committee, in dealing on 18 March with the prospect of war if Roumania was attacked, had emphasised that 'Germany has for many months been virtually mobilised for war, both in the civil and military spheres. She has therefore a long start and it would be highly dangerous for us to deliver any form of ultimatum unless we had taken far-reaching preparatory measures to lessen the gap between our relative readiness to enter what might soon develop into a world war.'[10] The same Committee, on 27 March, urged that the government 'should not assume that to "knock Italy out of the war at the outset" was feasible', while the COS thought it unwise 'to place any substantial reliance on assistance, active or passive, from Poland'.[11] The only consolatory opinion was that Japan would probably hold her hand to see how the war developed in Europe and, in particular, the extent of British and French naval losses.[12]

An additional warning from the COS was that the government's diplomacy could be fatally disrupted by a Russo-German agreement, while its prospects would be greatly enhanced if Russia was an ally or at least a sympathetic neutral. Yet, during the spring and summer, persistent signs of some impending deal between Germany and Russia, so disturbing to the soldiers, were discounted by the politicians. It was curious that this should have been so, given that the chore of having to learn details of successive partitions of Poland would have featured in the schooling of ministers, and given their awareness that Russia and Germany alike had irredentist claims against Poland which might form the basis of a yet another partition between them. Nor did Ministers suffer from any delusion that ideological antagonism would rule it out.

One reason was Chamberlain's own antagonism towards communism, so strong as to make it difficult for him to take Russia at all seriously as a possible ally. Halifax did acknowledge the advantages and set out to reach an agreement, though he expected the collapse of Nazism to render it unnecessary. He had not anticipated the enthusiasm of those German Army leaders, whom he hoped would overthrow Hitler, for a war to recover lost lands from Poland as opposed to war in the West. Goerdeler's ideas should have alerted him to the possibility that they might give this priority over their resentment of Hitler's rule. He might then have appreciated the urgent need to counter the threat with the only form of deterrence likely to impress Nazis and generals alike. He and Chamberlain had reminders enough from Hoare, Stanley and Elliot, who continued to press the military and diplomatic case for urgency in coming to terms of some sort with Stalin. So did the COS. Although sceptical of the offensive capacity of an Army so ravaged by its political masters, they made clear to the Foreign Policy Committee how important such an agreement would be. It would present 'a solid front of formidable proportions against aggression', whereas failure to achieve an agreement 'might be regarded as a diplomatic defeat which would have serious military repercussions and might have the immediate effect of encouraging Germany to further acts of aggression and of ultimately throwing the U.S.S.R. into her arms'. 'Russia should not, in any circumstances, become allied with Germany. From the military point of view such an eventuality would create a most dangerous situation for us'.[13]

The Cabinet as a whole was responsible for botching the sensible compromise which Chamberlain and Halifax reached after the meeting with Colvin. Halifax had wanted an immediate warning to Hitler about Poland, but had settled for an agreed statement ready for issue in a crisis. At Cabinet, Zetland, also sensibly, argued that its issue should rather be a matter for that body to decide, not just the Prime Minister and Foreign Secretary. When the Foreign Office's draft of the statement was circulated, however, there were sharp differences of opinion over its wording, especially as between Halifax and Chamberlain. Faced with a clash between its two most powerful members, the Cabinet responded in the way of committees the world over. Finding a compromise unobjectionable to either became the most urgent task. This took the form of a milder statement (to satisfy the Prime Minister) to be issued immediately (to please the Foreign Secretary). So this substituted statement, which differed only in tone, was not to be kept in reserve to deal with a crisis but issued promptly as though the current situation was critical. Ironically, the judgment of the COS that there was no sign of a crisis was passed in to Chatfield just before the meeting ended. The upshot was that Halifax got the immediate warning to Hitler, which he had preferred, in only slightly less challenging language, while the attempt to give it a more casual and informal tone by the device of an answer to a question in the Commons was defeated by the excited expectations that aroused. The occasion was instead one of high drama, and Greenwood promptly characterised the Prime Minister's statement as the most important delivered to the House since 1914.

As in September 1938, the government, so frequently accused till then of insufficient urgency in responding to developments in Europe, had rushed to make a sudden, dramatic and arguably premature intervention in face of an emerging crisis. Each intervention has been open to interpretation as either inept and dangerous, or timely and well-judged. Yet, controversial though these events remain among historians, the popular perception that the obtuse and faint-hearted men of Munich redeemed themselves by their apt and courageous Polish guarantee has been so enduring that there has scarcely been an international crisis since without these events being recalled as a warning and an example to governments. On the present reading, ministers should have been confining themselves, in 1938 and 1939 alike, to coalition-building and organisation for war for the purposes of deterrence and defence. After all, even the immediate prospects, if deterrence failed, were thought, wrongly, to be grim. On the day that Chamberlain made his announcement about Poland, two of his colleagues recorded Service advice that air raid casualties in Great Britain as a whole during the first two or three weeks of war might run to 17,500 killed and 35,000 wounded every day, requiring perhaps 433,000 hospital beds by the fourth week. Only about 80,000 beds were available in England and Wales, and about 2000 in Scotland. Nor would there be enough doctors and nurses to cope.[14]

The role of historians in all this was not purely retrospective. At a Chatham House conference in March 1938, H.N. Fieldhouse had helpfully predicted that present British policy would lead to a war with Germany, Italy and Japan in which Great Britain would face destruction before America intervened. That intervention would bring debt, the sale of British securities to America, and the lasting transference of naval, commercial and financial power to Washington.[15] In February 1938, R.W. Seton-Watson imagined four possible developments in the

European situation. Firstly, and ideally, a real and sustained understanding between Great Britain, France and Germany, but not at the expense of other countries, would mean peace for a generation. This was currently unavailable. Secondly, a precarious balance of France and Great Britain against Germany and Italy, with Russia excluded from the comity of nations, would simply mean chronic tension and uncertainty and was contrary to the interests of the two Western Powers. Thirdly, and what he feared, was an arrangement between Germany and Russia, either on Weimar lines or at the expense of Poland, which would facilitate a German bid for the Adriatic, the Middle East and a colonial empire. Finally, what should, in his view, be the aim of British policy was an understanding with France and Russia, though not at the expense of other states. This would have the support of the smaller Powers and of the United States, and it would be able to preserve an armed peace because it would have overwhelming force on its side. This combination would have to hold out until the disordered finances of the dictators brought them to a more reasonable frame of mind.[16]

E.L. Woodward delivered a lecture to the Imperial Defence College on 24 October 1938, the text of which reached the Foreign Office on 24 November and was circulated to the Cabinet. He had been surprised that no one in the Royal Navy, let alone the other Services, had contacted him after the publication of his book on German naval expansion before 1914, and he was convinced that no politician had ever read it.[17] He had, in April 1938, written a series of articles for *The Spectator*, arguing that rearmament must precede appeasement. He now took the opportunity to offer the Services his advice from a historical perspective. He saw no need to hurry into a war, which might create more problems than it solved. As long as Great Britain maintained naval supremacy, German domination of the continent could not be extended to the rest of the world. If the country was organised sufficiently, it would be possible to deter any Power from risking war at all. In any case, war against Germany should be postponed for a few years; time was on the side of the democracies, not the dictatorships. Hitler had now reached a point, much like Napoleon after 1809, when any further extension of his power might weaken rather than strengthen him. It should also be remembered that Great Britain's obsession with Napoleon III in the 1860s had prevented anticipation of a greater danger from Prussia. He did not indicate which other future enemy he had in mind; possibly he saw Japan as the more immediate, Russia as the longer-term threat. He was, nevertheless, convinced that militarism was rooted in German culture and that their renewed bid for domination was certain and had to be robustly resisted.

He blamed British leaders for their slowness to grasp this and rearm.[18] Hankey dismissed this case for postponing a confrontation as 'shockingly defeatist' and resented its circulation by the Foreign Office in the Confidential Print. To judge by the hasty spring 'guarantees', he need not have worried. To judge by the course of the war, these complementary diagnoses were sound enough in recommending more time to build a coalition and arm its members.

Instead, the ignominious failure of the Czech guarantee was followed quickly by worthless guarantees to Poland and Roumania. Admittedly, the national mood had changed so radically as to give any British guarantee a manifest substance it had lacked before 15 March, and what the word signified had undergone a sudden change. Traditionally, it had been used to mean a collective pledge to maintain indefinitely some arrangement made by international treaty. During the second half of March 1939, it came to mean, in the thinking of British diplomats and politicians, a unilateral pledge to maintain in the immediate future the independence of another state even at the cost of war. Yet, because of the word's recent associations, Cabinet ministers initially shrank from using it at all in public. Chamberlain did not employ it in his statement of 31 March, nor did his colleagues in the ensuing debates. Within the confines of the Foreign Office, however, it was freely used in this new sense from the time of the Anglo-French conversations, whenever officials referred to the various pledges under discussion. Unconvinced and undeterred, Hitler invaded one of the 'guaranteed' states, whereupon Great Britain and France honoured their pledges and entered upon a general European war which the guarantees had been designed to prevent. The 'guarantee' had thereby sustained its reputation as an equivocal diplomatic device, dangerous in its unpredictable consequences.

List of Abbreviations

CAB	Cabinet Office papers in the National Archives of Scotland, West Register House, Edinburgh
CID	Committee of Imperial Defence
COS	Chiefs of Staff
DBFP	Documents on British foreign policy (HMSO)
DCOS	Deputy Chiefs of Staff
DDF	Documents diplomatiques Francais
DGFP	Documents on German foreign policy
DP(P)	Defence plans (policy)
EHR	English Historical Review
FO	Foreign Office papers in the Public Record Office, Kew
FPC	Foreign Policy Committee
H.C.	House of Commons (debates)
H.L.	House of Lords (debates)
JCH	Journal of Contemporary History
JIC	Joint Intelligence Committee
JPC	Joint Planning Committee
RIIA	Royal Institute of International Affairs
WO	War Office

Notes

Chapter 1 Diplomacy by guarantee

1. Cabinet 16(39), 30 March 1939, CAB 23/98.
2. DBFP 3/4/573, 584.
3. DBFP 3/2/937.
4. DBFP 3/2/1224.
5. 339 H.C. Deb. 5s. cols. 29–162.
6. David Dilks (ed.), *The Diaries of Sir Alexander Cadogan, O.M., 1938–1945* (1971), 3 October 1938, p. 112.
7. DBFP 3/2/app. 4.
8. DBFP 3/2/928.
9. *Diaries of Sir Alexander Cadogan*, 3 October 1938, p. 112.
10. 339 H.C. Deb. 5s. cols. 303–4.
11. 339 H.C. Deb. 5s. cols. 364, 430–1.
12. 339 H.C. Deb. 5s. col. 44.
13. 110 H.L. Deb. 5s. cols.1303–4.
14. H.W.V. Temperley and L.M. Penson, *Foundations of British Foreign Policy 1792–1902* (1938), pp. 81–3.
15. Sir Ernest Satow, 'Peacemaking, old and new', *Cambridge Historical Journal*, 1 (1923–25), 295–318.
16. Temperley and Penson, *Foundations*, p. 40.
17. R. Millman, *British Policy and the Coming of the Franco-Prussian War* (1965), pp. 116, 133.
18. Lillian M. Penson, 'Obligations by Treaty: Their Place in British Foreign Policy, 1898–1914', in A.O. Sarkissian (ed.), *Studies in Diplomatic History and Historiography, in Honour of G.P. Gooch, C.H.* (1961), p. 87.
19. Millman, *British Policy*, p. 74.
20. Gordon Martel, *'The Times' and Appeasement: The Journals of A.L. Kennedy, 1932–1939* (Cambridge, 2000), pp. 46–7.
21. 110 H.L. Deb. 5s. cols. 1413–4.
22. 339 H.C. Deb. 5s. cols. 229–30, 303–4.
23. CHJ, 2 (1926) pp. 151–70.
24. DBFP 3/3/325; DDF 2/12/390.
25. *Diaries of Sir Alexander Cadogan*, 24 November 1938, p. 126.
26. DBFP 3/3/423.
27. DBFP 3/3/413–4.
28. DBFP 3/3/420, 427.
29. DBFP 3/3/444.
30. DBFP 3/3/500.
31. DBFP 3/4/19.
32. DBFP 3/4/42, 86.
33. DBFP 3/4/90, 91, 167, 171.

34. 345 H.C. Deb. 5s. col. 223.
35. DBFP 3/3/414.
36. 342 H.C. Deb. 5s., 28, 30 November, 5, 12, 15, 19, 21 December 1938; 343 H.C. Deb. 5s., 31 January 1939; 344 H.C. Deb. 5s., 20, 22, 27 February 1939; 345 H.C. Deb. 5s., 13, 14, 15 March 1939.
37. 34th mtg., FPC, 6 December 1938, CAB 27/624.

Chapter 2 The outlook from Whitehall

1. DBFP 3/3/1–78.
2. DBFP 3/3/61, 97.
3. A.M. Cienciala, *Poland and the Western Powers, 1938–39* (London, 1968), pp. 2–4.
4. DBFP 3/3/83.
5. DBFP 3/3/76.
6. DBFP 3/3/77.
7. DBFP 3/3/85n, 93, 137.
8. DBFP 3/3/84–5n, 90–4.
9. Count Edward Raczynski, *In Allied London: The Wartime Diaries of the Polish Ambassador* (London, 1962), p. 9.
10. DBFP 3/3/1370.
11. Cabinet 51(38), 31 October 1938, CAB 23/96.
12. DBFP 3/3/184 Maisky did not mention this in his own report to Moscow of the conversation. DVP 21/414.
13. *Diaries of Sir Alexander Cadogan,* 10 December 1938, pp. 128–9.
14. 339 H.C. Deb. 5s., 6 October 1938, col. 551.
15. DBFP 3/2/1228 app.
16. Lord Strang, *Home and Abroad* (1956), p. 147.
17. Keith Feiling, *Life of Neville Chamberlain* (1947), p. 370.
18. Richard Cockett, *Twilight of Truth: Chamberlain, Appeasement and the Manipulation of the Press* (1989), pp. 85–6.
19. DGFP D/4/253, 260.
20. DGFP D/4/255, 264.
21. DGFP D/4/254.
22. DGFP D/4/253.
23. R.F.V. Heuston, *Lives of the Lord Chancellors* (1964), p. 599.
24. DGFP D/4/260; *Documents and Materials Relating to the Eve of the Second World War* (Moscow, 1948), vol. II, Dirksen Papers (1938–39), no. 29.
25. *Diaries of Sir Alexander Cadogan,* 4 October 1938, pp. 112–3.
26. *Diaries of Sir Alexander Cadogan,* 7 November 1938, p. 123.
27. Memoranda given to Halifax by Cadogan, with a covering note, on 9 November 1938, C14471/42/18, FO 371/21659.
28. *Diaries of Sir Alexander Cadogan,* 9 October 1938, p. 114.
29. Memorandum, 8 or 9 November 1938, C14471/42/18, FO 371/21659.
30. Filed with the FO memoranda at FO 371/21659.
31. DBFP 3/3/285; FRUS 1938, pp. 85–6.
32. David Kaiser, *Economic Diplomacy and the Origins of the Second World War* (1980), p. 291.
33. Cabinet 49(38), 19 October 1938, CAB 23/96.

34. For example, among Richard Overy, David Kaiser and Tim Mason, 'Germany, "Domestic Crisis" and War in 1939', *Past and Present*, 122 (1989), pp. 200–40.
35. Cabinet 49(38), 19 October 1938, CAB 23/96.
36. CP 257, CAB 24/280.
37. D. Dilks, introduction to *Diaries of Sir Alexander Cadogan*, p. 3.
38. Colin L. Smith, *The Embassy of Sir William White at Constantinople, 1886–1891* (1957), p. 16.
39. Memorandum, 10 November 1938, CP 257, CAB 24/280.
40. Ibid.
41. *The Memoirs of Lord Gladwyn* (1962), pp. 58–71.
42. Glyn Stone, *The Oldest Ally* (1994), p. 62.
43. CID 328th mtg., 30 June 1938, CAB 2/8.
44. Ibid.
45. CID memo.1474-B, CAB 4/28; CID 334th mtg., CAB 2/8.
46. Stone, *The Oldest Ally*, pp. 72–3.
47. Aaron S. Klieman, 'Bureaucratic politics at Whitehall in the partitioning of Palestine, 1937' in Uriel Dann (ed.), *The Great Powers in the Middle East* (1988), pp. 128–53; Clyde Sanger, *Bringing an End to Empire* (1995), pp. 159–75.
48. Anthony Clayton, *The British Empire as a Superpower* (1986), pp. 487–507; Charles Townshend, *Britain's Civil Wars: Counterinsurgency in the Twentieth Century* (1986), pp. 85–113.
49. CP 250(38), 5 November 1938, CAB 24/280.
50. DBFP 3/3/326.
51. DBFP 3/3/355–8.
52. Cabinet 50(38), CAB 23/96.
53. DBFP 3/3/370 and 456.
54. C8153/85/18, C8154/85/18, C8250/85/18, C8637/85/18, FO 371/21673.
55. DBFP 3/3/279 and app. II(i); C12819/G, FO 371/21673.
56. DBFP 3/3/295; minutes, 9 November 1938, C13715/85/18, FO 371/21673; P. Stafford, 'The visit of Chamberlain and Halifax to Rome: a reappreciation', *EHR*, 98 (1983), pp. 61–100.
57. C12819/G, FO 371/21673.
58. Cabinet 53(38), 7 November 1938, CAB 23/96.

Chapter 3 The challenge of barbarism

1. *Annual Register*, 1938, 19.
2. S.W. Roskill, *Hankey, Man of Secrets* (1970–74), Vol. III, 84–5.
3. Ruth Dudley Edwards, *Victor Gollancz: A Biography* (1987), pp. 283–4, 296–300.
4. *The Times*, 14 November 1938.
5. DBFP 3/3/313.
6. Sir Philip Gibbs, *Across the Frontiers* (1938), pp. 263–4, 281–2.
7. Gibbs, *Across the Frontiers* (1939), pp. 311–2.
8. *Diaries of Sir Alexander Cadogan*, 13–14 November 1938, p. 125.
9. L. London, *Whitehall and the Jews, 1933–1948: British Immigration Policy, Jewish Refugees and the Holocaust* (2000), pp. 99–100; William D. Rubinstein

and Hilary L. Rubinstein, *Philosemitism: Admiration and Support in the English-Speaking World for Jews, 1840–1939* (1999), pp. 94–5.
10. 32nd mtg., FPC, 14 November 1938, CAB 27/624.
11. Cabinet 55(38), 16 November 1938, CAB 23/96.
12. R. Eatwell, 'Munich, public opinion and the Popular Front', *Journal of Contemporary History*, 6 (1971), no. 4, pp. 122–39; Cook and Ramsden, *By-elections in British Politics* (1997), pp. 112–29.
13. Zetland Papers, MSS Eur. D. 609/9.
14. 32nd mtg., FPC, CAB 27/624.
15. C14561/62/18, FO 371/21665.
16. 338th mtg., CID, 17 November 1938, CAB 2/8.
17. Gordon Waterfield, *Professional Diplomat* (1973), pp. 208–12; Franz G. Weber, *The Evasive Neutral: Germany, Britain and the Quest for a Turkish Alliance in the Second World War* (Missouri: University of Missouri Press, 1979), pp. 20–1; S. Deringil, *Turkish Foreign Policy during the Second World War: An Active Neutrality* (Cambridge, 1989), pp. 2–3, 39–40.
18. 33rd mtg., FPC, 21 November 1938, CAB 27/624; John S. Koliopoulos, *Greece and the British Connection, 1835–1941* (1977), pp. 94–6.
19. John Herman, *The Paris Embassy of Sir Eric Phipps: Anglo-French Relations in the Foreign Office, 1937–1939* (1998), p. 144.
20. DBFP 3/3/325; DDF 2/2/390.
21. DBFP 3/3/458n.
22. DBFP 3/3/461–2, 464–6, 468–71, 473–84.
23. *Correspondence and Papers of Arthur Cecil Murray, Viscount Elibank, 1909–62*, MS 8809, National Library of Scotland.
24. Klemens von Klemperer, *Mandate for Resistance: The Case of the German Opposition to Hitler* (1969), p. 112.
25. Klemperer, *Mandate*, p. 115; Arthur P. Young, *Across the Years* (1971), pp. 44–6; Sidney Aster (ed.), *The X Documents* (1974), pp. 156–62, 233.
26. DBFP 3/3/298, 312.
27. Klemperer, *Mandate*, pp. 113–4.
28. Minutes by Sargent, 12 December, and by Cadogan, 13 December 1938, C938/15/18, FO 371/22961.
29. Sidney Aster, *1939: The Making of the Second World War* (1973), p. 5; Klemperer, *Mandate*, pp. 114–7; *Diaries of Sir Alexander Cadogan*, 10–11 December 1938, pp. 128–9.
30. For e.g., Patricia Meehan, *The Unnecessary War: Whitehall and the German Resistance to Hitler* (1992).
31. Iain Morrow, *The Peace Settlement in the German–Polish Borderlands* (1936), pp. 419–56; DBFP 3/4/app. vii.
32. DBFP 3/4/app. VII (i), minutes by Collier, 7 December 1938.
33. DBFP 3/4/app. VII (ii and iv).
34. DBFP 3/4/app. VII(vii).
35. DBFP 3/4/app. VII(x).
36. DDF 2/13/91; DBFP 3/4/app. VII(xii, xv).
37. DBFP 3/4/app. VII(xiii).
38. DBFP 3/4/app. VII(xiv–xvi).
39. DBFP 3/4/app. VII(xvii).
40. DBFP 3/4/app. VII(xvi and xix, encls.).

41. DGFP D/5/376; RIIA *Survey of International Affairs*, 1938, vol. 3, p. 363.
42. DGFP D/5/376–9.

Chapter 4 The prospect of war

1. DBFP 3/3/422.
2. DBFP 3/4/app. vii(xiii).
3. DBFP 3/4/app. vii(xv).
4. 342 H.C. Deb 5s. cols.1580–1.
5. DBFP 3/3/475.
6. DBFP 3/3/425.
7. DBFP 3/3/427.
8. *Diaries of Sir Alexander Cadogan*, 12–13 December 1938; DBFP 3/3/426.
9. *Struggle for Peace*, pp. 371–8.
10. Nigel Nicolson (ed.), Harold Nicolson, *Diaries and Letters, 1930–39* (1966), p. 382; *Diaries of Sir Alexander Cadogan*, pp. 129–30; Harvey, *Diplomatic Diaries*, p. 228; *The Economist*, 17 December 1938.
11. *Diaries of Sir Alexander Cadogan*, p. 130; Harvey, *Diplomatic Diaries*, p. 228.
12. C.P. 284(38), CAB 24/281.
13. Cabinet 59(38), 14 December 1938, CAB 23/96.
14. Nicholas Pronay and Philip M. Taylor, '"An improper use of broadcasting": the British Government and clandestine radio propaganda operations against Germany during the Munich crisis and after', *Journal of Contemporary History*, 19 (1984), 357–84.
15. DRC 14, 28 February 1934, CAB 4/23; Gaines Post, Jr., *Dilemmas of Appeasement: British Deterrence and Defense, 1934–1937* (Ithaca and London, 1993), pp. 309–17.
16. DBFP 3/1/164.
17. 341st mtg. CID, 15 December 1938, CAB 2/8.
18. B. Bond (ed.), *Chief of Staff: The Diaries of Lieutenant-General Sir Henry Pownall* (1972), I, 14 November 1938, p. 170.
19. Eugenia C. Kiesling, *Arming Against Hitler: France and the Limits of Military Planning* (1996), pp. 177–8.
20. *Diaries of Sir Alexander Cadogan*, 15 December 1938, p. 130.
21. CID 342nd mtg., 16 December 1938, CAB 2/8.
22. 1499-B, CAB 4/29.
23. 342 H.C. Deb. 5s. cols. 2517–26.
24. Cabinet 60(38), 21 December 1938, CAB 23/96; C.P. 293(38), CAB24/281.
25. COS memo. 809 (J.P.), 19 December 1938, CAB 53/43; 265th mtg., COS, 21 December 1938, CAB 53/10.
26. 265th mtg., COS, 21 December 1938, CAB 53/10.
27. 343rd mtg., CID, 22 December 1938, CAB2/8.
28. Chamberlain to Chatfield, 22 December 1938, CHT/6/4; Chatfield, *It Might Happen Again* (1947), pp. 160–2.

Chapter 5 Resolving to resist

1. *Diaries of Sir Alexander Cadogan*, p. 132.
2. C835/15/18, FO 371/22961.

3. DBFP 3/3/app. viii.
4. DBFP 3/3/519, 541.
5. His emphasis; DBFP 3/3/505, encls. 1 and 2.
6. DBFP 3/3/515.
7. DBFP 3/3/505, encl. 2.
8. WO 190/745.
9. DBFP 3/3/515.
10. Minutes at C173/15/18, FO 371/22960.
11. DBFP 3/3/496.
12. William C. Mills, 'Sir Joseph Ball, Adrian Dingli, and Neville Chamberlain's "secret channel" to Italy, 1937–1940', *International History Review*, XXIV (2002), 278–317.
13. DBFP 3/3/500; *Diaries of Sir Alexander Cadogan*, 10–14 January 1939, pp. 135–9; Harvey, *Diplomatic Diaries*, 10–14 January 1939, pp. 238–44; P. Stafford, 'The visit of Chamberlain and Halifax to Rome: a reappreciation', *EHR*, 98 (1983) 61–100.
14. Note by Lt. Col. L. Hollis, 18 November 1938, JPC memo. 329, CAB 55/13.
15. Asa Briggs, *History of Broadcasting in the United Kingdom* II (London, 1995, rev. edn), pp. 138–9.
16. JPC memo. 329, annexes 1–3; Richmond's original script in encl. to annex 3, CAB 55/13; Arthur J. Marder (ed.), *Portrait of an Admiral: The Life and Papers of Sir Herbert Richmond* (London, 1952), pp. 20–43.
17. JPC memo. 337, CAB 55/14.
18. JPC memo. 337, annex. II for revised version, CAB 55/14.
19. 267th mtg., COS, 13 January 1939, CAB 53/10.
20. DBFP 3/3/531–4, 541.
21. DBFP 3/3/529.
22. Minutes on Vereker's despatch at C528/15/18, FO 371/22961.
23. DBFP 3/3/535.
24. Harvey, *Diplomatic Diaries*, 15–16 January 1939, p. 245.
25. A.P. Young, *The X Documents*, ed. by Sidney Aster (London, 1974), pp. 156–62.
26. DBFP 3/3/541; C552/15/18, C564/15/18, C835/15/18, FO 371/22961.
27. Cadogan, *Diaries*, 17 January 1939, pp. 139–40.
28. 35th mtg., FPC, 23 January 1939, CAB 27/624.
29. COS memo. 828, 23 January 1939, CAB 53/44.
30. DBFP 3/4/5.
31. COS memo. 830 (JP), 24 January 1939, CAB 53/44.
32. 269th mtg., COS, 24 January 1939, CAB 53/10; COS memo., 24 January 1939, CAB 53/44.
33. Cabinet 2, 25 January 1939, CAB 23/97.
34. D.C. Watt, 'Misinformation, misconception, mistrust: episodes in British policy and the approach of war, 1938–1939' in Michael Bentley and John Stevenson (eds), *High and Low Politics in Modern Britain* (London, 1983), pp. 214–54.
35. 270th mtg., COS, 25 January 1939, CAB 53/10.
36. JPC draft memo., COS 830 (JP), 24 January 1939; COS memo. 830, 25 January 1939, CAB 53/44.
37. Martin Wight, 'Switzerland, The Low Countries and Scandinavia' in Arnold Toynbee and Frank T. Ashton-Gwatkin (eds), *The World in March 1939* (London, 1952), pp. 151–65.

38. 36th mtg., FPC 26 January 1939, CAB 27/624.
39. DBFP 3/4/13, 16, 17, 31, 35, 76.
40. *The Struggle for Peace*, pp. 381–9.
41. JPC memo. 331 app. 1, 26 January 1939, CAB 55/14.
42. DCOS memo. 77, 23 January with memo. by Inskip of 20 January; DCOS 78, undated narrative, CAB 54/5.

Chapter 6 Continental commitment

1. N. Baynes, *The Speeches of Adolf Hitler, 1922–1939* (1942) II, pp. 1567–78.
2. 343 H.C. Deb. 5s. cols. 42–3.
3. Cabinet 3(39), 1 February 1939, CAB 23/97.
4. Minutes by Cadogan and Chamberlain, 4 and 6 February 1939, C1474/16/18, FO 371/22988.
5. 37th mtg., FPC, 8 February 1939, CAB 27/624.
6. C1402/5/18, FO 371/22964.
7. Cadogan, *Diaries*, 6 February 1939, p. 147.
8. 343 H.C. Deb. 5s. col. 623.
9. 268th mtg., COS, 18 January 1939, CAB 53/10.
10. DBFP 3/4/79.
11. JPC memo. 351, CAB 55/14; COS 827 (JP), 25 January 1939, CAB 53/44.
12. COS memos. 829–30, 24–25 January 1939, CAB 53/44.
13. Cabinet 5(39), 2 February 1939, CAB 23/97.
14. Memo. by Chamberlain, 18 February 1939, C.P. 49 (39), CAB 24/283; Cabinet 8(39), 22 February 1939, CAB 23/97.
15. Chatfield, *It Might Happen Again* (1947), p. 170.
16. Ibid.
17. Sir Frederick Leith-Ross, *Money Talks* (1968), pp. 183–91.
18. Scott Newton, *Profits of Peace: The Political Economy of Anglo-German Appeasement* (1996), pp. 97–9.
19. Minutes, 6 February 1939, C1316/16/18, FO 371/22988.
20. Minutes, 7 February 1939, C1316/16/18, FO 371/22988.
21. DBFP 3/4/app. II.
22. Minutes, 31 January–2 February 1939, C1195/16/18, FO 371/22988.
23. Minutes, 2 February 1939, C1277/15/18, FO 371/22963.
24. Beaumont-Nesbitt to Strang, 8 February 1939; minutes by Roberts and Kirkpatrick, 14 February 1939, C1822/3/18, FO 371/22958.
25. Minutes, 1–2 February 1939, C1278/15/18, FO 371/22963.
26. Cabinet 6(39), 8 February 1939, CAB 23/97.
27. Cadogan, *Diaries*, 9 February 1939, p. 148.
28. Minutes by Roberts, 8 February 1939, C1544/16/18, FO 371/22988.
29. COS memo. 832, 1 February 1939, CAB 53/44.
30. Note of a meeting at the Dominions Office, 17 February 1939, C2622/15/18, FO 371/22966.
31. COS memo. 837, 7 February 1939, CAB 53/44.
32. 276th mtg., COS, 15 February 1939, CAB 53/10.
33. C. P. 293 (38), CAB 24/281.
34. 266th mtg., COS, 5 January 1939, CAB 53/10; COS memo. 824, 14 January 1939, CAB 53/43.

35. Cabinet 7(39), 15 February 1939, CAB 23/97.
36. COS memo. 847 (JIC), 20 February 1939, CAB 53/45.
37. DBFP 3/4/109.
38. DBFP 3/4/app. 1 (iii).
39. DBFP 3/4/app. 1 (iii).
40. DBFP 3/4/app. 1 (iv).
41. *The Times*, 23 February 1939.
42. DBFP 3/4/118; D. Dilks, in *Diaries of Sir Alexander Cadogan*, pp. 151–3.
43. Minutes, 20 February 1939, C2139/15/18, FO 371/22965.
44. Ashton-Gwatkin's report at DBFP 3/4/app. II.
45. Brocket to Halifax, 28 February 1939, C2575/15/18, FO 371/22966; letter to *The Times*, 8 March 1939.
46. DBFP 3/4/app. II (2) (a).
47. Ashton-Gwatkin's record of this conversation sent by Holman to Strang on 23 February, recd. 25 February 1939, C2346/8/18, FO 371/22950.
48. Ibid.
49. Minutes by Vansittart, 20 February 1939, C2209/15/18, FO 371/22965.
50. Minutes, 25 February 1939, C2345/8/18, FO 371/22950.
51. Minutes, 20 February 1939, C2209/15/18, FO 371/22965.
52. Minutes, 21 February 1939, C2139/15/18, FO 371/22965.
53. Minutes, 23 February 1939, C2243/15/18, FO 371/22965.
54. DBFP 3/4/162.
55. Minutes, C2533/15/18, FO 371/22966.
56. Cabinet 10(39), 8 March 1939, CAB 23/97.
57. N.J. Crowson, *Facing Fascism* (1997), pp. 108–14.
58. R. Rhodes James (ed.), *Chips: The Diaries of Sir Henry Channon* (1967), 7 March 1939, p. 229.
59. *The Times*, 10 March 1939.
60. *The Times*, 11 March 1939.
61. *Diaries of Sir Alexander Cadogan*, 11 March 1939, p. 155.
62. *Diaries of Sir Alexander Cadogan*, 13–14 March 1939, pp. 156–7; Harvey, *Diplomatic Diaries*, 14 March 1939, pp. 161–2.
63. DBFP 3/4/254.
64. 345 H.C. Deb. 5s. col. 224.
65. Minutes by Roberts, 13–14 March 1939, FO 371/22922.

Chapter 7 The challenge of annexation

1. Minutes, 6 March 1939, FO 371/22997.
2. Cabinet 11(39), 15 March 1939, CAB 23/98.
3. DBFP 3/4/265.
4. Minutes by Peake, 15 March; Sargent, 15 March; Cadogan, 16 March 1939, C3313/19/18, FO 371/22993.
5. DBFP 3/4/268.
6. DBFP 3/4/298.
7. DBFP 3/4/268, 270, 276.
8. Minutes, 16 March 1939, C3136/15/18, FO 371/22966.
9. 345 H.C. Deb. 5s. cols. 435–40.

10. 345 H.C. Deb. 5s. cols. 458–62, 464–7, 470–2, 477–80, 486–9, 508–12, 514–9.
11. 345 H.C. Deb. 5s. cols. 489–94, 500–5, 523–8.
12. 345 H.C. Deb. 5s. cols. 533–59.
13. 111 H.L. Deb. 5s. cols. 932–6.
14. DBFP 3/4/288, 301, n. 2.
15. Runciman Papers, WR 357, University of Newcastle Library.
16. Minutes by Sargent and Cadogan, 17 March, on Hoare, tel. 37, 16 March 1939, R1733/1733/67, FO 371/23752.
17. *The Struggle for Peace*, pp. 413–20.
18. CID memo. 1530-B, 23 February 1939, CAB 4/29.
19. Rebecca Haynes, *Romanian Policy towards Germany, 1936–40* (2000), pp. 68–90.
20. V.V. Tilea, *Envoy Extraordinary: Memoirs of a Romanian Diplomat*, ed. by Ileana Tilea (1998) pp. 213–6; S. Aster, *The Making of the Second World War* (1973), pp. 61–5; D. Lungu, *Romania and the European Great Powers, 1933–1940* (1989), pp. 155–6.
21. DBFP 3/4/395.
22. Cadogan, *Diaries*, 17 March 1939, p. 160.
23. DBFP 3/4/395.
24. L. Atherton, 'Lord Lloyd at the British Council and the Balkan front, 1937–1940', *IHR*, 16 (1994), p. 36.
25. DBFP 3/4/389.
26. DBFP 3/4/390.
27. COS 282nd mtg., 18 March 1939, CAB 53/10; JPC 242nd mtg., 18 March 1939, CAB 55/3.
28. COS 283rd mtg., 18 March 1939, CAB 53/10.
29. DBFP 3/4/397, 399.
30. DBFP 3/4/398.
31. Cabinet 43(38), 25 September 1938, CAB 23/96.
32. Cabinet 12(39), 18 March 1939, CAB 23/98.
33. DBFP 3/4/406, 407, 423–6.
34. DBFP 3/4/447.
35. DBFP 3/4/421.
36. C3858/15/18, FO 371/22967.
37. C3859/15/18, FO 371/22967.
38. Cabinet 13(39), 20 March 1939, CAB 23/98.
39. Harvey to Wilson; Cadogan to Halifax, 20 March 1939, C3858/15/18, FO 371/22967; DBFP 3/4/448.

Chapter 8 The quest for coalition

1. Record of ministerial meetings, 21 March 1939, CAB 21/592; COS memo. 863, 22 March, 1939, CAB 53/46
2. Record of ministerial mtg., 21 March 1939, CAB 21/592.
3. Memo. of 34th mtg., on 21 March 1939, DCOS 80, 23 March 1939, CAB 54/5.
4. Record of ministerial mtgs., 21 March 1939, CAB 21/592.
5. Cadogan, *Diaries*, 20 March 1939, pp. 161–2; DBFP 3/4/446.

6. DBFP 3/4/447, 471.
7. DBFP 3/4/457, 472.
8. Peter Jackson, 'France and the Guarantee to Romania, April 1939', *Intelligence and National Security*, 10 (1995), 242–72.
9. DBFP 3/4/458.
10. DBFP 3/4/463.
11. DBFP 3/4/465.
12. DBFP 3/4/479.
13. Cabinet 14(39), 22 March 1939, CAB 23/98.
14. DBFP 3/4/481.
15. Note (30 March) to Harvey on the meeting, C4415/G, FO 371/22968.
16. DBFP 3/4/497.
17. DBFP 3/4/402.
18. DBFP 3/4/484; Cadogan, *Diaries*, 22 March 1939, pp. 162–3.
19. DBFP 3/4/507.
20. PREM 1/329.
21. DBFP 3/4/498.
22. Minutes by Speaight (27 March), Strang (28 March), Sargent (29 March), Cadogan (30 March), C3946/19/18, FO 371/22996.
23. DBFP 3/4/476.
24. DBFP 3/4/522.
25. Harvey, *Diplomatic Diaries*, p. 268.
26. Cadogan, *Diaries*, pp. 163–4.
27. 38th mtg., FPC, 27 March 1939, CAB 27/624.
28. DBFP 3/4/538.
29. COS Paper, European Appreciation, 1939–40, 2 February 1939, CID/DP(P)44, CAB 16/183.
30. 246th mtg., JPC, 28 March 1939, CAB 55/3.
31. 285th mtg., COS, 28 March 1939, CAB 53/10.
32. R.J. Minney (ed.), *The Private Papers of Hore-Belisha* (1960), pp. 186–7.
33. Cabinet 15(39), 29 March 1939, CAB 23/98.
34. Piotr S. Wandycz, 'Colonel Beck and the French: Roots of Animosity?', *International History Review*, 3 (1981) pp. 115–27.

Chapter 9 The guaranteeing of Poland

1. DBFP 3/4/561, 563.
2. L. Atherton, 'Lord Lloyd at the British Council and the Balkan Front, 1937–1940', *International History Review*, 16 (1994), 25–48.
3. Ian Colvin, *Vansittart in Office* (1965), pp. 298–311; Cadogan, *Diaries*, 29 March 1939, pp. 164–5; Harvey, *Diplomatic Diaries*, 29 March 1939, p. 271. Halifax's remark to Cadogan that the Prime Minister had 'agreed' to the idea of an immediate declaration implied that it was put to him by Halifax, not the other way round.
4. Sidney Aster, *1939: The Making of the Second World War*, (1973) p. 101.
5. Colvin, *Vansittart in Office*, pp. 308–9.
6. Aster, *1939*, p. 93.
7. War Office, Summaries of Information (New Series), FO 371/22996.

8. DBFP 3/4/547.
9. Phipps to FO, 8.15 p.m. 27 March, recd. 9.30 a.m. 28 March 1939, C4189/54/18, FO 371/23015, citing the American Ambassador, William C. Bullitt.
10. DBFP 3/4/449; minutes by Sargent, 29 March 1939, C3948/19/18, FO 371/22996.
11. Minutes by Speaight and Makins, 29 March 1939, FO 371/23016.
12. Minutes by Kirkpatrick, Sargent and Cadogan, 30 March 1939, C4621/15/18, FO 371/22968.
13. DBFP 3/4/564.
14. Minutes, 30 March, on Kennard's tel. 91, 29 March 1939, recd. 9.30 a.m. 30 March, C4364/54/18, FO 371/23015.
15. C4655/3356/18, FO 371/23062.
16. Minutes by Cadogan, 31 March 1939, C4760/13/18, FO 371/22958.
17. Minutes by Roberts, 30 March 1939, C4289/3356/18, FO 371/23062.
18. Minutes by Kirkpatrick, 30 March 1939, C4472/3356/18, FO 371/23062.
19. Minutes, 30–31 March 1939, C4417/15/18, FO 371/22968.
20. Minutes, 14 April 1939, C5032/54/18, FO 371/23016.
21. Annex to minutes of 286th mtg. of COS, 30 March 1939, CAB 53/10.
22. Cabinet 16(39), 30 March 1939, CAB 23/98.
23. 345 H.C. Deb. 5s. cols. 2215–6.
24. DBFP 3/4/566.
25. DBFP 3/4/568.
26. 39th mtg., FPC, 30 March 1939, CAB 27/624.
27. DBFP 3/4/566 and 568.
28. Sidney Aster, 'Ivan Maisky and parliamentary anti-appeasement, 1938–39', in A.J.P. Taylor (ed.), *Lloyd George: Twelve Essays* (1970), pp. 342–3.
29. DBFP 3/4/573.
30. DBFP 3/4/584.
31. 40th mtg., FPC, 31 March 1939, CAB 27/624.
32. Manchester Guardian, 31 March 1939, p. 11.
33. Cabinet 17(39), 31 March 1939, CAB 23/98.
34. DBFP 3/4/589.
35. 345 H.C. Deb. 5s. cols. 2415–20.
36. Gordon Martel, *'The Times' and Appeasement: The Journals of A.L. Kennedy, 1932–1939* (2000), p. 286.

Chapter 10 Diplomacy by drama

1. George A. Kelly, A Theory of Personality: The Psychology of Personal Constructs (N. Y., W. W. Norton, 1963).
2. Cf. D. Gillard, 'British and Russian Relations with Asian Governments in the Nineteenth Century' in Hedley Bull and Adam Watson (eds), *The Expansion of International Society* (1984), pp. 87–97.
3. INKP 1/2, 30 August 1939; Wallace Diary, 31 August 1939.
4. W.N. Medlicott, *British Foreign Policy since Versailles* (1940) p. 9; T.F.D. Williams, 'Negotiations leading to the Anglo-Polish Alliance', *Irish Historical Studies*, 10 (1957), pp. 59–93, 156–92.
5. Anna M. Cienciala, *Poland and the Western Powers, 1938–39* (1968), p. 226.

6. Thomas Sakmyster, *Hungary's Admiral on Horseback: Miklos Horthy, 1918–44* (1994), pp. 221–7; Rebecca Haynes, *Romanian Policy towards Germany, 1936–40* (2000), pp. 67–98.
7. 2nd mtg., SAC, 13 March 1939, CAB 16/209.
8. 4th mtg., SAC, 4 April 1939, CAB 16/209.
9. COS memo. 856, 20 March 1939, CAB 53/46.
10. 242nd mtg., JPC, 18 March 1939, CAB 55/3.
11. COS memo. 856, 20 March 1939, CAB 53/46.
12. Note by Chatfield, 29 March 1939, commenting on a memorandum by Churchill; recd. by Chamberlain, 30 March 1939. CHT 6/4.
13. 295th mtg., COS, 16 May 1939, CAB 53/11; 47th mtg., FPC, 16 May 1939, CAB 23/97.
14. Memo. by Elliot and Colville, 31 March 1939, CP 77(39), CAB 24/284.
15. *International Affairs*, XVII (1938), 408–17.
16. R.W. Seton-Watson, *Britain and the Dictators: A Survey of Post-War British Policy* (1938), pp. 404–5.
17. E.L. Woodward, *Short Journey* (1942), p. 242.
18. A copy of the lecture in the Confidential Print, C 14420/95/62, in the Templewood Papers, TP c. VIII 5, Cambridge University Library, has passages intriguingly marked by Hoare, but without comment.

Bibliography

Articles

Adamthwaite, Anthony, 'The British Government and the media, 1937–1938', *Journal of Contemporary History*, 18 (1983), 281–97.

Alexander, Martin S. and William J. Philpott, 'The Entente Cordiale and the next war: Anglo-French views on future military co-operation, 1928–1939', *Intelligence and National Security*, 13 (1998), 53–8.

Alexandroff, Alex and Richard Rosecrance, 'Deterrence in 1939', *World Politics*, 29 (1977), 404–423.

Andrew, Christopher, 'Secret Intelligence and British foreign policy, 1900–1939', in Christopher Andrew and Jeremy Noakes, *Intelligence and International Relations, 1900–1945* (Exeter, 1987), 9–28.

Ashton-Gwatkin, Frank, 'Thoughts on the Foreign Office, 1918–1939', *Contemporary Review*, 188 (1955), 374–78.

Aster, Sidney, 'Ivan Maisky and parliamentary anti-appeasement, 1938–39' in A.J.P. Taylor (ed.), *Lloyd George. Twelve Essays* (London, 1974).

Aster, Sidney, '"Guilty Men". The case of Neville Chamberlain' in Robert Boyce and Esmonde Robertson (eds), *Paths to War, New Essays on the Origins of the Second World War* (London, 1989), 233–68.

Atherton, Loiuse, 'Lord Lloyd at the British Council and the Balkan front, 1937–1940', *International History Review*, 16 (1994), 25–48.

Baugh, Daniel A., 'Confessions and constraints: the Navy and British defence planning, 1919–39' in N.A.M. Rodger (ed.), *Naval Power in the Twentieth Century* (London, 1996), 101–19.

Buffotot, Patrice, 'The French High Command and the Franco-Soviet Alliance, 1933–1939', *Journal of Strategic Studies*, 5 (1982), 546–59.

Chanady, A. and J. Jensen, 'Germany, Romania and the British guarantee of March–April 1939', *Australian Journal of Politics and History*, 16 (1970), 201–17.

Cienciala, Anne M., 'Poland in British and French policy in 1939. Determination to fight – or avoid war', *Polish Review*, 34 (1989), 199–226.

Dilks, David, '"We must hope for the best and prepare for the worst". The Prime Minister, the Cabinet and Hitler's Germany, 1937–39', *Proceedings of the British Academy* (1987).

Eatwell, R., 'Munich, public opinion and the Popular Front', *Journal of Contemporary History*, 6 (1971), 122–139.

Ferris, John R., '"Indulged in all too little?" Vansittart, intelligence and appeasement', *Diplomacy and Statecraft*, 6 (1995), 122–75.

Forbes, Neil, 'London banks, the German standstill agreements and "economic appeasement" in the 1930s', *Economic History Review*, 2nd series, 40 (1987), 581–7.

Greenwood, Susan, '"Caligula's Horse" revisited: Sir Thomas Inskip as Minister for the Co-ordination of Defence, 1936–1939', *Journal of Strategic Studies*, 17 (1994), 17–38.

Harris, J.P., 'The British General Staff and the coming of war, 1933–9', *Bulletin of the Institute of Historical Research*, 59 (1986), 196–211.

Headlam-Morley, Sir James, 'Treaties of guarantee', *Cambridge Historical Journal*, 2 (1926), 151–70.

Holland, R.F., 'The Federation of British Industries and the international economy, 1929–39', *Economic History Review*, 2nd series, 34 (1981), 287–300.

Jackson, Peter, 'France and the guarantee to Romania, April 1939', *Intelligence and National Security*, 10 (1995), 242–72.

Kliemann, Aaron S., 'Bureaucratic politics at Whitehall in the partitioning of Palestine, 1937' in Dann, Uriel (ed.), *The Great Powers in the Middle East, 1919–1939* (1988), 128–53.

Lammers, Donald S., 'Fascism, Communism and the Foreign Office', *Journal of Contemporary History*, 6 (1971), 66–86.

Lammers, Donald S., 'From Whitehall after Munich: the Foreign Office and the future course of British foreign policy', *Historical Journal*, 16 (1973), 831–56.

Lungu, Dov B., 'The European crisis of March–April 1939: the Romanian dimension', *International History Review*, 7 (1985), 389–414.

MacDonald, Callum A., 'Economic appeasement and the German "moderates", 1937–1939. An introductory essay', *Past and Present*, 56 (1972), 105–135.

MacDonald, Callum A., 'Radio Bari: Italian wireless propaganda in the Middle East and British counter-measures, 1934–1938', *Middle Eastern Studies*, 13 (1977), 195–207.

Maiolo, J.A., 'The knockout blow against the import system: Admiralty expectations of Nazi Germany's naval strategy, 1934–9', *Historical Research*, 72 (1999), 202–28.

Manne, Robert, 'Some British light on the Nazi-Soviet Pact', *European Studies Review*, 11 (1981), 83–102.

Mills, William C., 'Sir Joseph Ball, Adrian Dingli, and Neville Chamberlain's "secret channel" to Italy, 1937–1940', *International History Review*, 24 (2002), 278–317.

Morewood, Steven, 'Appeasement from strength: the making of the 1936 Anglo-Egyptian Treaty of Friendship and Alliance', *Diplomacy and Statecraft*, 7 (1996), 530–62.

Overy, R.J., 'Hitler's war and the German economy: a reinterpretation', *Economic History Review*, 2nd series, 35 (1982), 272–91.

Overy, R.J., David Kaiser and Tim Mason, 'Germany, "domestic crisis" and war in 1939', *Past and Present*, 116 (1987), 138–68; 122 (1989), 200–40.

Overy, R.J., 'Strategic intelligence and the outbreak of the Second World War,' *War in History*, 5 (1998), 451–80.

Parker, R.A.C., 'The pound sterling, the American Treasury and British preparations for war, 1938–1939', *English Historical Review*, 98 (1983), 261–79.

Peden, George, 'A matter of timing: the economic background to British foreign policy, 1937–1939', *History*, 69 (1984), 15–28.

Peden, George, 'The burden of imperial defence and the continental commitment reconsidered', *Historical Journal*, 27 (1984), 405–23.

Penson, Lillian M., 'Obligations by treaty: their place in British foreign policy, 1898–1914' in A.O. Sarkissian (ed.), *Studies in Diplomatic History and Historiography in honour of G.P. Gooch, C.H.* (1961), 76–89.

Prazmowska, A.J., 'War over Danzig? The dilemma of Anglo-Polish relations in the months preceding the outbreak of the Second World War', *Historical Journal*, 26 (1983).

Prazmowska, A.J., 'Poland's foreign policy, September 1938–September 1939', *Historical Journal*, 29 (1986).

Pronay, Nicholas and Philip M. Taylor, '"An improper use of broadcasting." The British Government and clandestine radio propaganda operations against Germany during the Munich crisis and after', *Journal of Contemporary History*, 19 (1984), 357–84.

du Reau, Elisabeth, 'Gouvernement et haut commandement francais devant la perspective de guerre, septembre 1938–septembre 1939', *Guerres mondiales et conflits contemporains*, 166 (1992), 149–66.

Roberts, Henry L., 'The diplomacy of Colonel Beck' in Gordon Craig and Felix Gilbert (eds), *The Diplomats, 1919–1939*, 579–614 (New Jersey, 1963).

Satow, Sir Ernest, 'Peacemaking, old and new', *Cambridge Historical Journal* I (1923–25), 23–60.

Satow, Sir Ernest, 'Pacta Sunt Servanda or International Guarantees', *Cambridge Historical Journal*, 1 (1923–25), 295–318.

Stafford, Paul, 'The visit of Chamberlain and Halifax to Rome: a reappreciation', *English Historical Review*, 98 (1983), 61–100.

Stafford, Paul, 'Political autobiography and the art of the plausible: R.A. Butler at the Foreign Office, 1938–39', *Historical Journal*, 28 (1985), 901–22.

Strang, Bruce, 'Two unequal tempers: Sir George Ogilvie-Forbes, Sir Neville Henderson and British foreign policy, 1938–39', *Diplomacy and Statecraft*, 5 (1994), 107–37.

Thomas, Martin, 'To arm an ally: French arms sales to Romania, 1926–1940', *Journal of Strategic Studies*, 19 (1996), 231–59.

Toynbee, A.J., H.N. Fieldhouse, Viscount Cecil of Chelwood, Marquess of Lothian and R.A. Butler 'The issues in British foreign policy' and 'The future of British foreign policy', *International Affairs*, XVII (1938), 307–417.

Toynbee, A.J., Lord Rankeillov, Victor Raikes, Graham Hutton, C.K. Webster, H.W. Nevinson and Wilson Harris, 'After Munich: the world outlook', *International Affairs*, XVIII (1939), 1–28.

Wandycz, Piotr S., 'Colonel Beck and the French: the roots of animosity', *International History Review*, 3 (1981), 115–27.

Wark, Wesley, 'Three military attaches at Berlin in the 1930s: soldier statesmen and the limits of ambiguity', *International History Review*, 9 (1987), 586–611.

Wark, Wesley, 'Something very stern: British political intelligence, moralism and strategy in 1939', *Intelligence and National Security*, 5 (1990), 150–70.

Watt, D. Cameron, 'Anglo-German naval negotiations on the eve of World War II', *Journal of the Royal United Services Institute*, 103 (1958), 201–7, 384–91.

Watt, D. Cameron, 'Appeasement reconsidered', *The Round Table*, 53 (1963), 358–371.

Watt, D. Cameron, 'The historiography of appeasement' in Alan Sked and Chris Cook (eds), *Crisis and Controversy: Essays in Honour of A.J.P. Taylor* (London, 1976).

Watt, D. Cameron, 'Misinformation, misconception, mistrust: episodes in the British policy and the approach of war, 1938–1939' in Michael Bentley and John Stevenson (eds), *High and Low Politics in Modern Britain* (Oxford, 1983).

Watt, D. Cameron, 'British intelligence and the coming of the Second World War in Europe' in Ernest R. May (ed.), *Knowing One's Enemies. Intelligence Assessment before Two World Wars* (Princeton, N.J., 1985), 237–70.

Watt, D. Cameron, 'The *Sender der deutschen Freiheits-partei*: a first step in the British radio war against Nazi Germany', *Intelligence and National Security*, 6 (1991), 621–6.

Weinberg, Gerhard L., 'Hitler and England, 1933–1945: pretence and reality', *German Studies Review*, 8 (1985), 299–309.

Weinberg, Gerhard L., 'The German Generals and the outbreak of war, 1938–1939' in Weinberg (ed.), *Germany, Hitler and World War II: Essays in Modern German History, 1938–1939*, (1995) 129–45.

Wight, Martin, 'Switzerland, the Low Countries and Scandinavia' in Arnold J. Toynbee and Frank Ashton-Gwatkin (eds), *Survey*, 151–65.

Williams, T. Desmond, 'Negotiations leading to the Anglo-Polish Alliance', *Irish Historical Studies*, X (1956–7), 59–93, 156–92.

Woodward, E.L., Lecture given on 24 October 1938 at the Imperial Defence, College Templewood Papers, T.P.c. vii5, Cambridge University, Library.

Woodward, E.L., 'Some Reflections on British Policy, 1939–45', Stevenson Memorial Lecture, *International Affairs*, 31 (1955), 273–90.

Young, Robert J., 'The aftermath of Munich: the course of French diplomacy, October 1938–March 1939', *French Historical Studies*, 8 (1973), 305–22.

Young, Robert J., 'Spokesmen for economic warfare: the Industrial Intelligence Centre in the 1930s', *European Studies Review*, 6 (1976), 473–89.

The foregoing account of how *exchanges* of view within governing circles over a period of six months led to an agreement to 'guarantee' Polish independence is based mainly on such records of those exchanges as are available in Cabinet and Foreign Office papers. Private thoughts confided to diaries and letters have been used more sparingly, except in the case of David Dilks's edition of Sir Alexander Cadogan's *Diaries* (London, 1971), so rich in detail as to be indispensable throughout. So has been the authoritative bibliography in Donald Cameron Watts's *tour de force How War Came: The immediate origins of the Second World War, 1938–1939* (London, 1989). A selection of books and articles particularly relevant to the present discussion appears below. Cabinet papers were consulted at the National Archives (Scotland), West Register House, Edinburgh, and Foreign Office papers at the National Archives, Kew. Printed works were consulted at the National Library of Scotland, Edinburgh, and in the libraries of the Universities of Glasgow and Edinburgh. The location of private papers used is indicated within the text.

Books

Adamthwaite, Anthony, *France and the Coming of the Second World War* (London, 1977).

Alexander, Martin S., *The Republic in Danger: General Maurice Gamelin and the Politics of French Defence, 1933–1940* (Cambridge, 1992).

Andrew, Christopher and David Dilks (eds), *The Missing Dimension: Governments and Intelligence Communities in the Twentieth Century* (London, 1984).

Annual Register (1938 and 1939).

Aster, Sidney, *1939. The Making of the Second World War* (London, 1973).

Baynes, Norman, *The Speeches of Adolf Hitler, 1922–1939* (London, 1942).

Bell, P.M.H., *The Origins of the Second World War in Europe* (London, 1986).

Bell, P.M.H., *France and Britain, 1900–40: Entente and Estrangement* (London, 1996).

Bond, Brian (ed.), *Chief of Staff: The Diaries of Lieutenant-General Sir Henry Pownall*, vol. 1, 1933–1940 (London, 1972).

Bond, Brian, *British Military Policy between Two World Wars* (Oxford, 1980).

Boyce, Robert (ed.), *French Foreign and Defence Policy, 1918–1940: The Decline and Fall of a Great Power* (London, 1998).

Boyce, Robert and Esmonde Robertson (eds), *Paths to War: New Essays on the Origins of the Second World War* (London and Basingstoke, 1989).

Briggs, Asa, *The Golden Age of Wireless, 1927–1939, vol. II of The History of Broadcasting in the United Kingdom* (Oxford, rev. edn, 1995).

Bullen, Roger (ed.), *The Foreign Office, 1782–1982* (London, 1984).

Bullitt, O.H. (ed.), *For the President, Personal and Secret: Correspondence between Franklin D. Roosevelt and William C. Bullitt* (Boston, Massachusetts, 1972).

Butler, R.A., *The Art of the Possible* (London, 1971).

Cain, P.J. and A.G. Hopkins, *British Imperialism: Crisis and Deconstruction, 1914–1990* (London and New York, 1993).

Carley, Michael J., *1939: The Alliance that Never Was and the Coming of World War II* (London, 1999).

Chamberlain, Neville, *The Struggle for Peace* (London, 1939).

Charmley, John, *Lord Lloyd and the Decline of the British Empire* (London, 1987).

Chatfield (A.E.M.), Baron, *It Might Happen Again* (London, 1947).

Cienciala, Anne M., *Poland and the Western Powers, 1938–1939. A Study in the Interdependence of Eastern and Western Europe* (London, 1968).

Clayton, Anthony, *The British Empire as a Superpower* (London, 1986).

Cockett, Richard, *Twilight of Truth: Chamberlain, Appeasement and the Manipulation of the Press* (London, 1989).

Cohen, Michael J. and Martin Kolinsky (eds), *Britain and the Middle East in the 1930s: Security Problems*, 1935–39 (London, 1992).

Colvin, Ian, *Vansittart in Office* (London, 1965).

Colvin, Ian, *The Chamberlain Cabinet* (London, 1971).

Cook, C. and J. Ramsden, *By-elections in British Politics* (London, 1997).

Cowling, Maurice, *The Impact of Hitler: British Politics and British Policy, 1933–1940* (Cambridge, 1975).

Cretzianu, Alexandre, in Sherman David Spector (ed.), *Relapse into Bondage: Political Memoirs of a Romanian Diplomat, 1918–1947*, ed. Sherman David Spector (London, 1998).

Cross, John, *Sir Samuel Hoare: A Political Biography* (London,1977).

Crowson, N.J., *Facing Fascism: The Conservative Party and the European Dictators, 1935–1940* (London, 1997).

Dann, Uriel (ed.), *The Great Powers in the Middle East, 1919–1939* (New York and London, 1988).

Degras, Jane (ed.), *Soviet Documents on Foreign Policy, 1917–1941*, vol. III, 1933–1941 (London, 1953).

Deist, W., M. Messerschmidt, H.E. Volkmann and W. Wette, *Germany and the Second World War*, vol. I, *The Build-up of German Aggression* (Oxford, 1990).

Dennis, Peter J., *Decision by Default: Peacetime Conscription and British Defence, 1919–1939* (London and Durham, North Carolina, 1972).

Deringil, Selim, *Turkish Foreign Policy during the Second World War: An Active Neutrality* (London, 1989).

Dilks, David (ed.), *The Diaries of Sir Alexander Cadogan, O.M., 1938–1945* (London, 1971).

Dilks, David (ed.), *Retreat from Power: Studies in Britain's Foreign Policy of the Twentieth Century*, vol. I, 1906–1939 (London, 1981).

Dockrill, Michael, *British Establishment Perspectives on France, 1936–40* (London, 1999).
Dockrill, Michael and Brian McKercher (eds), *Diplomacy and World Power: Studies in British Foreign Policy, 1890–1950* (London, 1996).
Documents and Materials Relating to the Eve of the Second World War, vol. II (Ministry of Foreign Affairs, Moscow, 1948).
Documents Diplomatiques Francais, 1932–1939, IIe Serie, 1936–1939, tome XV, 16 mars–30 avril 1939 (Paris, 1981).
Documents on British Foreign Policy, 1919–1939, Third Series, vol. III (1938–9) and vol. IV (1939), (London, 1950–1).
Documents on German Foreign Policy, 1918–1945, Series D, vols V–VII (London, 1954–7).
Doerr, Paul, *British Foreign Policy, 1919–1939* (Manchester, 1998).
Douglas, Roy (ed.), *1939: A Retrospect 40 Years On* (London, 1983).
Edwards, Ruth Dudley, *Victor Gollancz: A Biography* (London, 1987).
Feiling, Keith, *Life of Neville Chamberlain* (London, 1947).
Ferris, John, *Men, Money and Diplomacy: The Evolution of British Strategic Foreign Policy, 1919–1926* (London, 1989).
Forbes, Neil, *Doing Business with the Nazis. British Trade and Finance, 1931–1939* (London, 2000).
Foreign Relations of the United States. Diplomatic Papers (1938–1939) (Washington, 1955).
Foster, Alan J., *An Unequivocal Guarantee? Fleet Street and the British Guarantee to Poland, 31 March 1939* (London, 1991).
Francois-Poncet, Andre, *The Fateful Years, 1931–1938* (transl. London, 1949).
Fry, Michael G. (ed.), *Power, Personalities and Policies: Essays in Honour of Donald Cameron Watt* (London, 1992).
Gafencu, Grigore, *The Last Days of Europe* (transl. London, 1947).
Gannon, Franklin Reid, *The British Press and Nazi Germany* (Oxford, 1971).
Gibbs, N.H., *Grand Strategy*, vol. I, *Rearmament Policy* (London, 1976).
Gibbs, Sir Philip, *Across the Frontiers* (London, 1938, 1939).
Gilbert, Martin, 'Sir Horace Wilson', *History Today*, 32 (October1982) 3–9.
Gilbert, Martin and Richard Gott, *The Appeasers* (London, 2nd edn,1967).
Gladwyn, Lord, *The Memoirs of Lord Gladwyn* (London, 1972).
Gordon, G.A.H., *British Seapower and Procurement between the Wars: A Reappraisal of Rearmament* (London, 1988).
Hamill, I., *The Strategic Illusion: The Singapore Strategy and the Defence of Australia and New Zealand* (Singapore, 1981).
Haynes, Rebecca, *Romanian Policy towards Germany, 1936–40* (London, 2000).
Herman, John, *The Paris Embassy of Sir Eric Phipps: Anglo-French Relations and the Foreign Office, 1937–1939* (London,1998).
Heuston, R.F.V., *Lives of the Lord Chancellors* (London, 1964).
Hollis, Sir Leslie, *One Marine's Tale* (London, 1956).
Hoptner, J.B., *Yugoslavia in Crisis, 1934–1941* (New York, 1962).
Howard, Michael, *The Continental Commitment: The Dilemma of British Defence Policy in the Era of Two World Wars* (London, 1972).
Irving, David (ed.), *Breach of Security* (London, 1968).
Ismay, Lord, *The Memoirs of General The Lord Ismay* (London, 1960).

Jackson, W.G.F. and Dwin Bramall, *The Chiefs: The Story of the United Kingdom Chiefs of Staff* (London, 1992).
James, Robert Rhodes (ed.), *Chips: The Diaries of Sir Henry Channon* (London, 1967).
Kaiser, David, *Economic Diplomacy and the Origins of the Second World War: Germany, Britain, France and Eastern Europe* (New Jersey, 1980).
Kennan, George F., *From Prague after Munich: Diplomatic Papers, 1938–1940* (Princeton, N.J., 1968).
Kershaw, Ian, *The Hitler 'Myth': Image and Reality in the Third Reich* (London, 1989).
Kiesling, Eugenia C., *Arming Against Hitler: France and the Limits of Military Planning* (Kansas, 1996).
King-Hall Newsletter, vols 5–6 (London, 1938–39).
Klemperer, Klemens von, *German Resistance against Hitler: The Search for Allies Abroad, 1938–1945* (Oxford, 1992).
Kolinsky, Martin, *Britain's War in the Middle East: Strategy and Diplomacy, 1936–42* (London, 1999).
Koliopoulos, John S., *Greece and the British Connection, 1935–1941* (Oxford, 1977).
Lamb, Richard, *Mussolini and the British* (London, 1997).
Leith-Ross, Sir Frederick, *Money Talks. Fifty Years of International Finance* (London, 1968).
London, Louise, *Whitehall and the Jews, 1933–1948: British Immigration Policy and the Holocaust* (Cambridge, 2000).
Lungu, Dov B., *Romania and the European Great Powers, 1933–1940* (Durham, North Carolina and London, 1989).
McKercher, B.J.C., *Transition of Power: Britain's Loss of Global Pre-eminence to the United States, 1930–1945* (Cambridge, 1999).
Mackiewicz, Stanislaw, *Colonel Beck and His Policy* (London, 1944).
Maiolo, Joseph A., *The Royal Navy and Nazi Germany, 1933–39: A Study in Appeasement and the Origins of the Second World War* (London, 1998).
Marder, Arthur J. (ed.), *Portrait of an Admiral: The Life and Papers of Sir Herbert Richmond* (London, 1952).
Marguerat, Philippe, *La IIIe Reich et le petrole roumain, 1938–1940* (Leiden, 1977).
Martel, Gordon, *The Times and Appeasement: The Journals of A.L. Kennedy, 1932–1939* (London, 2000).
May, Ernest R. (ed.), *Knowing One's Enemies: Intelligence Assessment before the Two World Wars* (Princeton, N.J., 1984).
Medlicott, W.N., *British Foreign Policy since Versailles* (London, 1940; 2nd edn 1968).
Medlicott, W.N., *Britain and Germany: The Search for Agreement, 1936–1937* (London, 1969).
Meehan, Patricia, *The Unnecessary War: Whitehall and the German Resistance to Hitler* (London, 1992).
Millman, Brock, *The Ill-Made Alliance: Anglo-Turkish Relations, 1934–1940* (London, 1998).
Millman, R., *British Policy and the Coming of the Franco-Prussian War* (London, 1965).
Minney, R.J., *The Private Papers of Hore-Belisha* (London, 1960; reprinted 1991 with preface by B. Bond).

Mommsen, Wolfgang and Lothar Ketternacker (eds), *The Fascist Challenge and the Policy of Appeasement* (London, 1983).

Morris, Benny, *The Roots of Appeasement: The British Weekly Press and Nazi Germany during the 1930s* (London, 1991).

Morrow, Iain, *The Peace Settlement in the German–Polish Borderlands* (London, 1936).

Neville, Peter, *Appeasing Hitler. The Diplomacy of Sir Neville Henderson, 1937–39* (London, 2000).

Newman, Simon, *March, 1939. The Making of the British Guarantee to Poland* (Oxford, 1976).

Newton, Scott, *Profits of Peace. The Political Economy of Anglo German Appeasement* (London, 1996).

Nicolson, Harold, *Diaries and Letters, 1930–39*, Nigel Nicolson (ed.), (London, 1966).

Orde, Anne, *The Eclipse of Great Britain: The United States and British Imperial Decline, 1895–1956* (London, 1996).

Parker, R.A.C., *Chamberlain and Appeasement. British Policy and the Coming of the Second World War* (London, 1993).

Peden, George, *British Rearmament and the Treasury, 1932–1939* (Edinburgh, 1979).

Post, Gaines, *Dilemmas of Appeasement: British Deterrence and Defence, 1934–1937* (Ithaca, 1993).

Powers, Barry, *Strategy without Slide-Rule. British Air Strategy, 1914–1939* (London, 1976).

Pratt, Lawrence R., *East of Malta, West of Suez. Britain's Mediterranean Crisis, 1936–1939* (Cambridge, 1975).

Prazmowska, Anita, *Britain, Poland and the Eastern Front, 1939* (Cambridge, 1987).

Preston, Adrian (ed.), *General Staffs and Diplomacy before the Second World War* (Toronto and London, 1978).

Raczynski, Count Edward, *In Allied London: The Wartime Diaries of the Polish Ambassador* (London, 1962).

Ramsden, John, *The Making of Conservative Party Policy* (London, 1980).

Reynolds, David, *The Creation of the Anglo-American Alliance, 1931–1941. A Study in Competitive Co-operation* (London, 1981).

Roberts, Andrew, *The Holy Fox: A Life of Lord Halifax* (London, 1991).

Roberts, G. *The Soviet Union and the Origins of the Second World War* (London, 1995).

Roskill, S.W., *Hankey, Man of Secrets*, 3 vols (London, 1970–4).

Roskill, S.W., *Naval Policy between the Wars*, vol. II (1930–39) (London, 1976).

Royal Institute of International Affairs, *Survey of International Affairs* (London, 1938–9).

Rubinstein, William D. and Hilary L., *Philosemitism: Admiration and Support in the English-speaking World for Jews, 1840–1939* (London, 1999).

Sakmyster, Thomas L., *Hungary, the Great Powers and the Danubian Crisis, 1936–1939* (Athens, Georgia, 1979).

Sakmyster, Thomas L., *Hungary's Admiral on Horseback: Miklos Horthy, 1918–44* (1994).

Sanger, Clyde, *Bringing an End to Empire* (Liverpool, 1995).

Seton-Watson, R.W., *Britain and the Dictators: A Survey of Post-War British Policy* (London, 1938).

Seton-Watson, R.W., *From Munich to Danzig* (London, 1939).

Shaw, Louise Grace, *The British Political Elite and the Soviet Union, 1937–1939* (London, 2003).

Shay, Robert Paul, Jr., *British Rearmament in the 1930s. Politics and Profits* (Princeton, N.J.,1977).

Sherman, A.J., *Island Refuge. British Refugees from the Third Reich, 1933–1939* (London, 1973).

Shorrock, W.I., *From Ally to Enemy: The Enigma of Fascist Italy in French Diplomacy, 1920–1940* (Kent State, 1988).

Slessor, Sir John, *The Central Blue* (London, 1956).

Smith, Colin, *The Embassy of Sir William White at Constantinople, 1886–1891* (London, 1957).

Smith, M., *British Air Strategy between the Wars* (Oxford, 1984).

Stewart, Graham, *Burying Caesar. Churchill, Chamberlain and the Battle for the Tory Party* (London, 1999).

Stone, Glyn, *The Oldest Ally: Britain and the Portuguese Connection, 1936–1941* (London, 1994).

Strachan, Hew, *The Politics of the British Army* (Oxford, 1997).

Strang, Lord, *Home and Abroad* (London, 1956).

Strong, Sir Kenneth, *Men of Intelligence* (London, 1970).

Szembek, J., *Journal, 1933–39* (Paris, 1952).

Taylor, P.M., *The Projection of Britain: British Overseas Publicity and Propaganda, 1919–1939* (Cambridge, 1981).

Temperley, H.W.V. and L.M. Penson (eds), *Foundations of British Foreign Policy. From Pitt (1792) to Salisbury (1902)* (London, 1938).

Tilea, Viorel Virgil, *Envoy Extraordinary: Memoirs of a Romanian Diplomat*, Ileana Tilea (ed.), (London, 1998).

Toscano, M., *Designs in Diplomacy* (Baltimore, 1970).

Townshend, Charles, *Britain's Civil Wars. Counterinsurgency in the Twentieth Century* (London, 1986).

Tree, R., *When the Moon Was High* (London, 1975).

Wark, Wesley K., *The Ultimate Enemy. British Intelligence and Nazi Germany, 1933–1939* (London, 1985).

Waterfield, Gordon, *Professional Diplomat. Sir Percy Loraine of Kirkharle, Bt., 1860–1961* (London, 1973).

Watt, Donald Cameron, *How War Came. The Immediate Origins of the Second World War* (London, 1989).

Weber, Franz G., *The Evasive Neutral. Germany, Britain and the Quest for a Turkish Alliance in the Second World War* (Columbia, 1979).

Wingate, Sir Ronald. *Lord Ismay. A Biography* (London, 1970).

Winterton, Earl, *Orders of the Day* (London, 1953).

Woodward, E.L., *Short Journey* (London, 1942).

Woolf, Leonard (ed.), *The Intelligent Man's Way to Prevent War* (London, 1933).

Woolf, Leonard, *Barbarians at the Gate* (London, 1939).

Woytak, Richard A., *On the Border of War and Peace. Polish Intelligence and Diplomacy in 1937–1939 and the Origins of the Ultra Secret* (Boulder, Colorado, 1979).

Young, Arthur P., Across the Years (London, 1971).

Young, Arthur P., *The X Documents. The Secret History of Foreign Office Contacts with the German Resistance, 1937–1939*, App. by S. Aster (London, 1974).

Young, Robert J., *In Command of France. French Foreign Policy and Military Planning, 1933–40* (Cambridge, Massachusetts, 1978).

Young, Robert J., *France and the Origins of the Second World War* (London, 1996).

Index

1851 Convention, 155
1914–18, events of, 179
19 September declaration, 2, 9
21 May 1938, premature warning, 164
1938 September crisis, British handling of, 185
30 September 1938, Munich Agreement, 14
3 October 1938, British policy on Czechoslovakia, 178
11 October 1938, 18
12 January 1939, Chamberlain–Mussolini meeting, 12
14 March 1939, Great Britain's moral obligation confirmation, 13
1939 March crisis, British handling of, 185
31 March 1939, British policy on Poland, 178
30 January Hitler's speech, 95

accommodation, policy of, 29
active resistance, new policy of, 121
Addison, doubt of, 121
Admiralty proposal, 34
aerial bombardment, Cadogan's dismissal of, 74
aggression, 40
- collective judgment of, 9
- German technique of, 1
- unprovoked, 115
- warding off, 16

air attack, covert precautions against, 138
air defence, priority to, 62, 63
air raids, 47
alliance, wide-ranging, 145
allies
- arms stock of, 144
- importance of, 131

America's support, to Great Britain, 49
Anglo-American relations, damage to, 119
Anglo-American Trade Agreement, 46
Anglo-French guarantee, deterrent effect of, 152
Anglo-German declaration, 92
Anglo-Italian Agreement, 16 April 1938, 32, 58
annexation and predominance, distinguishing, 28
annexation, of Bohemia and Moravia, 122
Anti-Comintern Pact, 1936–7, 137, 161
anti-German bloc, 28
appeasement, 186
- alternative to, 54, 78
- British foreign policy of, 16
- destroying hopes of, 119
- policy of, 120, 180
- pursuit of, 43
- reopen path to, 96

Arab and Jewish aspirations, reconciling, 32
Arab hostility, 105
- consequences of, 69

Arab nationalism, 45
Arab revolt, 42
Arab world, satisfying, 25
arms
- free supply of, 45
- limitation, willingness, 96
- race, 114
- stock, of allies, 144

Ashton-Gwatkin, Frank
- clandestine contacts of, 43
- German predominance assessment by, 22

assurances, Hitler's betrayal of, 124
Ataturk, Kemal, 46
Austria, annexation of, 36, 179
autarkic practices, 29

autarky, 56
  difficulties of, 102
Axis Powers, 48, 65, 81, 105

Backhouse, views of, 72, 98, 105
balance of payments, deteriorating, 102
balance of power, 24
Balkan Entente, 140, 142
Balkan tobacco, consumer resistance to, 46
Balkans, 21, 27
Balutis, Bronius, 52
barbarism, 36
Barlow, Alan, Sir, 183
BBC, 60
Beck, Jozef, Colonel, 15, 16
  anxiety of, 168
Beck–Hitler meeting, 82
Belgian guarantee, 7
Belgium, saving, 71
Benes, Eduard, 2
Berlin and Warsaw, secret negotiations between, 165
Birmingham
  Chamberlain's 28 January speech at, 92, 96, 108
  Chamberlain's 17 March speech at, 123, 124
Bismarck, 7, 29
Bismarck's maxim, 17
bitter pill, sugar-coating, 2
Black Sea naval base, construction of, 30
Blackburn, Chamberlain's address at, 107
Bohemia and Moravia, annexation of, 122, 181
bombing offensive, sudden, 75
Bonnet, Georges, 3
Brest–Litovsk settlement, 78
Bridgwater by-election, result of, 43
Britain–France cooperation, 97
  need of, 46
Britain–Germany economic relationship, 102, 106
British Army
  continental commitment for, 101
  continental role for, 62, 63
  Hore-Belisha's views on, 61–62
British Cabinet, policy concerns of, 182
British commercial policy, 27
British diplomatic impotence, 55
British disapproval, demonstration of, 118
British empire
  strategy, 17, 30, *see also* British strategical calculations, Italy in; Collier, Laurence; Ashton-Gwatkin, Frank; Jebb's policy on; Secret Intelligence Service (SIS) memorandum
  vulnerability of, 17
British financial strength, 100
British foreign policy decision, unexpected, 1, 13
British foreign policy, of appeasement, 16
British imperial communications, 45
British interests and territories overseas, protecting, 62
British intervention
  list of events requiring, 93, 96
  thwarting, 66
British military aid, to France, 58
British military strategy, Poland in, importance of, 132
British ministers
  approach change of, 61
  Hitler's views on, 41
British naval supremacy, importance of, 186
British noninterference, dangers of, 88, 89
British policy
  American public opinion to, 42
  French worries of, 64
  pogrom's implications for, 40
British public mood, Nazi foreign policy effect on, 182
British public opinion, Chamberlain's concern for, 135
British rearmament
  defensive character of, 106
  need of, 23, 25, *see also* rearmament
British strategical calculations, Italy in, 79, *see also* British empire: strategy

British troop strength, ceiling on, 72
British–French dilemma, 150
broadcast talks, 80
broadcast warnings, importance of, 118
brutality and radical change, *see* Hitler's rule, characteristics of
business interests, private, encouraging, 30
by-election statistics, 113
by-election, post-pogrom, 43

Cadogan, Alexander, Sir, 2, 23
Canning, George, 5
Carol, King, 30
  aim of, 126
Carr, E.H., 80
casus belli, 97, 125
Chamberlain, Neville, 1, 3
  diplomacy of, 16, 19
  disappointment of, 20
  disillusionment of, 180
  distinction of, frontier violation versus attack on integrity and independence, 133
  imprudent claim of, 96
  miscalculation of, 59
  obsession of, favourite, 134
  questions of, 125, *see also* Birmingham
  shock and anger of, 123
  statement to Commons, 175
Chamberlain–Halifax opinion clash, 184
Chamberlain–Mussolini meeting, 12 January 1939, 12
Channel ports, saving, 71
Chatfield, Lord, 72
  concern of, 135
  questions of, 166, *see also* Chamberlain, Neville: questions of
Chelsea Constituency Association, 113
Chiefs of Staff (COS) views, 86, 105, 130, 142, 149, 166
  on intervention, 170
  on JPCs conclusions, 88, 99
  on Malta, 69
  on radio talk, 80
  on Russo–German agreement, 183
China, Japanese aggression on, 47
Christianity, enemy of, 40
Churchill, Winston, 4
Chvalkovsky, Frantisek, focus of, 11
coal agreement, 106
collective guarantees, reluctance to, 141
collective security, 24
collective versus joint and several guarantee, *see* guarantees, British definition of
Collier, Laurence, German predominance assessment by, 22
colonial claims, of Germany and Italy, 94
colonies, redistribution of, 84
Colvin, Ian, 157
combined resistance, 18
commitments of support, 87
Committee of Imperial Defence (CID), 31, 61, 72, 105
Commons debate, 1, 4, 13, 91, 96, 120
  draft of pre-arranged question and answer, 171
  on foreign policy, 67
concessions, use/misuse of, 22
conciliatory words, futile use of, 16
conquest and annexation, by Hitler, 26
conscription, 142, 155
Conservative Party, popularity of, 113
containment, diplomatic, limited, 23
continental affairs, British public dislike to intervention in, 7
continental predominance, 28
continental war, 70
co-operative thinking, 178
Corbin's criticism, 139
coup, 84
  by German generals, 50
  lack of evidence of, 159
crisis
  emerging, 185
  manufacturing, 85, 110

Czech guarantee, 145
  Anglo-French discord on, 48
  ignominious failure of, 187
  Opposition questions on, 114
Czech independence, fiction of, 119
Czechoslovakia
  British and French guarantee to, 2
    difficulties in honouring, 2
  British guarantee to
    ambiguity of, 4
    argument on, 3
  collapse of, implications of, 77
  disintegration of, 118
  forcible absorption of, 167
  German guarantee to, 12, 13
  German occupation of, 11
  Germany's plan for, 110
  Great Britain's promise on, 175
  Great Britain's strategic inaccessibility to, 3, *see also* limitrophe states
  guarantee to, British proposal of, 8
  redrawing frontiers of, 9, 14
  territory lost by, 10, *see also* Prague
  threat to, 36
Czechs and the Slovaks, rift between, 117

Daladier, Edouard, 3
Dalton's policy, 67
danger, impending, 12
Danubian states, 22
Danzig, 1, 66, 132
  German occupation of, 170
defence programme spending, 101
defence programme, accelerating, 63
defensive system, Franco-British alliance centred, 181
democracies, supine attitude of, 144
deterrence
  Great Britain's confidence on, 143
  policy of, 162
dictatorial tantrums, 19
diplomacy, personal, 91
diplomatic device, *see* guarantee
diplomatic history, 179
diplomatic propriety, 57
disarmament talk, 107
discontent, diverting, 75
disorder, murderous, 36
disputes, peaceful resolution of, 17
Djibuti railway, 68
Dominions, impact of British noninterference on, 90
Dutch ports, Germany's use of, 86

Eastern Europe, German predominance in, challenging, 46
Eastern quarrel, 66
economic appeasement, 30
economic imperialism, 22, 27
economic sanctions, 42
economy and politics, Great Britain's linking of, 108
emergency, declaration of, 138
encirclement
  German complaints of, 30
  policy of, 143
Ethiopia, recognition of Italian empire in, 32
Europe
  British goal of, 51
  Central, distribution of power and territory in, 19
  forceful domination of, Chamberlain's definition of, 96
  prolonged war in, averting, 106
  South-Eastern, redefinition of Great Britain's role in, 31
European affairs, Hitler's vision for Great Britain, *see* Hitler's formula, of Anglo-German relations
European appeasement, 18
  British public hope on, 39
  policy of, reason for abandoning, 34
European détente, 33
European disputes, 16
European frontiers, Central and Eastern, scepticism on guaranteeing, 115
European history, feature of, 29
European peace and security, threat to, 135
European quarrel, 144
European States System, 29, 118
  violent change to, 123

European war, 125, 150, 187
  avoiding, 76
  prospect of, 31
Evian Conference on Refugees, 42
expansionist policies, 22

Fieldhouse, H.N., predictions of, 185
First World War, 17
foreign affairs, public interest in, 43
Four Powers, 9, 14, 15, 16, 135
France
  British military aid to, 58
  credibility of, 11
  Germany–Italy simultaneous attack on, 99
  Great Britain's military support to, 180
  threat to, 87
France's moral recovery, 108
Franco–British co-operation, 108
Franco–German declaration, 47
  reluctance to invoke, 57
  test for, 51
Franco-German rapprochement, 33, 54
Franco–Italian antagonism, 54
Franco-Italian differences, settlement of, 113
Franco–Italian dispute, Great Britain's attitude to, 68
free negotiation, 171, 175
freedom, valuing, 125
French airfields, British use of, 72
French belief, on British military support, 71
French disagreement, on British proposal, 10
French military advice, 140
French military expectations, 64
French suspicion and resentment, arousing, 67
French worries, of British policy, 64
frontier violation versus attack on integrity and independence, Chamberlain's distinction, 133
Funk, Walter, 27
  suggestion of, 109

general election, 113
German aggression
  alternative means of countering, 154
  determination to resist, 132
  deterrence to, 77
  on Poland, 165, *see also* Poland
  plans of, 103
  resistance to, necessity of, 143
  rumours of imminent, 56
German air attack, 163
German armour, chinks in, 163
German Army leaders, disgruntled, preference of, 184, *see also* coup
German blackmail, French ministers to, vulnerability of, 65
German coastal advance, limiting, 71
German culture, 186
German customs union, 119
German economic predominance, 43, 150
German economy, Strang's views on, 44
German expansion, 1914, 145
German fear, of "encirclement", 133
German forces, disposition of, 170
German hostility, to Great Britain, 54
German military action, 1
German naval expansion, 186
German political and commercial predominance, resisting, 27
German predominance
  assessment of, Great Britain's, 21-22
  in Eastern Europe, 46
  modifying effects of, 30
German public, British efforts to reach, 60
German submarines, increase in number of, 74
German threat, retreat of, 112
German trade expansion, 110
German ultimatum, Tilea's report of, 159
Germany
  assurances of, nonreliability of, 123
  attitudes within, influencing, 78
  Balkan plans of, 109
  capacity of, Halifax's impressions on, 18

diplomatic containment of, 137
dissension and revolt within, 100
dissidence and economic difficulties in, signs of, 181
economic crisis in, expecting, 56
economic needs overshadowing political aspiration, 111–112
economic ultimatum to Roumania, 128
foreign debt of, 109
foreign policy of, 17
former colonies of, restitution of, 95
Great Britain's principal weapon against, 128
Great Britain's strategic interest to, clarifying, 135-6
hostile press campaign of, 20, 21
Italian and Spanish alignment with, 46
military strength implications, 23
plan of, assessing, 75
pre-emptive war against, 162
provoking internal revolt in, 76
provoking, 141
strengths of, assessing, 153
vulnerability of, 162
war against, principal justification for, 39
war aims of, 28
Germany–Britain, economic cooperation, 102, 106
Germany–Italy, joint planning by, 91
Germany–Soviet Union political deal, 104
Gibbs, Philip, Sir, 38
Godesberg meeting, 131
Goebbels, 35
aim of, 36
Goerdeler, Karl, 18, 43
ideas of, 184
programme of, 50
Gollancz, Victor, 37
Göring's impressions, on autarky, 102
Göring's suggestion, on post-Chamberlain era, 107
government action, public expectation of, 42
Great Britain
air attack on
coping, 72
vulnerability of, 47
America's support to, 49
draft statement, in support of Poland, 167–8
French support to, need of, 58
German attack on, impending, 65
German hostility to, 54
migration quota, 42
obligation versus France's obligation, comparison of, 87
optimism on Hitler, shattering of, 122
passivity of, 41
policy oscillations of, 181
Portugal's affiliation with, 31
strategy, in defending Roumania, 129
war entanglement, reason for, 26
Great War, 40, 179
Greece, alliance preference of, 46
guarantee
acceptance of 'word', 145
advantages of, 7
British definition of, 6-7
French disagreement with, 9
drawbacks of, 153
ending embarrassment of, 112
evolution of 'word', 187
impacts of, 5
British guarantee to Belgium, 6
insignificance of, 117
moral, worthlessness of, 116
value in diplomacy, 12

Hainan Island, occupation by Japan of, 105
Halifax, 1
conclusions post-Munich Agreement, 29
impressions on Germany's capacity, 18
mood of, 40
premature telegrams and responses of countries, 132-3
Hankey, Maurice, Sir, 36
Harvey, Oliver, 33

Headlam-Morley, James, Sir, 8
hegemony, 23
Henderson's interpretation, of Leopold's address, 106
Henderson's view, support for, 112
historians, role of, 185
history, diplomatic, 179
Hitler('s)
  betrayal of assurances, 124
  characteristic of, 75
  cramping, 23
  despairing condemnation of, 116
  deterring, policy flaws in, 182
  formula of Anglo-German relations, 20
  Great Britain's hopes on, 56
  Great Britain's optimism on, shattering of, 122
  hostility of, evidence, 74
  intentions of, Chamberlain's misinterpretation of, 180
  militarily restraining, 131
  move by, policy for anticipating, 84
  peaceful intent of, 106
  plan for Great Britain, 41
  readiness to exercise restraint, 18, 19
  removal and Sudeten crisis, 49
  revolt against, possibility of, 158
  rule, characteristics of, 35
  views on
    British ministers, 41
    Western democracies, 44
  violation of international order, 124
  warning to, 92-3
Hitler–Beck meeting, 82
Hoare, Samuel, Sir, 3
  radical plan of, 162
Holland and Switzerland, German plans to attack, 83
Holland
  conquest of, 111
  German occupation of, possibility of, 91
  strategic importance to Great Britain, 86, 89
Hore-Belisha's memorandum, 70
Hore-Belisha's views, on British army, 61–62
hostile press campaign, Germany's, 20, 21
House of Commons, mood of, 176
Hungarian takeover, of Ruthenia, 117
Hungary and Czechoslovakia, arbitration between, 10
Hungary, guilty of unprovoked aggression, 117
Hungary's independence, threat to, 120

Iberian peninsula, 22
ideological antagonism, 184
Imperial Conference, 1937, 104
imperial interests, latent threats to, 106
Imperial Tobacco Company, 46
imperialism, economic, 22, 27
imperialist powers, emergence of, 17
Inskip, Thomas, Sir, 4
International Banking Consortium, 109
international conduct, new rules of, 40
international order, Hitler's violation of, 124
international policing, 23
international politics, development of, 26
international trade, revival of, 113
intervention, premature, 185
intimidation, Nazi leaders interest in, 35
inundation, 88
Italian and Spanish alignment, with Germany, 46
Italian claims, from France, 64
Italian Fascism, 40
Italian propaganda, 79
Italo–British conflict, 69
Italy, foreign policy of, 17
Italy–Britain, rapprochement, 48

January speculations, 97
Japan
  aggressive intent of, 105
  naval control to, denying, 104
Jebb's policy on countering German dominance, 24

Jewish immigration, into Palestine, 105
Jewish population, possible exodus, 42
Jews, onslaught against, 35, 37
Joint Planning Committee (JPC), 85, 138, 153
  pessimism of, 99
  radio talk script approval by, 80
  resentment of, 128
journalists, expulsion of, 36
JPC, *see* Joint Planning Committee
Judaism, enemy of, 40

Kelly's theory, George, 178
Keynes, Maynard, John, 37
Kirkpatrick, Ivone, 65
Kitchener, quote of, 70
Kristallnacht, events of, 35, 181

Labour Party, views of, 172, 174
land warfare, 71
League of Nations, 17
leak of information, advantages, 91
Left Book Club, 37
Lenin's international order, 28
Leopold's address, Duke, 106
liberal ideas, defending, 37
Liechtenstein broadcasting station, 68
limitrophe states, 12
Lithuania, German ultimatum to, 141
Lithuania's hold on, Memel, 51
Litvinov
  proposal of, 142
  views of, 133
Lloyd, Lord, 7
Locarno Treaty, 8
London
  air attack on, 65
  bombing of, 111
Low Countries, preventing conquest of, 62
Luxembourg broadcasting station, use of, 61

Machiavellian, 24
Maconachie, Richard, Sir, 80
Maginot Line, 26, 99, 151
Maisky's argument, Ivan, 18
Malaxa, Nicolae, 126
Malta's defences, British importance of, 69
Mander, Geoffrey, 8
maritime deterrence, 105
maritime states, 45
Mason-MacFarlane, 75
  alarm notes of, 103
  radical plan of, 162
mediation, between Warsaw and Prague, 15
Mediterranean, forces in, mutual reduction of, 69
Mein Kampf, 18
Memel Convention, 1924, 51
Memel status, case for international concern, 66
Memel statute, Lithuanian failures to respect, 54
Memel
  Germany's intention to occupy, 130
  Lithuania's hold on, 51
Middle East
  British forces in, security of, 105
  Great Britain, importance to, 81
militarism, *see* German culture
military action, pretext for, 26
military geography, 3
military guarantees, 28
moral guarantee, 145
  worthlessness of, 116
moral obligation, 6
Munich Agreement, 1-2, 10, 14, 29
  Chamberlain's policy post-, 180
  Hitler's disregard, 119, 124
  Mussolini's contribution to, 32
  threat of war and, 43
Munich Declaration, 110
  German contempt for, 54
  Hitler's interpretation of, demonstrating, 53
murderous disorder, 36
Muslim world, undermining reputation in, 81

Mussolini
British concessions to, Halifax's fears of, 67
British policy to, explaining, 172
conversations with, Halifax's formula for, 68
deal with, Chamberlain's inclination for, 64
indifference to British overtures, 78
Mussolini–Hitler bond, breaking, 24

Napoleon, post 1809, 186
National Socialism, 36
Naval Agreement, Great Britain and Germany's, 57
naval blockade, 104
Nazi atrocity, press reports of, 38
Nazi leadership views, on economic cooperation, 109
Nazi regime destruction, speculation of, 100
Nazi regime
destabilising, 169
serious dissent within, 51
threat of, challenging assumption of, 179
Nazi thesis, 119
Nazism
destruction of, 131
subverting, broadcast propaganda for, 68
neutrality, policy of, 90
Nicolson, Harold, 4
no confidence motion, 67
non-aggression pacts, 3
noninterference, US preference for, 144
November pogrom, 40, 159

obsession, problems of, 186
Ogilvie, Frederick, 60
Ogilvie-Forbes, George, Sir, 12
Opposition speeches, on Government policy, 121
overseas supplies, danger to, 71

Palestine problem, resolving, 25
Palestine
implication of conference on, 81
Jewish immigration into, 105
partition of, 32
peace and conciliation, 92
peace, short-lived, purchasing, 77
peaceful change, preference for, 17
peaceful negotiation, 51, 76, 180
persecution, 39
personal attacks, avoiding, 155
personal constructs, 178
pogrom, November, 40
pogrom's implications, for British policy, 40
poison gas, banning, 21
Poland and Roumania, worthless guarantees to, 187
Poland and Russia, open alliances with, policy of, 131
Poland('s)
allies support to, 163
COS advise on, 170
British support to, 1, 13
diplomacy of, military dimension of, 146
German aggression on, definition of, 165, 174
German attack on, rumours of, 157
German press attacks on, 161, 167
Great Britain's inescapable commitment to, 177
need of Russian arms, 140
public statement in support of, merits/demerits of, 166
recovering lost land from, *see* German Army leaders, disgruntled, preference of
unilateral declaration in support of, 173
vulnerability to German attack, 141, 147
weakness of, 142
policy oscillations, Great Britain's, 181
Polish Corridor, abolishing, 50
Polish disquiet, 141
Polish neutrality, guarantee of, 161
Polish resentment, 141
Polish ultimatum, Prague's acceptance of, 16

Polish–Roumanian Mutual Guarantee Pact, British–French guarantee to, 145, 156
political aims, incompatible, 109
post-Munich Europe, preserving, 24
power politics, 36
power
  distribution of, 29
    unequal, 52
Powers, minor, corralling, 28
Prague
  German occupation of, 12
    Great Britain's views on, 118, *see also* Czechoslovakia
predator states, 22
predatory activities, 12
pre-emptive war, 23, 162
premature war, dangers of, 86
Private Notice question, 173
promise of support, British and French, 115
propaganda, role of, 60, 78, 95
provocation, avoiding, 66
Prussian garrison, 7
public expectation, of government action, 42
public hostility, 62
public opinion, defeatist tendencies in, 114
public outrage, scale of, 116
puppet government, 119

racial purity, 119
rainbow story, 113
rearmament
  British, 96, 106, 143, 151
  end to, 50
  gaining time for, 155
  importance of, 186
  level, 23
  over-rapid, problems of, 19
  scale of Britain, France, America, 114
  task of, 92
rebuff, Ribbentrop's, 54
rebuffs, 53, 134, 137
Red Army, 82
regime change, in Berlin, 50
repercussions, moral and political, 86
resistance
  active, new policy of, 121
  allied, draft declaration on, views on, 140
  collective
    problems in, 144
    urgent need of, 134
  determination for, 111
Ribbentrop('s)
  assurance, 110
  claim, 143
  hostile press campaign goal, 21
  rebuff, 54
Richmond, Herbert, Sir, 80
Rome visit, 79, 92, 180
Roosevelt
  message from, 49
  diplomatic weight of, using, 85
Roosevelt's New Year message, interpretation of, 92-3
Roumania
  Germany's economic ultimatum to, 128
  Germany's plan on, 75
  political or economic independence of, threat to, 130
  strategic implications for Great Britain, 128
  territorial integrity of, Germany's guarantee on, 126
  wheat from, purchasing, 27
Roumanian oil supplies
  Germany's control of, 92, 149
    preventing, 160
rumours
  false, 181
  omitting reference to, 173
  use of, 88
Russia
  importance of, 147, 152, 172, 184
  open association with, opposition to, 148
  reasons for excluding, 149
  role of, 176
Russian arms supplies, arranging, 156
Russian arms, Poland's need of, 140
Russian assistance, form of, 146
Russian Communism, 40
Russian danger, retreat of, 113

Russian policy approach, *see* combined resistance
Russo-German agreement, improbability of, 183
Ruthenia, disputes over, 10
Ruthenia, Hungarian takeover of, 117

Salazar, Antonio, 31
Sargent, Orme, Sir, 43
Sargent's views, on German expansion–British resistance, 77
Saudi Arabia, Great Britain's influence in, 45
Scandinavian states, 90
scientific enquiry, 40
seapower, of Great Britain, 71
season and military action, 83
Secret Intelligence Service (SIS) memorandum, 24-5
self-determination, 52
  national, 29
Seton-Watson, R.W., political projections of, 185-6
Siegfried Line, 153, 166
  breaching, 150
Simon's questions, 151
Sinclair, Hugh, Sir, 24
Slovak crisis, 114
Slovak revolt, 110
South-Eastern Europe, redefinition of Great Britain's role in, 31
South-Eastern European governments, affiliation of, 28
Spa Conference 1920, 14
Spain, civil war in, 31, 46
  ending of, 113
spineless and afraid, *see* Hitler's views on, British ministers, 41
Steward, George, role of, 20
Strang' draft, 19
Strang's views, on German economy, 44
strife, internal nationalist, 118
Study of History, 36
submarine tonnage, 57
Sudeten crisis, 29
  Hitler's removal and, 49
Sudeten territory, 15
Suez Canal Company, Italy's demand on, 48
support
  promise of, British and French, 115
  unconditional, 1
Sword, E.R., Lt. Col., 146

territorial adjustments, 29
  by free negotiation, 168, *see also* free negotiation
territorial changes, 50, 66, 180
  British policy on, 78
territorial concessions, 68
territorial revision, British policy on, 52
Teschen episode, 16
threat versus negotiation, 14, 16
Tilea's premature report, 126
Tilea's story, repudiation of, 130
tobacco formula, 46
tolerance and open-mindedness, 37
Toynbee, J., Arnold, 36
Trade and Payments Agreement, November 1934, 102
Trans-Olza, Poland's claim on, 14
treasury advice, 183
treaties
  revision of, 52
    violent, 29
Treaty of Locarno, 8
Treaty of Versailles, 51, 122, 160, 180
turkeys, Hungarian, importing, 30
tyranny, 39

Ukraine
  Germany's attack on, improbability of, 82
  Germany's plan on, 75-6
Ukrainian separatism, promoting, 66
ultimatum
  definition of, 127
  Kennard's confirmation of absence of, 173
unemployment, 102, 107

vassal states, 24, 28, 76
verbal distinctions, 6
Vereker, George, 82

Versailles settlement, 19, 23
  Germany's demand for revision of, 29
  peaceful revision of, 67
Vienna settlement, 1815, 5
vote of censure, 59

War Office, 103
war
  averting, 115
  glorification of, 36
  Great Britain's diplomatic role in averting, 179
  Greenwood's anticipation of, 176
  imminence of, 62
  long drawn, implications of, 132
  non-preference to, 29
  premature, 86
  preparations, 71–73
  scares, 114
  talk, 81
  two-front, 182
    risking, 164
warning and deterrence, policy of, 125
Warsaw and Prague, British offer of mediation between, 15
Warsaw's relaxed attitude, 160
weaker states, post-Munich era for, 16
Western civilisation
  future of, 36
  threat to, 39
  call to protect, 37
Western democracies, Hitler's views on, 44, 79
Western Powers, view of, 163
Woodward, E.L., views of, 186
Woolf, Leonard, 36
world domination, Germany's march for, 135

Yugoslav suspicions, 149

Zetland, Lord, 43
Zionist aspirations, 82